JOSE MARAVALL

Dictatorship and Political Dissent

WORKERS AND STUDENTS
IN FRANCO'S SPAIN

ST. MARTIN'S PRESS
NEW YORK

© *Jose Maravall* 1978

All rights reserved. For information, write:
St. Martin's Press, Inc., 175 Fifth Avenue, New York, N.Y. 10010
Printed in Great Britain
First published in the United States of America in 1979
ISBN 0–312–20012–9

Library of Congress Cataloging in Publication Data

Maravall, Jose.
  Dictatorship and political dissent.

  Bibliography: p.
  Includes indexes.
    1. Trade-unions—Spain—Political activity.
  2. Students—Spain—Political activity.   3. Dissenters—Spain.   4. Spain—Politics and government—
  1939–1975.   I. Title.
  HD6762.M266   1979   322.4'2   78–12879
  ISBN 0–312–20012–9

Nous prendrons jour malgré la nuit

PAUL ELUARD

Contents

Acknowledgements

A small part of the material has been used in articles published in *Sociology* and in *Government and Opposition*, and I wish to thank the editors for giving me permission to include it in this book. Also, different papers related to the book were discussed in seminars at St Antony's and Balliol Colleges, Oxford; at the London School of Economics and Westfield College, University of London; at the Universities of Reading, Kent, and Warwick, and I benefited very much from comments and criticisms raised on these occasions. Finally, and although they cannot be held responsible for its weaknesses, I must say that the book owes very much to discussions with and help from John Goldthorpe, Frank Parkin, Duncan Gallie, Chelly Halsey, John Rex, Salvador Giner, Raymond Carr, and Ubaldo Martínez-Lázaro.

Jose Maravall
August, 1977

1 Introduction

The present book has grown out of two pieces of research on contemporary Spanish politics: on the working-class movement and the student movement.[1] The decision to bring the two researches together in a single book was intellectually justified on the grounds that, together, they presented a wider analysis of politics under nondemocratic regimes, and under Francoism in particular, and also that they were both concerned with the general question of the emergence of underground political movements in Spain from 1939 to 1975. The basic theoretical coherence of the different parts of the book should, therefore, provide some insights into both the sociology of nondemocratic regimes and the dynamics of political movements of dissent, taking Spain as a specific case. It must be noted that the main purpose of the book is not to give a comprehensive descriptive account of Francoism nor even of dissent against the dictatorship. This type of general introduction to Spanish politics may be found in other publications. What is intended here is an analysis in depth of certain questions; questions such as: to what extent does economic development in autocracies produce social and political contradictions that foster organized movements of dissent? What have been the main sources of working-class militancy and have they been associated with particular economic or political characteristics? Can it be said that political militancy is transmitted between generations? How does the pattern of recruitment in secret organizations change over the different phases of evolution of these organizations? The context is the Francoist dictatorship from 1939 to 1975 and I would hope that the answers to the theoretical questions will, more or less directly, shed some light on Spanish politics in this period. It is therefore, perhaps, convenient to make a few general introductory remarks on the Francoist state in connection with the political sociology of dictatorships, totalitarianism, authoritarianism, and Fascism.

Analysis of non-democratic states has significantly changed in recent years. The dominant influence of theories of 'totalitarianism' in the 1950s and 1960s has been displaced by a number of Marxist and *Marxisant* contributions[2], which have tried to offer an interpretation of Fascism as a product of an economic crisis of capitalism, a political crisis in the system of class domination, and a reaction on the part of large sectors of a socially threatened petty bourgeoisie. These interpretations see an underlying similarity between strictly Fascist movements and states and other reactionary movements and states in capitalist societies. These new contributions pose the taxonomical problem of where can Francoism be 'located', and whether internal changes in the Francoist state from 1939 to 1975 can be interpreted in accordance with the continuities between different dictatorial states (Fascism, Bonapartism, military dictatorships, etc.).

The discussion of the Francoist state within the context of theories of 'totalitarianism' has mainly involved the question of whether the totalitarian syndrome was applicable to such a state, particularly after the internal changes within the Francoist system during the 1950s and after. Friedrich and Brzezinski (1956: 22) defined totalitarianism as a state where six interrelated traits would be present, namely (i) an official ideology 'to which everyone is supposed to adhere, at least passively'; (ii) 'a single mass party, typically led by one man'; (iii) a system of terror, through party and/or police control; (iv) a monopoly or near-monopoly of control of all effective mass media; (v) a monopolistic control of means of armed combat; (vi) a central control and direction of the economy. The difficulty of fitting Francoism within this conception of 'totalitarianism' has led to the construction of another typological cell: 'authoritarianism'. It is Linz in particular who has defined the traits of authoritarianism: a political system 'with limited, non responsible, political pluralism; without elaborate and guiding ideology (but with distinctive mentality); without intensive or extensive political mobilization (except for some points in their development), and in which a leader (or occasionally a small group), exercises power within formally ill-defined limits, but actually quite predictable ones.'[3]

These conceptions of 'totalitarianism' and 'authoritarianism' have been criticized on the grounds that they are simple taxonomical niches with no underlying theory, and that they ignore the economic and class basis of political domination. Only on these grounds is it possible to locate Fascism and state-socialism in the same cell, neglecting their fundamental economic, social, and ideological characteristics. Fascism should, on the contrary, be seen as a specific historical product in the context of a capitalist economy and a system of capitalist class domination, where private property, private profit, and private capital accumulation are central institutions of the economy, and where systematic labour-repressive policies are consistent with sharp class divisions. Second, due to the economic and class differences between Fascism and state-socialism, the goals of state policies in the two cases do not bear any resemblance and they are associated with opposing claims to legitimacy. It is also alleged that the concept of 'totalitarianism', by being simply a residual category for everything which is not pluralist capitalism, is an example of Cold War manicheism: stressing an alleged similarity, it makes anti-Communism a logical continuity from anti-Fascism. It is finally said that while it is difficult not to see some of the traits of the Friedrich/Brzezinski syndrome in pluralist democracies (e.g. traits 5 and 6), it is, however, hardly possible to apply the whole 'syndrome' to specific historical cases (Kitchen 1976: ch. 3; Lane 1976: 44–54).

A considerable problem that theories of non-democratic capitalist states have faced is that of the relationship between Fascism and other kinds of states. Poulantzas in particular has coined the term 'exceptional capitalist state' to denote the genus, within which Fascism would be one species, together with Bonapartism and military dictatorships.[4] The concept, however, seems inappropriate in at least two respects. First of all, it assumes that this state is the non-modal capitalist state, that is, that parliamentary democracy is the modal type. Second, this assumption of the non-modal character of the 'exceptional state' within capitalism, is based on a functionalist argument: parliamentary democracy would 'fit' the normal requirements of capitalism better, and an exceptional state only emerges when some abnormal require-ments (relating to the conditions of capital accumulation and to political stability) have to be met through exceptional functions. Not only is this teleological argument logically weak, it also has great difficulties in explaining why Fascism (or other exceptional states) persists once the abnormal requirements have been fulfilled (that is, when capital accumulation and class domination have been strengthened).

If the concept of the exceptional capitalist state appears to be unacceptable because of these two difficulties, it is still suggestive in that it stresses the necessity of singling out the common characteristics of the different forms of non-democratic capitalist regimes. These common characteristics have to be interpreted within a theoretical framework that also explains changes and transitions from one type of regime to another as well as the relationship between capitalist dictatorships and capitalist democracies. The common denominator of dictatorial capitalist states is obviously their origins and their policies.

An economic crisis in the capitalist system is an important antecedent of such states. This economic crisis is itself related to a threat to the traditional structures of class domination: both are due to a strong working-class movement *and* to a slump in the process of capital accumulation. A second factor which is at the origin of dictatorial capitalist states is the disaffection of important sectors of the ruling class from the existing system of parliamentary democracy. Finally, the crisis which forms the background of such states includes a situation of political uprootedness among sectors of society that do not participate through the existing channels of political representation and/or feel threatened by the social and economic crises (petty-bourgeoisie, small peasantry, lumpen-proletariat). In this situation of crisis, a social-political movement produces the collapse of the existing political system. This movement may vary – sometimes it is little more than a military insurrection, sometimes it results from the mobilization of the uprooted groups. What is important is that to a certain extent the movement is beyond the control of the traditional dominant groups, although it emerges to re-establish law and order.

The new state also shows a distinct autonomy from the traditional ruling groups, because of its relatively independent origins, its dictatorial character, and because of the crisis within these traditional ruling groups. However, this state does not challenge capitalism: on the one hand, it creates and generates new conditions for an intensive capitalist accumulation and growth; on the other, it produces a re-alignment of the ruling groups. These changes of an economic and social kind take place within a non-democratic political context; working-class organizations are destroyed while the institutions of pluralist democratic representation (parties, parliaments, and the electoral mandate) are abolished. Dictatorial capitalist states are thus labour-repressive systems without democratic institutions.[5]

There were important similarities between Italian Fascism and the Francoist state:[6] the earlier period of economic crisis and intense class confrontation, the destruction of parliamentary democracy and working-class organizations, the compromise between the different groups of the ruling class, the labour-repressive policies and the involvement of the state in a process of intensive capital accumulation, the creation of a corporatist-organicist state. Some of these traits will be discussed in following chapters, and only a few brief remarks will now be made about the strictly political context of Francoism as anti-democratic and repressive. One of the fundamental ideological programmes that served as the basis for the new Francoist state declared:

'Our state will be a totalitarian instrument in the service of the integral homeland ... The system of political parties will be abolished, with all its consequences.'[7]

An 'organic democracy', based on the 'natural groupings of society-family, municipality and union'[8], was opposed to the 'anarchy' of elective pluralist democracy. Freedom of association, freedom of expression, and individual human rights were abolished. In 1937 the three main political groups associated with the military uprising of 1936, the *Falange*, the *Juntas de Ofensiva Nacional-Sindicalista* (JONS), and the *Comunión Tradicionalista* (Carlists), were unified into a single party (the *Movimiento Nacional*); all other political parties were suppressed and persecuted. No democratic trade unions were allowed; the working class was controlled through the official and state-led *Sindicatos*, which were organized on the same principles as the *corporazioni* of Fascist Italy. These principles were part of a corporatist-organicist conception of society,[9] and they included the union of workers and managers in mixed and single organizations for each branch of production, as well as representation of the workers based not on elections but on nomination by the regime. The *Cortes* (the Spanish Parliament) lost its legislative powers and its members were not linked to any mandate.[10] The laws of Political Responsibilities and of Repression of Communism and Free Masonry had led to massive post-war purges. The number of Republican prisoners' deaths through execution or disease has been estimated to have been over 200,000, and there were many other different forms of political sanctions, from prison to professional harassment (Jackson 1965: Appendix). The State had complete control, either direct or indirect, of the media of mass communications, which were used as means of systematic political indoctrination; information was severely controlled and only official images of political and social events were transmitted.

6 Dictatorship and Political Dissent

The totalitarian characteristics of the Spanish regime in the period 1939–45 are generally accepted. A totalitarian mobilization of Spanish society was sought by the regime. A single political party penetrated all sections of society and ideological indoctrination was attempted through every agency of socialization. This indoctrination started with the Youth Front (*Frente de Juventudes*) for children of seven years of age and upwards, and continued through adolescence and adulthood by way of the educational system, the political institutions, and the mass media. The Spanish regime would then correspond to the 'ideological political system' type described by Brzezinski and Huntington (1964). There was a high degree of direct ideological inducement, of normative and material control over ideas, of manipulation of institutions, and an extensive re-writing of history. The *Frente de Juventudes* was a copy of the *Gioventú Italiana del Littorio* of Fascist Italy and of the *Hitlerjugend* of National-Socialist Germany. Its creation in 1940 followed the same path as the 1936 unification of youth organizations under the Hitler Youth:

'... The German Youth, besides being reared within the family and schools, shall be educated physically, intellectually and morally in the spirit of National Socialism ... through the Hitler Youth.'[11]

The conflict that has often been noted between socialization within the family and purposeful indoctrination by social and political agencies under non-democratic regimes also existed in Spain and will be discussed in detail in chapters 4 and 6.

The adaptation of the regime to the Second World War led to a number of modifications within the state. Linz explains these modifications in terms of the relative importance of the different groups within the Francoist coalition, and of the increasing influence of non-Fascist conservative and Catholic elements. However, it is difficult to see the relative influences of the political groups independently of the course of the Second World War. In 1942, the Spanish parliament (the *Cortes*) had been re-introduced into the political system, but its composition followed the principles of the 'Organic State' and representation was by political nomination and not by democratic election.[12] In 1945, the *Fuero de los Españoles* (Spaniards' Bill of Rights) and the Law on National Referendum were promulgated, and in 1947 a Law of Succession of the Head of the State, which established a Monarchy.

The end of the World War also activated the opposition to the regime. A 'National Alliance of Democratic Forces' was set up in September 1944, with the participation of the Communist Party from

January 1946; at the end of 1944 there was infiltration in the valley of Arán of groups of *maquis* from the south-west of France, some of which reached Andalucía; in December 1946 and on May 1, 1947 attempts were made by the socialist trade union, UGT, to organize strikes in Bilbao. There was a widespread belief that the collapse of the regime was very likely after the victory of the Allies. Within the universities the main attempt was carried out in 1946 when the Republican student union, the FUE, was revived underground in a number of universities. At the beginning of 1947 the twelve members of the National Committee of FUE were arrested after a search in the *Lycée Français* in Madrid and were court-martialled.

Expectations of the rapid downfall of the regime because of international pressure were frustrated. The hold of the regime over the country was very strong, the exhaustion of the war and the purges had left the democratic forces very weak. Indeed, international isolation led to a reinforcement of political controls and of autarchic economic policies. By 1950 guerrilla activity (which had been stimulated by the French *maquis*) collapsed; in 1951 the surviving Communist Party members within Spanish universities were arrested. International pressure was not very strong either. The new Cold War alignments limited it and hopes of a military intervention were never fulfilled. The Francoist regime was also trying to reshuffle the internal coalition of forces, in order to adapt to the new external situation. The Catholic and the Monarchist sectors gained ground: in the reorganization of the Cabinet in July 1951, Vallellano represented the latter and Ruiz-Giménez the former. At the same time, the 'Opus Dei' was increasing its influence within the regime as a new technocratic group which defended a programme of economic reform and growth that was seen as compatible with the main institutions of Francoism. The degree to which this economic programme had deep unintended consequences will be discussed in chapter 2.

The internal changes in the coalition supporting the regime had two important consequences. On the one hand, they increased the tensions between the different groups, which could be detected in the contents of journals and magazines such as *La Hora* or *Alcalá*. Sectors of the *Falange* reacted against their gradual loss of influence, stressing their populistic Fascism against what they saw as their clerical-conservative antagonists: the populism of Falangist groups such as '*Alejandro Salazar*' and '*Ramiro Ledesma*' had a strong anti-capitalist fervour, and included demands for agrarian reform and nationalization of the banks. On the other hand, there was greater political involvement of liberal Catholic intellectuals, linked to the

8 Dictatorship and Political Dissent

Republic – such as Marañón, Marías, Giménez-Fernández, etc. The links between this group of intellectuals and the group of Catholic intellectuals who were in those years still within the regime but would be drawn into opposition in the mid-1950s (Ruiz-Giménez, Laín, Ridruejo, etc.) was one of the major characteristics of the initial stage of cultural dissent. Some of these intellectuals would move to left-wing positions in the 1960s (particularly Ruiz-Giménez and Aranguren) and would coalesce with influential socialist or communist academics and intellectuals (like Tierno-Galván or Sacristán).

The international position of the regime began to change. In 1951 diplomatic and economic isolation ended; in 1952 Spain was admitted to UNESCO; in 1953 the regime signed an economic and military agreement with the US; in 1955 Spain joined the United Nations and the Organization for European Economic Co-operation in 1959 (later the Organization of Economic Co-operation and Development). In the 1950s open manifestations of unrest began. In 1951 an increase in transport fares led to a boycott of transport in Barcelona in March, and in Madrid in April, and a university (Barcelona) was closed for the first time since the war. These were the prolegomena of the confrontations of 1956 which involved workers and students; thenceforward organized opposition to the regime was uninterrupted.

The evolution of the regime from 1945 has been interpreted by Linz in terms of a transition from 'totalitarianism' to 'authoritarianism': a limited pluralism and informal bargaining between groups developed, and policies encouraging passive acceptance of the regime replaced totalitarian mobilization. It must, however, be noted that no significant changes in individual rights, political freedoms, and democratic participation took place. Friedrich and Brzezinski interpret the transition as a gradual transformation

'... into a personal military dictatorship of essentially reactionary propensities ... As such, it rests upon military support and ecclesiastical sanction and a kind of negative legitimation of popular apathy, reinforced by some pseudo-democratic rituals, such as rigged elections and plebiscites.' (1956: 9, 314)

Thus, the *Ley de Principios del Movimiento Nacional* of 1958, which was a constitutional norm of the 'authoritarian' stage, declared that all particular interests were subordinated to the superior interest of the nation; that the political structure of the state was an 'organic democracy'; that the 'principles of authority and service' and of 'unity of power' were bases of the state; that political associations were forbidden; that the nation was Catholic and only the Catholic religion was allowed; that trade unions were organized by, and were at the service of, the state, their representatives were members of the *Movimiento*, and trade unions were 'total' (i.e. composed of managers and workers within each industrial union); that strikes were illegal; that the interests of workers and managers were subordinated to the interests of the state. From another perspective, the non-democratic characteristics of the alleged 'authoritarian' stage of the Francoist regime were manifested at the level of repression. The Bulletin of the European Committee for Amnesty reported some 600 political prison sentences, of an average five years in length, for the period 1958–61, which was a period when political opposition was virtually absent in both the working-class and student movements. Between 1968 and 1970 alone three states of emergency were declared. And as Linz accepts, one of the main characteristics of the regime in its alleged transition was the skilful management of the permanent threat of repression, which was always a Damocles' sword suspended over any political or para-political activities.

It is indeed difficult to interpret the changes in the Francoist system if the relationship between class, politics, and the economy is ignored. From 1967 to 1975 it was possible to find publications of all varieties of Marxism in Spain, and the degree of ideological sophistication that existed within the Spanish left, within the universities, within intellectual and political groups, was easily comparable with any other European society. Tolerance at the ideological level was unquestionable – it did not exist, however, at the level of political criticism of the regime or at the level of organizational politics. Here repression was very harsh: just as an isolated instance, democratic trade-union leaders were still being sentenced in December 1973 to up to twenty years in prison for organizing free labour unions. From 1965, roughly, two worlds seemed to exist in Spain: political inactivity opened the door to the material goods of an increasingly affluent society while it also became possible to indulge in ideological radicalism. This was the bright side of civilization, tolerance, and well-being. On the other hand, political activity against the regime led to the dark side: repression, fear, and persecution. Management by the regime of the boundaries between the two worlds was skilful and it conveyed an image of change, liberalization, and abundance. There was some resemblance between the political situation in Spain in the last decade of Francoism and the description that Cavaignac made of the political situation under another dictatorial state, the Bonapartist regime in France after 1848: 'Is not Paris, once so deeply shaken, now peaceful? Is not life now sweet and cosy? Is it not possible now to have dinner on time? It is not possible now to listen to good music after dinner?' (Pernoud 1962: 537). There was a relationship between repression, stability and order, well-being and relative tolerance, which was experienced in different ways (as repression or as well-being) according to which side one was on.

The changes within Francoism, both liberalization of economic policies after 1957 and greater ideological tolerance and pluralism after 1965, can be seen as transitions within the type of dictatorial capitalist state that is associated with the social, economic, and political stability of the system of class rule. In the early 1930s, Trotsky suggested the possibility of transitions from milder to harsher forms of non-democratic capitalist states (and *vice versa*), and argued that stabilized Fascism would experience a change from within: 'Fascism, once it becomes bureaucratic, approaches very closely other forms of military and police dictatorship . . . Fascism is regenerated into Bonapartism . . . Bonapartism of Fascist origin . . . distinguishes itself by its much greater stability.'[13] This still seems a useful insight into the factors that produce changes within non-democratic states. Francoism appears to be a suggestive case as it was a dictatorship with a rather unique degree of success by its own standards. An apparently contradictory repression, greater individual tolerance, and ideological pluralism seem to have been the product of a strengthened 'normality', of the consolidation of an economic and social order. There were other factors involved as well, though, and they will be discussed in the following chapters. These factors include unintended consequences that stemmed from a process of capitalist economic development and which produced contradictions in the institutional system; they include the persistence of what have been called 'islands of separateness' (Friedrich and Brzezinski 1956: part 6) within the system (in the families, the universities, the factories); finally, the long-term success of underground organizational politics was another crucial factor. These are issues that have to be analysed in order to interpret the emergence of two power-ful movements of dissent under Francoism within the working class and among university students.

The main questions that the following chapters will discuss, then, are, how was organized political dissent possible under the Francoist dictatorship, and can its study possibly be extended to a sociological interpretation of movements of political protest under repressive systems. The chapters will focus on the working-class movement (chapters 2, 3, 4) and the student movement (chapters 5, 6, 7). Why these two movements? Is there any connection between them?

As to the first question, there is little doubt that students and workers were the two crucial political movements working against the dictatorship. Nationalist demands, being as they are a major source of conflict and division in Spain, were never represented by an organized movement in the years of Francoism. They could only have been studied either at the level of a 'general grievance' (particularly in Catalonia) or at the level of a tightly-knit secret terrorist organization (the ETA). In the country as a whole there were only two organized movements of active dissent: the working-class and the student movements, which cross-cut geographical and national differences within Spain. It must also be said that the question of whether there was 'something else' in the politics of dissent under Francoism besides the working-class and the student movement, is largely irrelevant for the purposes of the present study. I have noted earlier that I do not intend to provide an overall and superficial guide to the curiosities of Spanish politics. The object of the book is to analyse what appear to me to be crucial sociological and political questions on social movements and dictatorships. I would finally hope that, indirectly, this discussion will reveal the dynamics of Francoism and of Spanish politics generally in this period of thirty-five years.

As to the second question, the working-class and the student movements were deeply interconnected. This may seem surprising and peculiar to an Anglo-Saxon reader, but this is more an ethnocentric reaction than an objective interpretation of the strong links that frequently exist between workers' and students' movements of resistance under dictatorships. If we look at the Spanish case, the links are visible at several levels. First of all, the crucial turning points of the two movements coincided chronologically. Thus, 1956 saw the first important industrial disputes and also the first expressions of student protest, which led to an important reshuffle in the government. 1962 was the beginning of what was to become an uninterrupted struggle both for the student and the working-class movements: this marked the beginning of a series of strikes (by miners, metal workers, and students), the creation of an underground student organization (FUDE) and the formation in Asturias, the Basque Country, Catalonia, and Madrid of illegal workers' committees as an alternative to the official trade unions. In 1965 two new illegal unions achieved large support from the working class (the Workers' Commissions) and from the students (the *Sindicato Democrático de Estudiantes*). In 1969 repression against both movements became harsher, and there were a number of states of emergency. This, in turn, led to the collapse of the SDE and a deep crisis in the Workers' Commissions, and to the return to a more strict underground struggle. Both the workers' and the students' movements re-emerged from their crisis considerably strengthened in 1973. The two movements obviously have their own history, to be analysed in chapters 2 and 5, but these crucial episodes indicate the links between them. The similarities in these episodes were associated with the dynamics of the regime but also with the policies of underground political parties.

The underground leftist parties were the backbone of the two movements from 1956 and they provided a strong link between working-class and student politics. The most influential parties were the Spanish Communist Party (PCE), the Spanish Socialist Workers' Party (PSOE), and the Popular Liberation Front (FLP), but in the 1970s two Maoist groups, the Workers' Party (PTE) and the Revolutionary Organization of Workers (ORT), replaced the FLP which had disintegrated in 1969. The strategic and tactical ideas of the two movements presented strong similarities: e.g., both movements carried out an underground struggle but they also used legal institutions (often through infiltration: the FUDE's and the Workers' Commissions' 'entryism' into the state-controlled student and labour unions). Also, the movements frequently organized joint actions – this was particularly so after 1967. The size of the Universities of Madrid and Barcelona (Madrid has about 150,000 students) contributed to the political importance of students. Finally, the leaders of both movements frequently occupied important positions in the secret leftist parties. Thus, of the twenty-seven national executive members of the Workers' Commissions, twenty had representative posts in the Communist Party, three in the PTE and three in the ORT; the general secretary and the majority of the executive of UGT were also important members of the PSOE. The great majority of the leaders of FUDE were members of a party, and FUDE itself was the product of a pact between the Communist and the Socialist parties and the FLP. The student leaders were often members of the provincial committee of the party, as representatives of the student section, and later on, after finishing their studies, they were often promoted within the party.

The political inter-connections between both movements can perhaps be illustrated by references to the student movement within the working-class movement (the opposite reference is much more predictable). The first reference is from an interview with a leader of the anarchist trade union, CNT:

'Today the students are in the vanguard of all revolutionary struggles. In the last twenty years they have become part of the vanguard of the working-class movement, they are by no means a 'liberal' movement of adolescents.' (interview no. 16)

The second reference is from very important political documents of the Workers' Commissions[14]. In these documents, the Workers' Commissions 'salute the student movement in which they see a constant, energetic and responsible force in the struggle for democracy'; they denounce the 'repressive measures of which they [the students] are the victims, measures as unjust and brutal as those exercised against ourselves'; they 'call upon all workers to struggle for the liberty of the students arrested and jailed'; and they declare to be 'in favour of still closer coordination between the workers' movement and that of the students ... Programmes can be put forward and agreements reached about forms of mutual assistance in common problems ... The carrying out of common actions, of strikes, distribution of propaganda, meetings, etc., should be uninterrupted.'

The main theoretical characteristic of this book is possibly the use of different but compatible approaches to the central problem of how political dissent is possible under a dictatorship. This issue is divided into several parts, which refer in particular to the possible contradictions between capitalist growth and autocratic institutions. We shall discuss the combination of economic and political factors that encouraged working-class dissent. Then there are the processes of political socialization; the policies of underground organizations and their management of secrecy, mobilization, and recruitment, the experiences of militancy and repression. This kaleidoscopic theoretical approach is associated with a very pragmatic methodology, combining macro- and micro-sociological information, quantitative and qualitative materials. The main sources of evidence included are as follows:

1 The use of newspaper reports on the working-class movement for information on strikes and on repression. This was possible after the 1966 Law on the Press, which led to an exhaustive coverage of strikes by the liberal and popular press. I used, in particular, the national daily newspapers *Ya*, *ABC*, *Madrid*, *Informaciones*, *Alcázar*, and *Pueblo*, for the period 1966–74, and obtained information on 2,287 strikes. This was 29.0 per cent of the total number of strikes according to official reports of the Ministry of Labour for the same period, and, there was a high degree of correspondence in the temporal and geographical distribution of both sets of data. The press reports provided the possibility of a much more disaggregated analysis, which is carried out in chapter 3, to study the patterns of militancy of different working-

class groups. The possibility of significant biases must obviously be accepted, but this is too good a source of information to ignore, particularly if, as it happens, it indicates a pattern of working-class struggle which is consistent with the evidence provided by other sources. Unfortunately, the opacity of politics under dictatorships is not easy to penetrate, and the best use must be made of whatever information is accessible.

2 Secondary sources which consisted in particular of the strike reports of the Ministry of Labour from 1963 to 1974 (on 9,370 disputes), as well as different opinion surveys (the FOESSA survey of 1970 and several surveys of the *Instituto de la Opinión Pública* in 1968 and 1969). These opinion surveys were re-processed with the help of Nuffield College Research Services Unit. The Ministry of Labour reports on strikes were also carefully reanalysed: the statistical results of this reanalysis are used in chapters 2 and 3. The Ministry of Labour data for the fifty Spanish provinces over the twelve-year period 1963–74 were used as the dependent variable in the analysis of industrial conflict which is presented in the first part of chapter 3.

3 Documents from the working-class and student organizations. In the case of the working class these documents were the main political texts of the three major secret trade unions under Francoism – UGT, USO, and the Workers' Commissions, and the documents were used directly as information on the ideology, strategy, and tactics of these organizations. They are analysed in chapter 4. In the case of the student movement, this documentary source was 564 leaflets and pamphlets collected by the *Instituto de Técnicas Sociales* between 1960 and 1970, and which the ITS made available to me.

4 Interviews with student and trade-union leaders. They consisted of long individual meetings which generally lasted three days, and produced two to four hours of tape-recorded information of a semi-structured character. These interviews are intensively used and long quotations are reproduced in chapters 4, 5, 6, and 7, and it seems convenient to say more about them.

The group of student leaders was chosen with the intention that it should be a representative sample of the leaders of the student movement from 1956 to 1970, besides being a satisfactory collection of 'strategic informants'.[15] At the same time, because of the qualitative nature of the evidence that I expected to obtain from the interviews, and because I wanted to discuss processes of socialization, I intended to make use of the 'life history' approach.[16] Two problems had then to be faced. First, the problem of the inferences that could be drawn from the information collected: this problem has existed in most of the researches dealing with intensive interviewing – that of Lane, Becker, Matza, Keniston[17] – and it was made worse by the fact that the movement was a clandestine one. Second, the problem of access: that is, of contacting informants and obtaining information within a close community.

The first step was to construct a population of leaders from 1956 to 1970 through a reputational method, checked by personal 'total immersion'[18], by the literature on the events, and the published names of students who had suffered different forms of sanctions in that period. The reputational method began with four individuals, whose political activity took place between 1956 and 1970. Each of them was selected as a representative member of the four main political groups within the Spanish student movement in that period: the Spanish Communist Party ('*Partido Communista de España*', PCE), the Spanish Socialist Party ('*Partido Socialista Obrero Español*', PSOE), a very influential left-wing socialist party ('*Frente de Liberación Popular*', FLP), and the group of radical militants without a party affiliation. Each of them was used intensively as an informant and as a representative interviewee (see Dexter 1970). As informants, they were asked about the characteristics of the movement, of the particular political parties, about events, strategies, and tactics, about procedures of recruitment, and they were asked to describe 'systematic' militants of the movement, giving details about their period of militancy, political affiliation, and the faculty where they studied. Systematic militancy was defined on two criteria: ideological (socialism) and positional (holding posts in legal and/or clandestine organizations – political parties or student unions). From the beginning, the strong consensus existing between the different informants about the population of radical militants/leaders was one of the salient facts of the development of the research: there was a constant overlapping of reported militants/leaders in the successive information provided by the different informants, which was an indication of the *gemeinshaftslich* character of the student movement during most of that period.

As the population of militants/leaders was being drawn up, it was structured in cells which were constructed using three criteria: the successive political periods (or stages of the movement), the different political groups, and the Faculties. These cells were the basis for the selection of each of the following forty-six interviewees/informants, as they indicated the composition of the student movement. The selection *between* cells was made so as to reach a representative sample (from the point of view of periods, political groups, and Faculties) of interviewees which would also be a group of representative 'informants'. The selection of an individual *within* a cell was made at random. I do not think that the random character of the selection was significantly hampered by the fact that the reputational reconstruction of the population and the development of the interviewing programme were carried out simultaneously. The majority of the population were known from the start, and in the first period of the interviewing programme, selection was made from the larger cells so as to maximize the random character of the ongoing selection. The reputational reconstruction of the population and the interviewing programme concluded when it became apparent that the limits of the population had been reached (no new information on militants/leaders was provided in the last eighteen interviews); and when the sample was considered to provide a satisfactory representation of the population (fifty individuals out of 232, whose internal distribution by the three criteria used – periods, political groups, and Faculties – strongly corresponded). All the interviewees were considered both as representative cases, providing accounts of personal experiences following a life history pattern, and as strategic informants, providing evidence on external processes, policies, and events. As for the problem of access, that is, of the necessary steps required to enter and study a secret political community, it was solved here by my personal political identity, which was known to the interviewees and by the political groups involved. Both the interviewees and the political groups were informed of the purpose of the research and about its eventual publication. There was not a single case of refusal to be interviewed but the whereabouts of two individuals in the initial interviewing sample were unknown, so others had to be substituted. The interviewing programme was carried out in June–September 1972, December 1972, January 1973, and May–September 1973. Among the student leaders that I interviewed was Francisco Sauquillo, who, with four other Communist lawyers, was later murdered by a Fascist gang on January 24, 1977. I hope that this book will be a testament to the struggle that he maintained against the dictatorship, together with many other militants of secret political organizations.

The group of trade-union leaders was intended to provide evidence only as strategic informants. Thus, the problem of the representativeness of the group in relation to an unknown population of trade-union leaders was not faced, and would indeed have been difficult to solve (this population must have been incomparably larger than that of student leaders and also much harder to reconstruct through a reputational method). My intention was to interview a group of politically representative trade-union leaders, and the selection of the group was done as follows.

The first step was to contact one important representative for each of the four unions that I wanted to study – UGT, USO, CNT, and the Workers' Commissions. I interviewed these first four contacts as representative informants, and I asked them to provide me with additional names of militants occupying important posts and who could supply me with relevant information. I obtained fifty-two names and I selected seventeen. The distribution of these seventeen leaders of working-class unions was as follows. Five represented the orthodox communist faction which was dominant within the leadership of the Workers' Commissions (they were also members of the PCE – the Spanish Communist Party). Three represented the minoritarian left-wing Communist faction within the Workers' Commissions (the PTE and the ORT, both with Maoist programmes). One was an independent member of the Workers' Commissions, that is, without party affiliation. Four were leaders of the socialist union UGT. Two were leaders of the socialist union USO. Two were representative militants of the anarchist CNT. However, these two final interviews concentrated in particular on the period 1939–60. From the 1950s, and until the summer of 1976, the CNT does not seem to have played an important role in the re-emergence of the Spanish working-class movement for several reasons: it was a vulnerable organization which suffered mass repression and was poorly suited to underground resistance; there were deep occupational changes in the areas where this union gathered most of its support; it opposed political parties and was militantly anti-communist, which made underground survival more difficult. Only from the second half of 1976 did the CNT start to recover influence, helped by the new conditions of tolerance of post-Francoism. All the interviewees held representative posts either at a national level (eight) or at the provincial level of Madrid (nine), and at least one national representative was interviewed for each of the groups. All those prospective interviewees who were contacted agreed to be interviewed, and each interview generally took three days (as in the case of students), providing between two and four hours of tape-recorded conversation. The themes covered national politics, the politics of the unions, and personal aspects of politics, and they are discussed in chapter 4. The interviewing programme was carried out between October 1975 and August 1976.

2 The re-emergence of a working-class movement under a dictatorship: economic growth and industrial relations in Spain

The present chapter will discuss the contradictions that rapid capitalist economic growth may generate within the core institutional areas of dictatorial states: and it will seek to show how these contradictions created new possibilities for working-class action under Francoism. The discussion will have to face a crucial problem: that of the relationship between, on the one hand, the development of a secret working-class movement *and*, on the other, the evolution of a capitalist economy and a dictatorial state.

In the earlier chapter, I stressed the need to analyse non-pluralist capitalist states by considering their policies in terms of their consequences for class domination and for the organization of capitalist production and accumulation. Political sociology has often interpreted processes of economic growth within non-democratic regimes as producing contradictions in the institutional order of society and as presenting a difficult challenge to the existing political power. From this perspective, the political control of change is a difficult task: due to an assumed structural interdependence between the different elements of the social system, a modification in one institutional area tends to influence others and to bring pressure towards generalized change. Isolated changes in the production system lead to dysfunctions with other institutional areas, and to a tendency to develop new unofficial social relations and institutions.[1] There are some clear similarities in functionalist, Marxist, and *Marxisant* conceptions of 'system contradictions' as an important source of social strain and political conflict (see Lockwood 1964 and Parkin 1972).

This discussion seems relevant in two respects: first, it could be said that 'system contradictions' associated with processes of capitalist growth may help to explain the transition from a rigid form of dictatorial state to a more 'flexible' one. Second, it would be possible to see connections between these contradictions and the resurgence of a working-class movement within a dictatorship that has destroyed working-class organizations and has set up a labour-repressive regime. The Spanish case provides good ground for a critical analysis of these questions, as it is a European society with a considerably developed economy, which grew at a fast rate under a dictatorial form of state. The Spanish experience of economic growth under Francoism may be considered as presenting a set of quasi-experimental conditions: *ceteris paribus*, the period 1939–55 as capitalist autarchy and stagnation without democracy, and the period 1955–75 as capitalist development without democracy.

1 The State and the economy

At the end of the Civil War, the new State attempted to reorganize the underdeveloped Spanish capitalist economy on the lines of an autarchic model. The goal was to transform the country into a self-sufficient economic unit, and this also included the protection of non-competitive and costly private industries. The autarchic model of the economy was particularly supported by 'protectionist' capitalist groups, but it was generally accepted by Spanish capitalism, first in the context of the Second World War, which immediately followed the end of the Spanish war, and later in the context of the economic and political isolation of Spain after the victory of the Allies in 1945. The State tried to implement the autarchic economic model with policies that sought to replace imports by national goods, using protectionist tariff barriers and quantitative restrictions on imports.

The autarchic economic policies were intended to promote rapid industrialization under economic protectionism, a labour-repressive regime, and a State-led mobilization of resources. The Second World War posed problems for the implementation of these policies, due in particular to the difficulties of importing basic capital goods and machinery that would provide the foundations of industrialization and later make the progressive substitution of imported manufactured goods possible. But the end of the Second World War and the subsequent political and economic isolation of the Spanish regime (1946–50) reinforced the autarchic economic orientation[2]. It was now also a defensive policy: besides being seen as an instrument for a sustained industrialization and for strengthening the Spanish capitalist elite, it appeared as the only alternative for the economic survival of the regime.

Under the autarchic framework that lasted roughly from 1939 to 1955, the new State tried to stimulate industrialization with a constant flow of money from the Bank of Spain. However, the flow of printed money did not produce intensive investment in manufacturing: it was often used for short-term speculative investments, while productive investment was being detracted by the low level of the internal aggregate demand, by the limited markets, and also by incongruencies in the tax system (e.g. the fact that capital allocated to the sinking fund was considered as profit). Private capital was not taking advantage of the internal political context, and Spanish capitalism remained in a weak and stagnant condition for more than fifteen years. An example of such weakness is that, in the 1950s, the average number of workers employed in an industrial plant was only eleven[3] and productivity did not increase. A typical capitalist strategy in the years of autarchy was first, to achieve a satisfactory tariff protection from foreign competition, second, to get a licence to import raw materials, and third, to achieve national predominance in a particular area of economic activity obtaining from the state a good share of the national production. Capitalist activity was not so much cost-orientated as demand-orientated: competition was almost non-existent, and the state machinery controlled imports, production, distribution, and prices in a rickety capitalist economy.

State intervention was to a large extent carried out through the *Instituto Nacional de Industria* (the National Institute for Industry), created in 1941 to carry out a similar economic role as the Italian IRI. Its main purpose was to intervene in economic areas that did not offer lucrative prospects to private capital or that required large investments, and this was justified by a *'principio de subsidiariedad'*. (principle of subsidiarity) according to which public funds were subsidiary to private capital, with the consequence that as soon as an economic activity became profitable it was taken over again by private firms. The activities of the INI extended to steel and metallurgy, chemicals, shipbuilding, electricity, mining, petrochemicals, oil refineries, synthetic fibres and cellulose, manure, foodstuffs, and transport. These economic activities of the INI were mostly financed by credits from the Bank of Spain and budget consignments, and they became a major source of inflation. From 1941 to 1949, the INI lacked economic planning, was poorly managed, and made a series of disastrous economic decisions: there was neither public control of its activities and of its use of huge public funds, nor questioning of the subordination of national resources to private profit through the 'principle of subsidiarity'.

The process of private capital accumulation was based on profit-making through labour-intensive production and inflationary pricing in an economy with a weak productive structure and scarce consumer goods. As has been said, this process of capital accumulation was protected by state intervention through the INI and by the constant creation of money by the Bank of Spain. But an additional factor in the nature of capitalist industrialization and capital accumulation under Francoism was the corporatist organization of the working class, following somewhat the model of Fascist Italy: the 'sindicatos verticales' had some similarities with the Italian 'corporazioni'. They were indeed a key element in the Francoist political system and a congruent development of the philosophy of the 'organic state'.

The workers were compulsorily affiliated into single organizations for each branch of production. These organizations were 'mixed', that is, workers and management were brought together into the same union. These organizations were also non-democratic: their representatives were not elected but nominated by the regime. The sindicatos were part of the state, they participated strongly in the Cortes (the non-democratic parliament) and had a minister within the Cabinet. The political centrality of this corporatist organization was explicitly underlined, as the 'organic' Nuevo Estado was defined as nacional-sindicalista ('national-syndicalist'). This definition may be found in the Programme of the Falange, where it is also stated that 'we shall assure the corporatist organization of Spanish society through a system of vertical unions in the different branches of production, at the service of national economic integrity' (point 9), and that 'our regime will make class struggle radically impossible, through the integration of every contributor within an organic totality' (point 11).

A constitutional law developed this corporatist conception. Thus, the Fuero del Trabajo (Labour Charter), promulgated in 1938 and with many similarities to the Italian Carta del Lavoro of 1927 and the Portuguese Estatuto do Trabalho Nacional of 1933, declared that 'the vertical unions are a corporation ... hierarchically ordered under the direction of the state ... whose posts of command will necessarily behove on militants of *FET y de las JONS* [Falange] ... [and they are] an instrument to the service of the state'. The Labour Charter also pointed out that 'the national production constitutes an economic unity at the service of the country' and that 'any individual or collective activity that in any manner disturbs or attacks the normality of production will be considered as a crime against the state'. Three additional laws passed in August 1939, January and December 1940, further implemented the subordination of the *sindicatos verticales* (the 'vertical' corporatist unions) to the single party and to the state.

Besides the regimentation of the working class within a labour-repressive system, the state took command of the regulation of industrial relations. Collective bargaining did not exist; a 1942 law created the *reglamentaciones de trabajo*: they were official norms produced by the Ministry of Labour, which set wages and work conditions and which were compulsory for every industrial branch and every single firm. The right to strike and the right to autonomous and democratic trade-unionization were suppressed, along with political parties, political expressions of dissent, and democratic political representation.

The costs of the war, military defeat, exile, and post-war repression[4] played their part in lowering resistance from the working class and the traditional left-wing unions and parties to the creation and functioning of this corporatist labour-repressive institutional structure after 1939. The two big labour unions – the anarchist CNT (*Confederación Nacional de Trabajadores*) and the socialist UGT (*Unión General de Trabajadores*) – had been dissolved after the civil war, outlawed, and their militants persecuted, as had also been the case with all working-class political parties. Attempts to organize an underground military resistance, in the form of the *maquis*, lost all possibility of success after 1945, once the Francoist regime survived the end of the Second World War. In October 1948, the socialist guerrilla came to an end. The socialist and anarchist organizations had difficulties in adapting themselves to the new conditions: the former because of a political error it committed by operating mainly in exile, waiting for the expected collapse of the Francoist regime in a post-Fascist Europe; the latter because of its short-term activity of terrorism after the civil war and as a result of an organizational structure little suited to clandestine struggle. This led to a gradual elimination of anarchist groups within Spain and to their progressive confinement to organizations in exile (see Romero-Maura 1971). The Communist Party (PCE) readapted itself more easily to the new situation – it was much smaller, better protected, with a rigidly centralized direction and important financial support. From the early 1950s the PCE was slowly rebuilding its organization in the interior of Spain, and developing a strategical and tactical programme which was based on the principle of struggle from within[5].

The 1950s brought a number of changes to Spanish politics. The new tensions in the international context – the Cold War, Berlin, Czechoslovakia, and Korea – ended Spain's isolation. In August 1950, the US Congress agreed to provide financial help for the Francoist regime. In 1951 the diplomatic and economic boycott came to an end and in 1953 an agreement between the US and the Spanish governments was an important landmark in a slow change of economic orientation within the Spanish regime, which consisted of a progressive shift away from autarchic industrialization to a liberalization of economic policies[6]. Increasing expansion of economic activity followed: there were greater credit facilities, foreign trade was normalized, and the growth of *per capita* income, which between 1941 and 1950 had been non-existent (in fact, there had been a slightly negative rate of −0.02), reached an annual rate of 3.3 between 1951 and 1960 (6.9 between 1955 and 1956) while the GNP *per capita* between 1951 and 1958 grew at an annual rate of 4.45 – higher than any other European society except West Germany and Italy (Fundación FOESSA 1970: 56). The population active in agriculture fell from 49 to 42 per cent between 1950 and 1960[7]. External migrations began to contribute to the growth of Spanish capitalism: on the one hand, they provided essential earnings to the balance of payments (second only to tourism, which also started to increase in the 1950s); on the other, they provided a safety valve for the policy of full employment that was part of the populist rhetoric of the regime. However, the related shortage of skilled manpower in Spain pushed wages up, particularly after 1962. Economic development in Spain in the 1960s was no longer based on wage-squeezing.

The reactivation of the Spanish economy influenced industrial relations. The labour market began to operate increasingly independent of governmental controls. Managerial strategies of linking productivity with wage increases resulted in a progressive gap between real and official wages, in a period where productivity and competition again became the main concern for important sections of management. Wage drifting was especially acute in Spain in the mid 1950s and contributed to the inflationary process. From a capitalist point of view, anti-inflationary policies required strict wage controls and work conditions and productivity more flexible than the official norms of the Ministry of Labour (the *Reglamentaciones de Trabajo*). Two decrees in 1956 were a first attempt to introduce some changes in the system of industrial relations and to attribute to management a greater margin of manoeuvre for informal agreements with the workers. The changes were intended to favour the more competitive firms and to stimulate productivity.

The new economic directions were reinforced by a cabinet change in February 1957. This reshuffle was an expression of a shift in the balance of power within the Francoist regime: finance capitalism had reached a position of economic hegemony in the heterogeneous social and political coalition of the dictatorship. The new government introduced reforms in the tax system and in the Public Administration; it unified the foreign exchange of the currency; it also tried to stimulate productivity, control wage increments and prices, and to this effect set up a system of collective bargaining which was seen as an important part of the economic policies. The participation of Spain in the international capitalist scene was also increased: Spain successively joined the International Monetary Fund, the World Bank and the OECD, and the government started negotiations with the European Economic Community. Finally, the new government started a policy of indicative planning whose first product in 1959 was a stabilization plan. This stabilization plan included devaluation of the peseta, restrictions on imports and financial help to exports, reduction in public expenditure, a credit squeeze, and a wages and salaries freeze[8].

The second half of the 1950s was not only a period of economic change, for it was then that the first overt manifestations of working-class struggle (and student dissent as well) took place. There had been a few scattered strikes before 1956 (particularly in 1947 and 1951) but they had never been on a large scale. These first industrial conflicts were isolated, often violent, and, of course, illegal. Political repression, the control of the corporatist bureaucracy, in a climate of difficult economic conditions, produced a sort of fatalistic radicalism in these first struggles, which were led by Asturian miners and metal workers from the Basque Country and Barcelona. At this stage there was no effective underground trade-union organization; UGT and CNT were being persecuted very harshly. Between 1940 and 1947 seventeen national executive committees of CNT were arrested and between 1939 and 1954 seven of the UGT. The nature of repression can be seen in the execution in 1948 of twenty-two miners members of the UGT in Asturias[9] in the mine '*Pozo Funeres*' by means of dynamite and petrol; and in the death of Tomás Centeno, the general secretary of this union, in February 1953 at the headquarters of the General Direction of Security in Madrid. Mobilization of the workers was very difficult to organize and the effects of the Stabilization Plan (including a wages freeze, greater unemployment, etc.) added to the difficulties. In 1962 the stabilization plan ended and the economy started again to expand. The annual rate of GNP growth between 1960 and 1965 was 9.2 – the rates of two other growing European economies, Italy and Portugal, were respectively 5.1 and 5.8 (OCDE 1966: 23). The annual rate of growth of the *per capita* income between 1960 and 1966 was 7.5 (Fundación FOESSA 1967: 56). Industrialization brought about radical changes in the social structure. The proportion of active population employed in agriculture fell from 42 per cent in 1960 to 30 per cent in 1966 and to 25 per cent in 1971. Between 1960 and 1968 more than one million people (in a population slightly over 30 millions) either rural proletariat, or small peasants, abandoned agriculture (Pérez-Díaz 1972; Barbancho 1967: 103–129). Redistribution of the population was dramatic: internal migrations between 1961 and 1968 totalled 2,949,466 men and women; the process of urbanization was very intensive (whereas in 1960 19.1 per cent of the population lived in cities of over 100,000 inhabitants, the percentage for 1965 was 32.7 per cent, higher than Italy, Sweden, or the USSR), and between 1960 and 1967 1,879,247 Spanish workers had emigrated to different European countries[10].

The state tried to foster and orientate economic growth following the French example of indicative planning and the first Development Plan was introduced in 1964. Growth was very high over the following decade, with an annual average around 7 per cent of GNP, while unemployment was never above 2 per cent, which was helped by the considerable emigration to other European countries that took place. Development was however very uneven: it did not include any reform of agriculture. The public sector was always managed according to the 'principle of subsidiarity' and to the interests of private capital. The tax system was cumbersome and regressive. There was no solution to the disequilibrium between supply of manufactured goods and aggregate demand (a disequilibrium due to fast-expanding private consumption and public expenditure and which produced an increasing balance of payments deficit). These characteristics of the process of development meant that inflation was always very high and that the regime had to use stop-go policies which included monetary restrictions and wage controls (particularly in 1967 and 1971).

It is in the new context of economic expansion and occupational *bouleversement* from the end of 1961 that the resurgence of an organized movement of working-class dissent must be placed. These changes brought about new conditions for working-class organization and struggle. The underground groups also became more active. At the beginning of the 1960s, the socialist UGT and the anarchist CNT formed a coalition with a Basque working-class organization (the STV, *Solidaridad de Trabajadores Vascos*): the *Alianza Sindical*. Later, in 1962, dissident elements of UGT and CNT established a new coalition with a small Catalan organization (the *Solidaridad de Obreros Cristianos de Cataluña*): it was known as the ASO (*Alianza Sindical Obrera*), and it also attracted a group from the Basque STV and found support from the International Federation of Metal Workers. At the same time the Spanish Communist Party was trying to set up a new trade union, the *Oposición Sindical Obrera* (OSO). The proliferation of groups of very different strength was perhaps the most salient characteristic of underground trade unionism in that period[11]. It was also, of course, a manifestation of weakness. But the new conditions that existed in Spanish society in the 1960s soon provided a better ground for the reorganization of the trade-union movement. This reorganization was going to take place from below, from the struggle at the shop-floor level and from the intensive use of collective bargaining.

2 The changes in the system of industrial relations

As has been noted, three institutional elements were fundamental to the Francoist regime. They were (a) the corporatist organization of the working class in the *Sindicatos Verticales* (with compulsory affiliation and appointments to representative posts made by political designation); (b) the prohibition of strikes (article 222 of the Penal Code defined strikes as acts of sedition); (c) the handing over to the Ministry of Labour of entire responsibility for regulating conditions of work, wages, productivity, and industrial relations (according to the '*Fuero del Trabajo*' of 1938 – which is a constitutional law – and the law of '*Reglamentaciones de Trabajo*' of 1942).

The general reorientation of the Spanish economy, from the mid-1950s, towards growth and integration within the capitalist world placed new stresses on these three central institutional features of the Francoist regime. Such strains were due to the dysfunction of these institutions in the new context, their incompatibility with the new requirements of an economy in a process of industrialization and development. This institutional maladjustment also brought about new conditions for the expression of working-class conflict. Confronted with these problems, the policy of the political regime consisted of attempts to keep institutional change to a minimum and always under control, thereby trying to isolate economic and political consequences.

The steps that the government took between 1953 and 1958 to modify the industrial relations system must be seen in this light. Such steps consisted, in particular, of the setting up of two new institutions: the '*jurados de empresa*' (which had certain similarities with shop steward committees) and a system of collective bargaining ('*convenios colectivos*').

The development of the '*jurados de empresa*' represented a modification in the corporatist organization of the working class, which had been such an essential feature of the regime in its first twenty years. The new system of collective bargaining was also a substantial change from the former regulation procedures with regard to conditions of work, wages, productivity, and industrial relations. Both innovations were closely linked: in order to negotiate an agreement there was a need for genuine worker representation. Unrepresentative delegates would hinder the compliance with, and the effectiveness of, any agreement, and the growth of productivity would be hampered. As a result of such logic, some managerial groups had begun pressing at that time for some democratization of the official trade unions[12]. The '*jurados de empresa*' were supposed to satisfy these demands: the official trade-union organization was still to remain 'vertical' and 'mixed', but there was a new autonomy and a new form of democratic representation at the shop-floor level.

The establishment of the system of collective bargaining had, as primary goals, an increase in productivity within industry and the introduction of rationalization in organization of work methods. Delamotte has discussed the importance of a system of collective bargaining for an economic policy that seeks to link wage claims with productivity increases. For this to be possible, there has to be a basic agreement between management and workers about the dependence of wage claims upon the prosperity of the firm (Delamotte 1962, vol. II: 204–14; Crozier 1962); collective bargaining must reflect this consensus. In Spain collective bargaining certainly did seem to have important consequences for the growth of productivity, but the powerlessness of the workers and the new powers of management seem to have been more important than any such consensus. A content analysis of 583 collective agreements completed in 1963 (50.5 per cent of the total of agreements for that year) shows that procedures for the control and stimulation of personal productivity were introduced in 475 cases, that is in 81.5 per cent of the total. The new economic policies, based on state indicative planning and wage controls, also required precise information about the existing wage levels within each branch of industry to stem wage drifting. The former '*Reglamentaciones de Trabajo'* were norms established from above and were generally out of touch with the real situation within firms in the 1950s. It had come to be the norm that management agreed to informal procedures of wage negotiation with the workers – in many cases with non-official representatives – as a way of increasing productivity and of dealing with industrial relations within the plants.

Both institutions – the *'jurados de empresa'*, as a form of works' committees, and the system of collective bargaining – could then be interpreted as being linked with the changes in the economy. They were instances of controlled institutional change and were intended to be a response to the new requirements of economic development and to the resulting institutional tensions. There is little doubt that the new liberalizing economic policies and the rate of economic growth created new demands which could not be met by the labour institutions that existed within the autarchic and corporatist organization of the economy. Both the *'jurados de empresa'* and the system of collective bargaining attempted to absorb the illegal but increasingly important shop-floor workers' representatives and the extra-legal, informal worker/management negotiations. Both tried to bridge the gap between official and obsolete institutions on the one hand and non-official institutional alternatives on the other.

From 1959 to 1964 there was rapid development in the new system of collective bargaining. In 1959, 179 collective agreements were established, covering 427,636 jobs, and by the end of the next five-year period 4,772 collective agreements had been negotiated[13]. This expansion of collective bargaining increased the strains within the old corporatist organization of the official trade unions. Most of the bargaining was taking place at the shop-floor level, drifting away from the control of the corporatist bureaucracy, both because of the interests of the workers and of management. Such shop-floor bargaining was especially intensive in the steel, metal, chemical, and building industries, and also in Barcelona, Biscaye, and Madrid (*Organización Sindical 1965*). These branches of industry and these geographical areas experienced at the same time a considerable strengthening of shop-floor organization and worker representation.

Although these innovations in the system of industrial relations were closely controlled, they had unintended consequences. In the first place, economic inflation in the 1950s and the Stabilization Plan of 1959 had created very strong wage grievances, which after 1962 (with the end of stabilization) produced an explosion in collective bargaining. In the second place, the strengthening of shop-floor workers' representation both legal (*jurados de empresa*) and illegal, progressively undermined the official trade-unions, as a result of the increasing gap between shop-floor representation and the national corporatist bureaucracy. Both phenomena reinforced each other: from 1962 onwards shop-floor representation (legal and illegal) and collective bargaining provided new conditions for the manifestation of claims, disputes, and antagonisms.

These institutional modifications came, then, to be important determinants of industrial conflict and dissent. They provided means for a working-class struggle that had not existed before under the Francoist regime and allowed for the reorganization of militant working-class groups. Collective bargaining created a margin – however limited – for the free expression of workers' interests and often became a useful tool for mobilization, pressure, and action. Deadlocks in collective bargaining arose frequently and a procedure of compulsory arbitration through the Ministry of Labour ('*Normas de Obligado Cumplimiento*') was established for these cases. Whereas 63,051 workers were involved in 1963 in this system of compulsory arbitration, the number increased to 438,288 in 1965. In 1966, 79 per cent of the workers from the steel and metal industries and 58 per cent of the miners had their conditions of work regulated by compulsory arbitration; in contrast, this was the case for only 7.4 per cent of agricultural labourers (Roldán 1966). The new system of collective bargaining was becoming a major factor in the reorganization of the working-class movement, whereas the shop-floor '*jurados de empresa*' was often used by underground groups as a legal platform for working-class mobilization. However, as a result of infiltration by militants from secret political groups, 1,800 '*jurados de empresa*' were dismissed from their posts between 1964 and 1966 – and the number increased in the following years.

3 The growth of organized working-class dissent

The working-class movement started to emerge again in 1962. The end of economic stabilization, the extension of collective bargaining promoted by management to increase productivity and by workers to advance wage claims, and the expansion of shop-floor organization from 1957 onwards contributed to the great increase in working-class activity. In the first months of the year a wave of strikes spread in Valencia, Barcelona, Madrid, Cartagena, and the Basque Country. In April, May, and June a second wave of strikes involved coal mining in Asturias, metal, chemical, electrical, and shipbuilding industries in the Basque Country, and metal industries in Barcelona. These strikes reached the mining zone of Linares, Puertollano, and Riotinto, and some of the metal industries of Madrid. At this stage the most dramatic strikes occurred in mining, where long and desperate confrontations took place. The crisis in coal mining was leading to a drastic conversion of the Asturian industry. Production was decreasing: for instance, whereas the volume in 1962 was 7,904,427 metrical tones, it was down to 7,140,056 in 1963. The level of redundancies was high: between 1959 and 1962 11.2 per cent of the employed labour force[14]. A general strike in the Asturian mines lasted from July 16 to September 20, 1962. In the country as a whole there were 425 industrial conflicts in 1962[15] and, even though most of them were very local and restricted, they heralded a significant change in the dynamics of industrial relations and of political life in Spanish society. The sudden explosion of industrial conflict made it impossible for the definition of strikes as acts of sedition (as they were defined in article 222 of the Penal Code, which was finally re-modelled in 1965) to be maintained and it led to a new decree which opened the way for a legalization of 'economic' (sic) strikes and instituted a complicated mechanism of compulsory mediation and arbitration.

1962 was also an important date for the development of a movement of works' committees elected in workshops, pits, building sites, and offices, and which were independent of the state-controlled trade unions. The movement had started in the Asturian mines; the first reported case took place during a very long strike in the mine La Camocha. When management wanted to negotiate, the miners elected a democratic committee. It progressively spread through the country, particularly in the metal industry of the Basque Country. These shop-floor committees were a major innovation in industrial relations in Spain. In steel, metal, and mining they took the lead in collective bargaining and in industrial conflicts. UGT and USO joined this movement and supported the factory committees against the official trade union by trying to turn them into an open challenge to the state-led *Sindicatos*.

A different view of factory committees soon emerged: the factory committees were seen as a possible embryo new trade-union movement, going beyond the traditional forms of trade-union organization represented by UGT and CNT. The new trade-union movement would develop from factory assemblies and factory committees and it would eventually become a single unified trade union. This conception was particularly defended by the Spanish Communist Party (PCE), which from 1963–64 stopped supporting OSO and jumped onto the bandwagon of the factory committees. What was to become the 'Workers' Commissions' was, thus, first a movement and later an organization. While in its first phase as a movement it consisted of autonomous shop-floor committees elected by the workers and which were compatible with existing democratic trade unions; in its second phase it became more of an organized trade union (although the difference between 'movement' and 'organization' was rather ambiguous). It was then that existing trade unions opted out – the UGT in particular, whereas USO remained within *Comisiones Obreras* for a longer period (until 1967). The Workers' Commissions were thenceforward dominated by the Communist Party, but left-wing Catholic organizations retained considerable influence (FST and AST – later to become a Marxist organization: the *Organización Revolucionaria de Trabajadores*, ORT). A turning point in the attempt to convert the Workers' Commissions from a movement into an organization was the formation in 1964 of the Workers' Commission of the Metal Industry of Madrid. This became the main catalyst in the process of development of a network of Workers' Commissions in different branches of industry and all over the country, which were coordinated by provincial inter-branch commissions and by a national executive. It is, however, true to say that the 'organized' Workers' Commissions did not absorb the movement of elected workers' committees, although both overlapped to a large extent.

One basic difference between the organized Workers' Commissions and the movement of workers' committees was that the former followed a strategic policy of infiltration and occupation of the official *jurados de empresa* (that is, the shop-floor legal committees which were, since the mid-1950s, the lower *échelon* of the state-controlled trade unions). The Communist Party had been trying to infiltrate the official trade unions during this period, and the Workers' Commissions successfully carried out this strategy. They were particularly effective in the metal industries of Madrid (mostly in the large factories of the south and south-west of the capital) and in those of Barcelona (mostly in the areas of the *Baix Llobregat* and the *Vallés*), but less so in Asturias and in the Basque Country, where UGT was relatively stronger and where a strategy of open boycott of the official trade unions found wide support. This was indeed one of the major differences between UGT, which defended the latter strategy of boycott, and *Comisiones*, which defended the former strategy of infiltration, and it will be discussed in greater detail in Chapter 4. *Comisiones* thus resulted from the attempt (particularly by the Communist Party) to try to form into a new and eventually single union both the autonomous workers' councils which had spread since the early 1960s *and* the groups of officially elected workers' delegates (*jurados de empresa*) who were seen as active or as truly representative (and which often included Communist Party militants). *Comisiones Obreras* were thus based on legal and illegal workers' committees. UGT, which had taken part in the movement of autonomous workers' councils, never accepted absorbtion into the structure of *Comisiones*, which was controlled by the Communist Party and whose intention was to relegate UGT to historical oblivion.

It is therefore not surprising that at first *Comisiones* were granted a semi-legal existence. They were seen as an extra-legal but not necessarily subversive organization of shop-floor representatives of the *jurados de empresa*, and some 'liberalizing' members of the regime considered them as a potentially promising development of the official trade unions. For *Comisiones*, however, activity at the level of the legal shop-floor committees was only an instrument in the struggle against the corporatist system and in the strengthening of their underground organization. It was a means for undermining the official trade unions from within and for acquiring greater influence among the working class through public activities[16]. This aim was clearly presented by one of the leaders of *Comisiones*, Julián Ariza:

> 'When wide sectors of the working-class movement participate in the union elections and defend the idea of using the premises and material means of the official union, we do so not because we accept its structure, its principles or its hierarchies. We do so to facilitate the exercise of workers' democracy ... The use of legality in this area demands, in fact, the exercise of trade-union rights and simultaneously negates the validity of the official scheme.'[17]

The elections for official trade-union representatives, in September 1966, were a great success for the Workers' Commissions and, as a result, the double struggle from within and from outside the official corporatist organization was intensified. This success, together with the possibilities for working-class mobilization, resulting from the new system of collective bargaining, and the strategic use of everyday claims and negotiations by all the underground trade unions, reflected the increase in working-class activity and rising industrial conflict from 1966. *Table* 1 shows the evolution of industrial conflict since that date[18].

The strength of working-class militancy from the late 1960s may be assessed in comparison with France, where in the 1970s the total of hours lost through strikes per year was around three million, in a situation where working-class organizations and militants were not persecuted and where strikes were not illegal. The consequence of this growing strength was that repression was intensified after 1967: states of emergency were declared in 1968 in the Basque Country and in 1969 and 1970 in the country as a whole. In 1968 the Supreme Court defined the Workers' Commissions as illegal and subversive organizations. Repression against secret working-class organizations was intensified on three levels: dismissal from jobs, dismissal from the official posts of shop-floor representation (the *jurados de empresa*), and direct political sanctions through the Public Order Court.

Table 1   Evolution of disputes between 1966 and 1974

	number of disputes	number of hours lost through strikes
1966	179	1,478,080
1967	567	1,887,693
1968	351	1,925,278
1969	491	4,476,727
1970	1,595	8,738,916
1971	616	6,877,500
1972	853	4,692,925
1973	931	8,649,265
1974	2,290	13,989,557
1975	3,156	14,521,901
1976 (first three months)	—	50,000,000 (estimate)

The stronger repressive policies of the government produced a deep internal crisis within the Workers' Commissions. As has been said, this organization had not followed a strategy based on a clandestine long-term struggle but had been operating at a quasi-public level. This had made it very vulnerable and, from 1968 onwards, its provincial and national committees were repeatedly harassed by police actions. The most spectacular arrest was that of the nine leading members of the national executive in 1972, which led to what was known as 'process 1,001' and which resulted in prison sentences ranging from six to twenty years. As a consequence, some groups within *Comisiones* demanded a strategic move to underground activity, greater effort in creating a less vulnerable organization, and also a shift from plant and factory struggle to a wider political arena[19]. This policy was defended by two Maoist organizations, the PTE (Workers' Party of Spain) and the ORT (Revolutionary Workers' Organization), against the Communist Party line. As a result of repression and of these internal divisions, the Workers' Commissions were weakened considerably between 1968 and 1973. Eventually the Communist Party was again able to impose its strategy of using legal platforms, quasi-public organization, and open mobilization of the workers, while an effort was also made to safeguard against repression by better organization at the grass-roots, by the wider involvement of militants in representation, and also by securing working-class support within the factories. The crisis in the Workers' Commissions at this period was particularly acute in the metal industries of Madrid, which had been one of the areas of working-class militancy since 1966. It must, however, be noted, and this is an important point, that the crisis in *Comisiones* did not result at all in a decrease in the workers' struggle: on the one hand, actions of solidarity against repression increased; on the other, the other organizations – UGT and USO in particular – were not affected by the internal difficulties of *Comisiones*.

Working-class conflict was particularly intensified in industrialized areas with large proletarian concentrations. This aspect of the struggle of the Spanish working class will be analysed later in Chapter 3. The Basque Country, Barcelona, Madrid, and Asturias provided 70 per cent of the total number of confrontations between 1963 and 1974. Industrial conflict was also especially intensive in the steel, metal, mining, and building industries. *Table 2* shows the distribution of industrial disputes by branches of industry for the period 1963–74.

Table 2   Distribution of industrial conflict by branches of industry between 1963 and 1974

branches of industry	N	%	active labour force	ratio ALF/average disputes per year
steel and metallurgy	4,172	44.5	991,700	2,850
mining	1,224	13.1	177,900	1,744
building	899	9.6	925,000	12,333
textile	553	5.9	713,400	15,509
chemicals	448	4.8	196,200	5,303

The growth of working-class militancy was based on the activity of steel and metal workers. Their weight within the working-class movement increased slightly after 1967: in the next eight years they produced 47 per cent of the confrontations. Conflicts were concentrated in medium-sized or big factories: between 1968 and 1974, 67.4 per cent of the total number of strikes were in plants employing more than 100 workers (whereas the proportion of these plants in Spanish industry was 1.3 per cent). *Table 3* provides the distribution of conflict by plant size in this seven-year period.

Table 3 Distribution of industrial conflict by size of the plant between 1968 and 1974

plant size	N	%	number of plants	ratio number of plants/average disputes per year
1–24	638	9.0	619,056	6,803
25–49	829	11.6	22,626	192
50–99	853	12.0	10,266	84
100–500	2,924	41.0	7,579	18
Over 500	1,883	26.4	1,267	5
Total	7,127	100.0	660,794	649

Industrial actions became more radical from 1967 onwards. *Figure 1* shows the evolution of the main types of industrial action in the twelve-year period of 1963–74. It can be seen that strikes and strikes-on-the-job increased as a proportion of the total number of actions: they

% of total actions
(N for the period = 9,370)

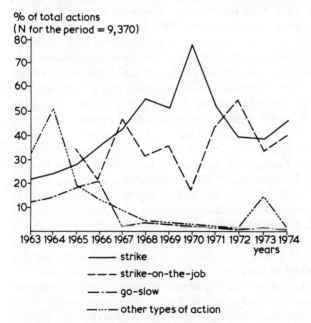

strike

strike-on-the-job

go-slow

other types of action

Figure 1 Evolution of types of action from 1963 to 1974

amounted to 30.3 per cent in the four years between 1963 and 1966, but the percentage increased to 86.6 in the period between 1967 and 1974.

The costs of strikes were, of course, great under a dictatorship which defined them as acts of sedition and which persecuted working-class organizations. Total strikes required good organization, competent leadership, and some protection from repression. They mostly took place in the strong enclaves of working-class militancy of Asturias, the Basque Country, and Barcelona. They were more difficult to organize in Madrid, where the objective of the illegal unions was to strengthen the organization of the movement and to mobilize the workers gradually with a careful display of action. In this situation, strikes-on-the-job had the advantage of surprise, of enabling workers to control the plant from within, of presenting fewer opportunities for repression. They were a good instrument for co-ordinated actions and for testing the strength of the movement; and they were easier to prepare and to carry out.

During this twelve-year period, strikes were the most frequent type of action (45.8 per cent), followed by strikes-on-the-job (29.2 per cent). There seemed to be some sort of relationship between these two actions: on the one hand, from 1967 to 1973 an increase in the one was also a decrease in the other; but on the other hand, it appears that in the same period a strike was often a confrontation that produced sympathetic strikes-on-the-job. From 1967 there were growing links between working-class actions in different factories, different branches, and different geographical areas. Thus, conflict became more offensive (through the increasing use of strikes) and also more solidaristic (through the co-ordination of actions in different places). Within the factories conflict became more endemic: in the central areas of working-class militancy (in the large factories of the steel and metal industries of the Basque Country, the metal industries of Barcelona and Madrid, and in the Asturian mines) there was constant simmering conflict, occasionally breaking onto the surface, and on which working-class organizations tried to capitalize.

In the last years of the Francoist regime there was a new type of action: the 'area general strikes' (*huelgas generales locales*). These involved workers in every branch of production in an area and they were organized to press for a set of economic and political demands, including the right to free and democratic trade unions. There were several important 'area general strikes' in 1973, most notably one in Pamplona (Basque Country), another in Sardanyola and Ripollés (Catalonia). By the end of the year these actions had become the most spectacular type of conflict: there were five in December (in the Basque Country, in the *Baix Llobregat* in Catalonia, and in Madrid, involving 1,719 factories and over 300,000 workers). One year later, December 11, 1974, 80 per cent of the active population of the Basque Country went on an 'area general strike' in solidarity with 140 political prisoners who were on hunger strike. More will be said in the following chapter about this type of action, but it must now be noted that it represented the wider and best organized form of working-class action under Francoism; that it was a major step in the long and difficult struggle towards a reorganized working-class movement; and that it was widely used at the end of the dictatorship and in the first months of the Monarchy (particularly in January and February 1976 when 20,000 workers were sanctioned and dismissed due to their involvement in strikes).

As it grew more intensive, industrial conflict after 1967 also became more politicized. Thus, from 1963 to 1967 economic demands were predominant (44.2 per cent of 1,676 cases), followed by claims related to collective bargaining (15.2 per cent), while solidarity claims were relatively rare (4.0 per cent). From 1967 onwards the situation changed: solidarity claims reached 45.4 per cent (of 7,694 cases), demands related

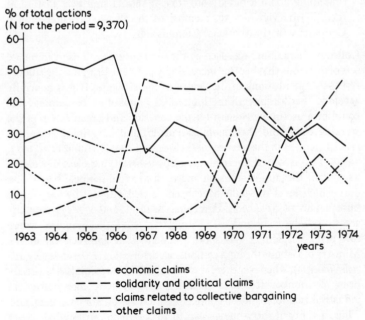

% of total actions
(N for the period = 9,370)

——— economic claims
— — — solidarity and political claims
—·—·— claims related to collective bargaining
—··—··— other claims

Figure 2   Evolution of types of claim from 1963 to 1974

to collective bargaining increased to 20.1 per cent, and economic demands dropped to 25.6 per cent. *Figure 2* shows the evolution of working-class demands over the twelve-year period[20]. Solidarity was not limited to the firm: it soon extended to an inter-industrial, and later to an inter-provincial level, as support for workers who already were in conflict in other firms or who had suffered sanctions. Politically orientated demands generally consisted of demands for free and democratic unions and for the right to strike.

This change in the nature of the demands demonstrates the difference in strength of the movement *vis-à-vis* the long earlier period of fear and inhibition. This difference was expressed in the following comment from one of the democratic union leaders whose reports are studied in Chapter 4:

'You see, workers were even frightened to sign letters . . . with purely economic demands, you see . . . with nothing political. Even in the early 1960s to sign a letter was seen as dangerous. It was a totally different situation from today! In 1955 there was a letter in my firm, in Isodel, which ended with something like "please do forgive us if our demand is too inconsiderate", and they were only claiming something about a bloody bus, that it should stop here instead of there.' (Interview no. 10, member of the Provincial Inter-branch Committee of the Workers' Commissions)

Collective bargaining was used by the secret organizations to stimulate sets of demands that became increasingly political, bringing the labour-repressive institutions to the centre of the struggle. It was generally accepted that 'despite all the limitations imposed on bargaining, this could be a useful instrument for the cohesion and organization of the working class' and that 'mobilizations around bargaining became a crucial element in the strategy of the working class' (Muñoz *et al.* 1973, 1974). This is why the re-emergent Spanish working-class movement used plant bargaining so much and tried to avoid national bargaining – at which level it would have been carried out by the corporatist bureaucracy of *Sindicatos*. Barcelona, Madrid, and Vizcaya were the areas, and the steel and metal industries were the branches where this plant bargaining was more frequent. The intervention of the Ministry of Labour through compulsory arbitration (*normas de obligado complimiento*), whenever there was a deadlock in bargaining, has already been mentioned. It was a clear example of state intervention in industrial relations and of political restrictions to workers' demands. Thus, a study of forty-one *normas* in 1971 (which represented 30 per cent of the total for that year and 32 per cent of the total number of workers affected by these compulsory arbitrations) shows that whereas collective agreements had on average increased wages between 12.6 per cent (for one-year agreements) and 16.6 per cent (for two-year agreements), the *normas* had increased wages by 10.0 per cent only. This form of state intervention through compulsory arbitration can, to a certain extent, be considered as an indicator of the degree of antagonism in industrial relations, and it should be possible to interpret the increase in the ratio of compulsory arbitrations to collective agreements from the beginning to the end of the 1960s as a manifestation of the growing strength of the working-class movement. This ratio increased from 2.6 to 20 per cent. However, in the 1970s, and because of the detrimental effect of state intervention on the demands of the workers, the democratic unions tried to avoid the *normas* (and deadlocks in bargaining), while at the same time they were still using collective bargaining as a tactical instrument. Hence, the Workers' Commissions declared that in collective bargaining they saw 'two possibilities which must be simultaneously used: the struggle for specific and immediate demands, which are so urgent for the workers, and the creation of a platform for mobilizing the workers in a revolutionary manner ... The agreements are a unitary platform of struggle.'[21]

In the 1970s the working-class struggle was characterized by the organization of 'area general strikes', to which reference has already been made, and also by the defence of sets of related claims that were called '*plataformas reivindicativas*' (platforms of demands). These programmes of demands were often defended by a series of solidaristic strikes or by co-ordinated and simultaneous waves of confrontations – the 'area general strikes'. The programmes were always very similar: they included, on the one hand, detailed demands referring to wage increases, employment, conditions of work, and, on the other, political claims (free and democratic trade unionism, amnesty, the right to strike, the right to organize assemblies in the plant, etc.). The *plataformas reivindicativas* provided the link between economic and political demands. This political aspect is expressed in the following call from the UGT for an 'area general strike' in January 1976, which, after a long exposition of the ongoing struggle, said: 'Comrades! The UGT summons you to the general strike from the 12th to win over our *plataforma reivindicativa*, to free all political prisoners, to achieve free trade unionism and all democratic freedoms'[22].

The response of the political regime to the growing strength of the working-class movement and to the extension of industrial conflict combined a double strategy of integration and repression. The strategy of integration consisted of partial reforms in the organization of the official trade unions and in legislation on industrial relations. This strategy included the legalization of 'economic' (*sic*) strikes in 1962, a reform of the Penal Code in 1965, the 'Organic Law of the State' (a constitutional reform) in 1966, and the new *Ley Sindical* of 1971. This new law introduced some autonomy with regard to the representation of the workers at the lower levels and a greater independence of workers and managers within the trade unions, but these remained nevertheless an 'instrument of the state', both vertical and compulsory.

Obviously, this strategy must be considered within the framework of a wider attempt to reorganize the regime. I have characterized the period 1955–75 of the Francoist regime as capitalist development without democracy; yet, however much the regime tried to keep the economic aspects of modernization isolated from its political aspects, some modifications were needed in order to avoid a complete lack of control over the increasing institutional tensions. These tension-management policies followed a minimalist strategy; the intention was to limit institutional changes and to keep control over them. For instance, in the political literature of the time it was usual to accept the need for 'administrative' reforms as opposed to 'political' reforms[23]. This was also one of the main reasons for the rise to political power of a new technocracy (from 1957 to 1974, the *Opus Dei*). This group urged and produced concrete policies for economic and administrative reforms.

The strategy of repression attempted to undermine the secret organizations through political persecution, trying to isolate them from the workers. Political repression against the organized working-class movement was indeed massive. An analysis of the information provided by the national press over the two months of January and February 1974 shows that 24,817 workers had their contracts and wages temporarily suspended and that 4,379 were dismissed from their jobs due to their participation in strikes. *Table 4* provides information on repressive measures taken by firms and the official trade unions over this period, but it does not include data on the third level of repression – police arrests.

The following chapter will analyse in greater detail variations in the nature of working-class conflict in the different areas of struggle. What the data from *Table 4* seem to indicate is, on the one hand, the greater use of repressive measures against militant workers in the Basque Country, which reflects the relevance of that area in the reorganization of the working-class movement in Spain; and on the other, the greater use of sanctions against official trade-union representatives (*enlaces* and *jurados de empresa*) in Madrid and Catalonia. This second set

Table 4   Repressive measures by geographical areas (January–February 1974)

geographical areas	suspension of contracts and wages		dismissals from jobs		dismissals from official trade-union posts	
	N	%	N	%	N	%
Andalucía	2,890	11.6	962	22.0	5	7.6
Asturias	783	3.2	359	8.2	4	6.1
Basque country	6,508	26.2	1,700	38.8	4	6.1
Catalonia	3,910	15.8	969	22.1	17	25.7
Galicia	3,772	15.2	90	2.1	—	—
Country of Valencia	2,583	10.4	53	1.2	6	9.1
Madrid	4,371	17.6	246	5.6	30	45.4
total	24,817	100.0	4,379	100.0	66	100.0

of figures can perhaps be seen as a rough indicator of the influence of the infiltrationist strategy of the Workers' Commissions in these two areas of Madrid and Catalonia, and of the relative strength of the non-infiltrationist strategy of the UGT in Asturias and the Basque Country. It also seems clear that the costs of the struggle, in terms of repression, were still very high indeed for the working class well into the 1970s.

4 Conclusions

A number of issues seem to be relevant in relation to the problem of the growth of social and political movements of dissent in authoritarian capitalist states. In particular, I have tried to link this problem to the question of institutional inconsistencies stemming from processes of economic growth.

Capitalist economic growth created new requirements, which could hardly be met by the institutional order of the dictatorship. This lack of institutional fit produced a situation of 'system malintegration', which was a condition for political dissent and conflict. Economic growth from the mid-1950s gave rise to new requirements for agreements on productivity and wage increases: one of these requirements was a form of workers' representation, which could not be found within the corporatist order that had existed from 1939 under conditions of economic autarchy and stagnation.

Such institutional weaknesses encouraged the growth of alternative institutions which tended to satisfy the new requirements. This was the case in Spain with the development of informal collective bargaining and workers' representation at the shop-floor level in the mid-1950s. At the same time, increasing industrialization and the consolidation of what Touraine[24] has called Phase B of capitalism created new conditions for the emergence of a working-class movement of dissent.

The dictatorial nature of the political system made it difficult to manage solutions to these new problems of 'system malintegration'[25]. The political regime tried to undertake slight modifications to the previous institutional structures, combining limited integrative policies with repressive measures. The main goal was to avoid the political challenge that might result from uncontrolled change. The regime tried to separate economic demands and instrumental representation of the workers from political demands and class actions. This strategy required the extensive use of repressive measures, the systematic persecution of working-class organizations, and harsh sanctions against militant workers. The strategic use of repression must be seen in the light of the description that Linz gives of the treatment of political opposition within his type of the authoritarian regime in general, and Spain in particular (Linz 1974). The regime allowed for the existence of a pseudo-opposition, which supported the state in its essentials. On the other hand, opposition that wholly challenged the regime and the foundations of the state had to lead a clandestine political life. At the same time the regime tried to carry out an integrative strategy which included modifications in the law on strikes, on corporatist trade unions, on collective bargaining, and on the *jurados de empresa*. This integrative strategy can be seen as part of an attempt to move towards a milder version of a labour-repressive system.

Working-class militancy was the result of these objective conditions produced by industrialization, productivity requirements, and bargaining, on the one hand, *and* of political factors on the other. Thus, Asturias, the Basque Country, and Barcelona were at the same time industrialized areas and also the main regions where working-class organizations (particularly communist and socialist) survived repression. This combination of economic and political factors will be examined in more detail in Chapter 3.

New forms of working-class organization and representation arose. Militant working-class groups were able to use collective bargaining and, to a certain extent the *jurados de empresa*, to strengthen their shop-floor support. This led to a movement of factory committees, and to particular attention to shop-floor militancy being paid by every working-class organization. A specific trade-union organization has been associated with this grass-roots movement: '*Comisiones Obreras*', but the traditional labour unions, and UGT in particular, also experienced a sharp growth resulting from the new dynamics in industrial relations. Conflict and dissent became progressively class- and politically-oriented. Whereas at the beginning of the 1960s the first waves of working-class conflict were due to wage claims and protests over conditions of work, they turned more and more into manifestations of working-class solidarity and political dissent.

This discussion has had to consider some aspects of the dynamics of authoritarian capitalist states. In the analysis of the Spanish case, it seems that certain consequences of capitalist economic development, such as the need for negotiation linked to productivity agreements, were an important factor in creating new conditions for organized dissent and conflict. The next chapter will study an additional factor: the survival and development of 'sanctuaries' of working-class militancy.

3 The sources of working-class dissent

In which areas did working-class militancy re-emerge under Franco-ism? Were they the pre-civil war areas of strong working-class organization, or were they new areas of working-class radicalism resulting from the process of industrialization that started in the late 1950s? This chapter will discuss the question of whether it is possible to interpret working-class militancy in Spain in the 1960s and 1970s in terms either of political continuity or of political discontinuity with the pre-Francoist era, and this requires a close analysis of the connection between political and economic factors in the areas where working-class struggle was particularly concentrated. Militancy will be analysed in terms of industrial conflict: under Francoism strikes had a political connotation as they were legally defined as acts of sedition, were seen as a challenge to the regime, and were harshly repressed.

Two problems are relevant here: the first is whether it was possible for working-class organizations to survive repression in these areas; the second is whether these areas had an industrial structure and a proletarian community that provided favourable conditions for collective action. The extent to which these areas of militancy were traditional or new may also have had consequences for the type of action used by workers in confrontations (e.g. strikes, go-slows, strikes-on-the-job) and for the type of demand that they put forward (e.g. solidarity, wage increases).

A few working-class centres often dominate working-class movements: their industrial and political attitudes and behaviour have a special influence, and they become the catalysts of a generalized pattern of conflict[1]. The influence of a few strategical groups increases in a non-democratic political context, where the political fragmentation of the working class is maximized and organizations are persecuted. In such a context, a movement can only re-emerge in those enclaves where working-class militancy could not be eradicated and where collective protection and support for organized actions exist. Thus, the working-class movement in Spain under Francoism was based over a long period of time on a few working-class pockets that produced the first isolated expressions of militancy after 1939 and that became the backbone of the working-class movement from the mid-1960s. Only in the decade of the 1970s did working-class militancy expand to other areas of the country, through the combined effects of the policies of illegal working-class organizations and of the occupational changes associated with rapid industrialization.

1 The areas of militancy old and new

Working-class struggle under the Second Republic (1931–39) was concentrated in the industrialized areas of Asturias, the Basque Country, and Catalonia. The working class in Asturias and Barcelona was especially militant, occasionally joined by the Basque Country workers. However, the agricultural proletariat was not only important demographically speaking; it was also a major political part of the working class. Thus, in the years 1932 and 1933, agricultural workers in some areas of Andalucía (Sevilla, Jaén, and Córdoba) produced as many strikes as Asturian miners and Catalan workers together. Peasant militancy persisted until the defeat of the Republic, although the wave of revolutionary strikes in 1934 was particularly strong in the mines of Asturias, in the metal industries and steel works of Vizcaya and Guipúzcoa, and in the metal and textile industries of Barcelona. Working-class militancy was predominantly of socialist and anarchist orientation. The socialist organizations (that is, the Spanish Socialist Workers' Party – PSOE – and the General Union of Workers – UGT) were particularly strong in the triangle of Madrid, Vizcaya-Guipúzcoa and Asturias, but they also had a strong influence in the agrarian region of Extremadura and the interior of Andalucía. In all these areas, the socialist vote in the legislative elections of November 1933 was high (between 30 and 47 per cent). Besides its strength among miners, steel, and metal workers, the UGT then had a strong appeal among the peasantry (the *Federación Nacional de Trabajadores de la Tierra*, the union of agricultural workers, had in 1932 445,414 members, out of a total membership of 1,041,539 for the UGT). As for the anarchist organization, the National Confederation of Labour (CNT), Catalonia and Andalucía in particular were their strongholds: Barcelona, and Sevilla, Granada, Málaga, and Cádiz[2]. *Map* 1 indicates the geographical distribution of influence of UGT (socialists) and CNT (anarchists).

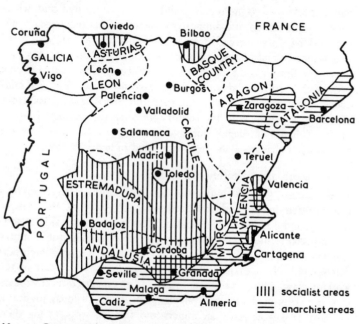

Map 1　Geographical distribution of Socialist and Anarchist influence before the Civil War.

The emergence of a working-class movement under Francoism appears to have had its origins very much in the same areas of working-class militancy of the 1930s, except for the Andalucían peasantry. Somehow, the industrialized regions of northern and north-east Spain were the only areas where working-class militancy could survive under the dictatorship and where conflict reappeared in the isolated and ill-organized bursts of strike activity in 1947, 1951, 1953, and 1956. When an organized working-class movement emerged from 1962 onwards, Asturias, the Basque Country (Vizcaya and Guipúzcoa), and Barcelona were its main pillars and most of the actions were concentrated there. Madrid also became in the 1960s an important area of working-class struggle, due to rapid industrialization which produced a large and new proletariat employed in car factories (Pegaso-ENASA, Chrysler), engineering, machine tool, and light metals factories, and it was in Madrid that the movement of the Workers' Commissions was born in the early 1960s. At the end of the decade there were other areas where the working-class movement became increasingly stronger: Pamplona and Vitoria in the two Basque provinces of Navarra and Alava; Valladolid in Castilla; Vigo and El Ferrol in Galícia; Sevilla in Andalucía. Although steel and metal workers, as well as miners, remained the core of the organized working-class movement in Spain in the 1970s, other sectors became more active.

In the twelve years between 1963 and 1974, 69.7 per cent of the total number of industrial conflicts (9,370) were in Asturias, the Basque Country (Vizcaya and Guipúzcoa only), Barcelona, and Madrid. *Table* 1 provides information on the distribution of working-class conflict over this period[3].

Table 1   Geographical distribution of industrial conflict in Spain between 1963 and 1974 (in percentages)

	Asturias	Barcelona	Basque Country (Guipúzcoa/ Vizcaya only)	Madrid	total four areas	100% total Spain (N)
1963	15.6	20.3	12.9	5.5	54.3	(777)
1964	15.2	10.7	30.1	5.3	61.3	(484)
1965	12.9	19.4	25.9	—	58.2	(236)
1966	20.0	14.0	30.0	6.1	70.1	(179)
1967	26.0	14.3	32.0	13.2	85.5	(567)
1968	40.4	8.8	19.6	4.0	74.6	(351)
1969	20.8	7.3	50.1	1.8	80.8	(491)
1970	8.0	9.7	39.6	4.5	61.8	(1,595)
1971	17.5	22.6	22.2	8.3	70.6	(616)
1972	10.7	15.8	26.8	9.5	62.8	(853)
1973	8.6	30.7	23.3	5.0	67.6	(931)
1974	3.1	31.2	40.2	5.4	79.9	(2,290)
totals	12.1 (1,130)	19.8 (1,858)	31.9 (2,990)	5.9 (549)	69.7 (6,527)	(9,370)

The four industrialized regions of Asturias, Barcelona, the Basque Country, and Madrid played a determinant role not only in the first period of the working-class movement, but also when it had developed and achieved a better organization and a planned strategy[4]. Thus, whereas from 1963 to 1965 these four areas had produced 57.1 per cent of disputes, the proportion increased to 79.3 per cent for the period between 1966 and 1969. However, industrial conflict then seemed to become slightly more diversified: in the five-year period of 1970–74, the four areas produced 70.2 per cent of the confrontations, while Andalucía provided 12.6 per cent and Navarra 4.8 per cent.

Two questions must now be considered: (1) the characteristics of the geographical areas where working-class conflict was particularly concentrated; (2) the characteristics of conflict in each of these areas. The social bases of the working-class movement in Spain were, on the one hand, the traditional strongholds of working-class militancy in the 1930s; on the other, the most industrialized areas in the country. These bases belong to what Linz and De Miguel have called 'the bourgeois Spain' (1966). Asturias is, to a certain extent, the exception from the point of view of the economy; the crisis in the coal industry was dramatic and had a considerable impact. The ranking of Asturias in the provincial scale of *per capita* income dropped in the 1960s and it became a province of emigration in that decade.

If we look first at the political characteristics, the four areas stand out as centres of political radicalism. The leftist vote in the 1931 municipal elections, which produced the collapse of the Monarchy and led to the second Republic, was for the country as a whole 45 per cent, but reached between 60 and 73 per cent in Asturias, Barcelona, and Madrid. The Basque Country is here the exception, with a much lower percentage, basically as the result of three factors: first, the absence of a left-of-centre vote due, among other reasons, to the very conservative political orientation of the Basque bourgeoisie (on the other hand the proportion of communist and socialist votes was higher in the Basque Country than in Spain as a whole and higher than that of Barcelona); second, the presence of Basque national parties that could not be classified simply as either leftists or rightist-orientated; finally, a high proportion of abstentions in Vizcaya and Guipúzcoa. It is difficult to make geographical/ecological estimations of political radicalism between 1939 and 1975, but perhaps electoral abstention can be used as a rudimentary indication; if so, it must be noted that this abstention was higher in Asturias, the Basque Country (except Alava), Catalonia, and Madrid. For instance, in the politically controlled elections for deputies in the Spanish Parliament[5] in October 1967, the proportion of abstentions for the country as a whole was 31 per cent, whereas the proportion for Vizcaya, Guipúzcoa, Asturias,

Barcelona, and Madrid reached between 45 per cent (Madrid) and 58 per cent (Vizcaya).

If we look now at the economic and social characteristics of the areas of working-class militancy, the four provinces with a higher *per capita* income in Spain were Vizcaya, Guipúzcoa, Madrid, and Barcelona[6]. The proportion of active population employed as wage earners in industry was highest in these areas[7], while industrial concentration of workers, measured by the proportion of workers employed in industrial firms of over 100 workers, was also comparatively higher in Vizcaya, Barcelona, Guipúzcoa, and Madrid[8]. The industrial density of these provinces was also strong: in 1958 the average number of industrial workers per square kilometre in Spain was 7.32, but reached 95.78 in Barcelona, 87.28 in Vizcaya, 64.33 in Madrid, and 57.56 in Guipúzcoa[9]. The rate of immigration in the 1960s was finally very high in Barcelona, Madrid, Vizcaya, and Guipúzcoa. They were by far the highest in the country[10].

Which were the most militant sectors of the working class in each of these areas and what were the characteristics of their struggle? *Table 2* indicates the predominant sectors for the four geographical areas[11] over a five-year period (1968–72). In Asturias miners were the central working-class group from the point of view of militancy, but the economic crisis of coal mines, together with new important steel works, led to an increasingly bi-sectorial conflict: whereas miners had produced 92.3 per cent of the total number of confrontations in 1968, the proportion decreased to 45.0 per cent in 1972, while that

Table 2 Main militant working-class sectors in Asturias, Barcelona, Basque Country, and Madrid – 1968 to 1972 (in percentages)

regions	industries	%
Asturias	{ miners	81.1
	{ steel workers	11.6
Barcelona	⎧ metal workers	40.9
	{ textile workers	23.1
	⎩ building workers	8.9
Basque Country, (Guipúzcoa and Vizcaya only)	{ steel and metal workers	72.7
Madrid	⎧ metal workers	42.2
	{ building workers	21.9
	⎩ bank employees	17.4

of steel workers increased from 6.3 to over 20 per cent in the same five-year period. Steel and metal workers[12] were overwhelmingly predominant in Guipúzcoa–Vizcaya and, to a lesser degree, so were metal workers in Barcelona and Madrid, where industrial conflict also involved textile workers, bank employees, and building workers. We must now turn to a specific analysis of industrial conflict in each of these strategic centres of the Spanish working-class movement.

So far the information on industrial conflict that I have used comes from the rather secretive annual reports of the Spanish Ministry of Labour which needed careful secondary analysis. The high degree of aggregation of these data makes it now impossible to use this information any further to study the particular sources of working-class dissent. I have therefore used information provided by the Spanish press from 1966 to 1974. This was possible because the new Press Law of 1966, which was presented as a main liberalizing innovation, allowed for a greater freedom of information and the major newspapers made a great effort, as part of their competitive sales policies, to provide wide information on 'labour problems'. Thus, while there was no relevant information on industrial disputes until April 1966, the national press reported 102 strikes for April to December 1966 and 324 for 1967. For the period 1966–74 I have gathered information about 2,287 industrial actions (an average of 254 per year). It also seemed convenient to use a source that was public, easily checked, and available for other studies.

It is obvious that this information must have had important biases, for two reasons: on the one hand political restrictions; on the other hand, the commercial interests of the press. But two other reasons seemed to recommend the use of this source: first, there was no better alternative for trying to lift some of the obscurity on the development of the Spanish working-class movement; second, there was no need to have information on the total of industrial disputes. A substantial number of cases could be quite satisfactory in order to get an image of some characteristics of the Spanish working-class movement.

Ministry of Labour reports also provided data for the nine years for which press information was used: the 2,287 disputes reported in the press over these years represent 29.0 per cent of the number provided by the Ministry of Labour (7,873). It is, however, the case that the press information concentrates somewhat on conflicts in specific geographical areas: thus 84.7 per cent of press news on conflicts refers to Asturias, Barcelona, the Basque Country, and Madrid, whereas these areas represent only 72.0 per cent of the Ministry of Labour data for that period. Consequently there is press information on 34.2

per cent of the Ministry of Labour's reported disputes in these crucial areas. The volume of information seems adequate to attempt a further step in the breakdown of the analysis, and to study industrial conflict among Asturian miners, steel and metal workers in the Basque Country, and metal workers in Barcelona and Madrid.

The main question that has to be examined is the survival of labour unions and political parties in these sources of working-class militancy. Was industrial action led by the traditional left-wing unions, UGT or CNT, or was it led by a new organization set up under Francoism, such as the Workers' Commissions? We shall then have to examine the industrial structure of each of the groups, in order to see whether this industrial structure was associated with organizational continuities or discontinuities. Finally, both political and industrial factors may help in interpreting variations in the nature of conflict in these groups, particularly in the types of action carried out and of political demands made. It would thus possibly be the case that solidarity claims and co-ordinated strikes were easier to carry out in traditional pockets of militancy, while new working-class groups, where support for secret organizations was still weak, had comparatively more strikes-on-the-job (a less costly and vulnerable kind of action) and more demands referring to collective bargaining (which would not require much influence from working-class organizations).

2 Industrial conflict in the Asturian mining industry

The Asturian coal miners have traditionally been a revolutionary symbol of the Spanish working class. They led an important and dramatic revolutionary attempt in 1934, under the Second Republic, and suffered devastating repression by the army, which the Lerroux government sent under the command of General Franco. After 1939 and until the mid-1960s, the miners were the major source of organized working-class dissent. The miners' strikes in 1956 and 1962 had a dramatic political impact, not only on other working-class groups, but on other sectors of the population – e.g. on the student movement, which organized a series of important demonstrations in support of the miners under the slogan 'Asturias in, *Opus* out' (*Asturias sí, Opus no*).

Most of the Spanish coal mining industry is concentrated in Asturias (70 per cent of the production of the country), and the industry has been centrally important to the economy of the area. The community was largely dependent on a single industry; the whole society was affected by industrial disputes and the population was polarized in two camps. Industrial, social, and private life overlapped and the internal cohesion of the working-class community was reinforced by social and cultural isolation and contributed to the formation of a typical subculture. Asturian coal mines are located in the central part of the province of Oviedo, in the valley of the rivers Nalón and Caudal. There are seventy-two mining companies, which in 1962 employed 44,250 workers; seventeen of these companies produce 90 per cent of the total output and employ 93 per cent of the labour force. A national enterprise was organized in the 1960s, Hulleras del Norte (HUNOSA), which was set up as the basic instrument for the economic reorganization of the industry. The state also intervened with a policy of 'concerted action' agreements for private companies, which consisted of financial help from the government and planned production targets over a number of years.

From the second half of the 1950s the economic crisis of Asturian coal mines was very severe[13] and it resulted in extensive redundancies. At the same time, according to a 1967 survey (SADEI 1967: vol. IV), there was a general lack of information among miners about the economic situation of Asturian mining and the reorganization programme that was being carried out by private enterprises and by nationalized enterprise. The crisis and the changes were seen as irrational and arbitrary. They affected a group of workers that had had a traditional pattern of occupational stability and self-recruitment.

Over the nine-year period of 1966–74, the press gave information on 254 confrontations. Strikes were often protracted and they generally involved many pits and mobilized large numbers of workers. Thus, in 1968 work was carried out normally on only 140 days and the annual deficit of HUNOSA was over £500,000, while in 1969 2 million hours were lost in strikes, which cost an estimated £1½ million (some £525 per worker).

The main course of action followed by miners was to strike (90 per cent of the total number of actions). The basic issues that sparked off the struggles were labour accidents (24 per cent); sympathy strikes (21 per cent); wage demands (20 per cent); redundancies and dismissals (16 per cent). The predominant issues and types of action are indicated in *Table 3*.

Labour accidents (very often deaths within the pits) generally led to demonstrations of solidarity and sympathy strikes. These strikes were often widely supported: such demonstrations of protest and mourning were frequently repressed, and this produced a heightening of conflict. A long spiral of conflict, in which one confrontation followed another, was the predominant characteristic of the miners' struggle. Confrontations often started over issues which were relatively minor to begin with, but which led to repression followed by long strikes of solidarity often lasting several months and involving several thousand workers.

Table 3   Predominant types of conflict among Asturian miners (1966–74)

type of action	issue	N	%
strike	labour accidents	62	24
strike	sympathy strikes	50	20
strike	wages	48	19
strike	redundancies	39	15

The evolution of conflict was very much related to the economic crisis. Over the decade of the 1960s the majority of strikes were of a defensive kind. Faced with unemployment, redundancies, and closures of pits, strikes were often a desperate struggle for survival. Only occasionally did the workers present an articulate alternative to the policy of the private companies and of the government. One of the few occasions was in 1970, when miners from HUNOSA and a large private company (*La Camocha*) and miners from other smaller private companies started a strike in protest against redundancies. This was immediately supported by 16,000 miners, in twenty-four other pits. In a single month the workers lost £1.7 million in wages, and the daily cost to the companies was £250,000. The companies suspended the contracts and wages of 11,229 miners. In March 1970 the miners presented an economic programme of reorganization of the industry, which called for the amalgamation into a single company of all profitable mines, a non-subsidiary state intervention (avoiding what amounted then to a nationalization of losses), and no redundancies.

The miners' long tradition of militancy and their homogeneity as a group made them a major political force within the Spanish working class[14]. They had been able to maintain their struggle under very difficult circumstances, in years of very harsh repression, and often in isolation. In the coal mines the leftist organizations (particularly the UGT, the Socialist Party, and the Communist Party) managed to survive repression within the cohesive and protective boundaries of the mining community. Between 1966 and 1974 the press reported 140 miners sacked from their jobs due to their leadership of strikes, and 51,249 suspensions of contracts and wages. There were no reports of official shop stewards (*enlaces* and *jurados de empresa*) having been sanctioned, as the official trade union was never effective in the mines and the workers did not carry out a strategy of infiltration – which is possibly connected to the relative strength of UGT among miners and the relative weakness of the Workers' Commissions.

3 Industrial conflict in the steel and metal industry of the Basque Country

Together with Asturian miners, the workers from the Basque steel and metal industries were for many years an almost isolated enclave of working-class militancy, as well as providing a relatively protected *milieu* for secret leftist organizations after 1939. The Spanish Communist Party (PCE), the Socialist Party (PSOE), and the UGT were able to retain their political influence among the Basque working class due to the fact that, particularly in Vizcaya, this working class had strong internal cohesion, was isolated from other social classes, and had a long tradition of militancy. Thus, the Basque workers, together with the Asturian miners, were the first to organize and mobilize.

Militancy extended from Vizcaya to Guipúzcoa and then, at the end of the 1960s, to Alava and Navarra. From 1969 onwards there was a pattern of co-ordinated actions covering the four Basque provinces. This extension of conflict to the whole of the Basque Country was a totally new phenomenon and one of the major political changes in the last years of Francoism. Working-class militancy spread from the traditional strongholds of radicalism in Vizcaya and, to a lesser extent Guipúzcoa, as a result of the activity of working-class organizations that survived repression and were able to gain strength and influence in the 1960s (UGT) or that were created in that decade within a new economic context and a less repressive system of industrial relations (USO and comisiones).

Table 4 Predominant types of conflict among Basque steel and metal workers (1966–74)

type of action	issue	N	%
strike	solidarity	274	58
strike-on-the-job	solidarity	53	11
strike	wages	24	5

No other part of the working class in Spain showed such a level of solidarity. Confrontations were also strongly political: they included demands for democracy and for amnesty. Thus, the state of emergency declared in the Basque Country in August 1968 was due to an uninter-rupted series of strikes and street occupations in many areas of Vizcaya and Guipúzcoa. From the late 1960s left-wing communist groups such as the ORT (Revolutionary Organization of Workers) increased their influence; what I could not find in the press reports, however, were strikes in direct political support of ultra-nationalist groups such as *Euzkadi Ta Askatasuna* (ETA). However, Basque workers mobilized extensively in protest against repression which very often was directed against these groups: for example there were strikes on the occasion of the Burgos trial of fifteen ETA militants in December 1970, and on the occasion of the trial of five ETA and six FRAP militants and of the subsequent execution of five of them in September 1975. Until recently, Basque nationalism has been rural and conservative, while the Basque working class has always had a very high proportion of immigrants and has been predominantly Communist or Socialist. From 1966 to 1974, the development of working-class conflict in the Basque steel and metal industry showed four characteristics. First of all, there was constant mutual support for workers in conflict, which produced a spiral of confrontations in which the workers achieved considerable co-ordination in their actions. Second, 'area general strikes' were often organized, and they were usually called for, by secret parties and labour unions. These strikes often had a political dimension and usually had their origins in issues of solidarity[15]. Third, there was an increasing use of '*plataformas reivindicativas*' (platforms of demands) as sets of basic claims, generally agreed upon by the workers in plant assemblies. The claims included calls for political amnesty and for democracy (in particular freedom of assembly, expression, association, and the right to strike), together with demands relating to work conditions and wages, and protests against cost of living increases. Finally, industrial conflict was concentrated in large firms: the average size of the work force of the seven firms most involved between 1966 and 1974 was 1,938.

The three secret labour unions, UGT, USO, and the Workers' Commissions were very strong within this working-class sector. However, the number of official trade-union representatives that the press reported as having been removed from their posts as a con-sequence of their participation in strikes was much lower than in Madrid and also than in Barcelona (only one every fifty-two strikes). The strategy of infiltration must have been less extended. On the other hand the average number of workers sacked per strike (four) was higher than in the three other working-class areas.

4 Industrial conflict in the metal industry of Barcelona

The metal workers of Barcelona were one of the earliest groups to organize and mobilize. They played a very important part in the strikes of 1962, but they did not seem to present the homogeneous and consistent resistance of the Asturian miners or of the Basque steel and metal workers. This was possibly due to the metropolitan and multi-industrial character of the area, as well as to the destruction of the anarchist labour union, the CNT, which had been the strongest working-class organization in Catalonia before the civil war. However, between 1966 and 1974 the press reported 461 actions, which represented 20.2 per cent of the total number of industrial disputes in the country for that period, and Barcelona appears to have been the second most militant area after the Basque Country.

The area that is considered here includes the municipality of Barcelona, and its *hinterland* (in particular the *comarcas* of the *Baix Llobregat* and *Vallés* and the urban centres of Hospitalet, Cornellá, Gavá, Sardanyola, Terrasa, Sabadell). According to the press reports, 81.2 per cent of industrial disputes in Barcelona were in the metal industry; textile workers were the second most active working-class group but their actions comprised only 6.5 per cent of the total of the area. In the 1960s 161,000 workers were employed in the metal industry, but the characteristics of the companies where they worked varied greatly: while some firms had over a thousand workers, many others were only small family workshops. Industrial conflict was located in the large firms. The 15 firms most involved in 1966–74 had on average 2,651 workers.[16]

Table 5   Predominant types of conflict among Catalan metal workers (1966–74)

type of action	issue	N	%
strike	wages	214	46
strike	solidarity	115	25
strike-on-the-job	deadlock in bargaining	33	7

Catalan metal workers were comparatively less mobilized than the three other working-class groups on issues of solidarity and were more interested in economic claims. Pay disputes led to major confrontations in the large firms that had a tradition of militancy. But wage-oriented strikes were, often enough, far from being moderate or parochial; first of all, the confrontations were frequently very acrimonious; second, a wage demand was frequently defended by workers from different factories who, following agreed tactics, took joint strike action. Thus, in December 1974, 500 shop stewards called for a general strike in the area of the *Baix Llobregat* to protest against the rising cost of living and to ask for higher wages. Twenty-five of the organizers were arrested, but a general strike in the area was organized successfully, involving over two hundred firms[17]. Strikes expressing working-class solidarity and support for other workers were often linked to wage-oriented strikes. This link frequently led to a spiral of conflict – the spiral would start with a pay dispute, which then resulted in sanctions against workers, and subsequently in a wave of demonstrations of solidarity[18].

Industrial conflict in Barcelona shared three characteristics with the other regions. One was that the workers' struggle was often manifested in a spiral of conflict, which gave rise to extensive working-class mobilization in shows of solidarity. Second, there was an increasingly co-ordinated use of strikes by workers from different factories, which after 1973 took the form of 'area general strikes'. Finally, instead of isolated claims, the workers produced and defended lists of demands, the *'plataformas reivindicativas'* (platforms of demands), particularly after 1974. An additional characteristic of the working-class movement in Barcelona was that the Workers' Commissions became the strongest organization since the early 1960s, while UGT and USO were much weaker. The Workers' Commissions were very successful in their strategy of infiltration within the official trade unions, occupying many posts at the shop-floor level and developing a struggle from these posts – thus it was official trade-union representatives who called the general strike of the *Baix Llobregat* in December 1974. Repression against the organized working-class movement included, therefore, sanctions against workers who had been elected to representative posts in the official trade-union elections. The press reported one elected trade-union officer dismissed, on average, every fourteen actions – allegedly for leading the dispute. Also according to press reports, 1,193 metal workers were sacked and 24,820 had their labour contracts and wages suspended. In comparison with reprisals against miners, sackings amongst Catalan metal workers were more frequent but there were fewer suspensions.

5 Industrial conflict in the metal industry of Madrid

Madrid had been one of the strongholds of Spanish socialism until

1939. As a whole the province of Madrid produced one of the highest votes for the left, under the Second Republic. In the municipal elections of April 12, 1931, which caused the fall of the Monarchy and the proclamation of the Second Republic, the proportion of elected leftist '*concejales*' in Madrid reached 70 per cent of the total elected, second only to Asturias with 73 per cent. In the legislative elections of February 16, 1936, which resulted in a triumph for the Popular Front, the coalition of the left gained the highest percentage of the vote in Madrid, Barcelona, and Sevilla. However, during the long period of the Francoist dictatorship, movements of dissent were particularly difficult to organize in Madrid, where all the State apparatus was concentrated and where repression against the dominant labour union, the UGT, had been massive. An added difficulty was that Madrid had not been a major industrial centre. It was easier for students to set up a powerful and organized movement, because of the great size of the University of Madrid and the political tradition of its students. So much so that until the mid-1960s, students were responsible in Madrid for most of the public opposition to the regime.

From the early 1960s onwards, rapid industrialization dramatically changed the occupational structure of Madrid and created a large proletariat. Thus, in 1965, the number of metal workers reached 115,000: an increase of 43.5 per cent on 1958. Madrid became in the 1960s the second industrial city of Spain, and the development of a modern metal industry was a central factor (see García 1965). An organized working-class movement started to emerge after 1964, and by 1967 it had extended to the major factories. The Workers' Commissions, which were set up in Madrid in 1964, were the most influential labour organization within the movement and they extended from Madrid to other parts of Spain. Repression against the Workers' Commissions, which started in 1968, was particularly strong against those of Madrid.

Between 1966 and 1974 the press provided information on 234 industrial confrontations in Madrid involving metal workers. This represented 10.2 per cent of the total volume reported for Spain as a whole over the same period. The working-class struggle in Madrid, appeared, however, to be more dispersed through various branches of industry than in the other three regions: disputes in the metal industry comprised only 49.2 per cent of all reported industrial conflicts. Building workers and bank employees also played a significant part in the working-class movement in Madrid – the former providing 23.8 per cent and the latter 10.3 per cent of all actions recorded by the press.

Table 6   Predominant types of conflict among Madrid metal workers
(1966–74)

type of action	issue	N	%
strike-on-the-job	solidarity	59	25
protest	solidarity	22	9
strike-on-the-job	deadlocks in bargaining	14	6

The use of strikes-on-the-job over solidarity issues shows a very careful mobilization strategy on the part of the secret unions. Such action was comparatively easy to effect and was adequate during a period of organizational weakness. Solidarity strengthened the movement. Again, large firms were the source of the movement: the average size of the workforce of the firms most involved was 2,739 workers. It must also be noted that metal workers in Madrid and Barcelona, the two areas where the new organization of the Workers' Commissions was more influential, mobilized more frequently than Asturian or Basque workers over problems of collective bargaining. Collective bargaining was, of course, the central task of official trade-union representation (*enlaces* and *jurados de empresa*), which was often infiltrated by militants of the Workers' Commissions. Official trade-union representatives in the metal industry of Madrid were more often dismissed from their posts than anywhere else, including Barcelona: one in every three disputes. On the other hand, the average number of workers sacked per conflict was lower than in the Basque and Catalan regions (one worker), and that of workers suspended per conflict lower than in the Asturian, Basque, and Catalan regions (three workers). Perhaps the most important characteristics of the actions of metal workers in Madrid were the new organization and new strategy that were born within this section of the working class and which had a considerable impact on the Spanish working-class movement as a whole.

6 The emergence of new areas of working-class militancy

As the working-class movement developed through the 1960s, other sectors emerged at the turn of the decade as consistent *foci* of conflict. These new groups were, in particular, the metal workers of Sevilla, of Galicia, and of Asturias; the bank employees of Madrid; and the building workers of Madrid. We must now examine the characteristics of working-class struggle in these new areas and compare them with those of the four strongholds already studied.

(i) In Sevilla, El Ferrol and Vigo in Galicia, and Asturias, groups of metal workers became politically active in the late 1960s. If we look at Sevilla the press reported 35 disputes for that period, involving metal workers (43 per cent of the total number of strikes in the area). During those years the province was facing an economic crisis that deeply affected the metal industry. Conflict was often of a defensive kind, as a fight against redundancies and against unemployment. There was also a strong solidarity between workers employed in different industrial activities (particularly between metal and building workers), and very often a claim presented by workers in a factory was supported by strikes in other factories and in other industries. Sixty-five per cent of the confrontations in the metal industry were strikes, while sit-ins and occupations of factories represented 15 per cent of the actions. The most frequent issue that mobilized these metal workers was solidarity (45 per cent of the issues), followed by redundancies (25 per cent), and wage claims (20 per cent). There were no press reports of official trade-union representatives having been sanctioned nor of collective suspensions of labour contracts and wages, but the average number of workers sacked per strike was very high (5.5).

The metal industry of Galicia in the north-west is concentrated in the cities of El Ferrol and Vigo, where shipbuilding has been a major industry for some time and where car factories (such as Citroën in Vigo) and engineering industries have been part of a process of industrialization (mostly in Vigo). There was no tradition of working-class struggle in Galicia, although the CNT had had some influence in La Coruña and Pontevedra around 1933. Between 1966 and 1974 the press reported thirty-three confrontations which consisted mostly of strikes. The incipient industrial struggle of this new working-class group culminated in 1972 when violent confrontations led by workers from the large shipbuilding companies and from Citroën-Hispania took place. Two actions were particularly important: the first, a co-ordinated strike in twenty-five firms[19], involving 15,000 workers, which resulted in 5,000 workers having their contracts and wages suspended and over a hundred official trade-union representatives removed from their posts. The second involved the occupation of the nationalized ship-building company Bazán after negotiation for a collective agreement failed. There was a clash with the police in which two workers were killed and several were injured, and twenty-five workers were sentenced to prison by the Court of Public Order, while the firm was occupied by the army. Repression here mostly involved dismissals of official union representatives and suspensions of labour contracts and wages.

In Asturias the economic crisis of the coal mines ran counter to the increasing economic importance of the steel industry, which consisted basically of two modern firms, a private one – UNINSA – and a nationalized one – ENSIDESA. Although secret unions were slow to penetrate these firms, particularly the latter, the press reported thirty-two conflicts for the period 1966–74, which represented 11.1 per cent of the total number recorded for Asturias.

There appear to have been small variation in the use of strikes by the three groups, but the importance of solidarity as a mobilizational issue was less among Asturian workers who most often went on strike as a result of fruitless negotiations with the management over a collective agreement. Also the economic crisis in Sevilla was reflected in the relative importance of confrontations over job redundancies between 1970 and 1974. If we compare conflicts in these new regions and in the four major traditional enclaves, there do not seem to be consistent differences producing distinct typical patterns. Strikes were less frequent in these new centres than in the traditional ones (with the exception of Madrid metal workers), but solidarity among metal workers in Sevilla and Galicia was lower only than among Basque workers. What is perhaps significant is that collective bargaining as an issue was associated with recent militancy (metal workers in Asturias and Galicia) and recent organization (metal workers in Madrid and Barcelona), while it was of much less importance in the strongholds of traditional unionism (Asturian mines and Basque steel and metal industries). This association may have been the result of relative political weakness, which would lead to mobilization on issues not immediately political, but it may also have been the product of the different attitudes held by the Workers' Commissions and USO (the new unions) and by UGT (the traditional union) towards infiltration of the legal machinery.

(ii) In the second half of the 1960s militancy among bank employees in Madrid increased. The three underground organizations, UGT, USO, and the Workers' Commissions, achieved substantial influence after 1967 and infiltration within the official trade union was very effective from the 1966 election onwards. The first stage in the development of opposition among these black-coated workers began with a protracted and bitter dispute that started in 1967 over a large sum of unpaid family allowances, and involved several banks. This dispute led to disciplinary measures against the workers' representatives which, in turn, provoked sympathy strikes and the extension of the conflict to several provinces. As a result, the organization of the employees was strengthened as well as the influence of leftist leaders, and bank employees became a rather militant group.

Overt hostility against the official trade unions was also very strong among bank employees: a collective letter sent to the official trade-unions' congress held in Tarragona in 1968 stated that 'we workers have the unalienable right to create our own labour organization ... We find ourselves without a labour union to protect and to defend us against the capitalism of the bank companies.' A national survey of bank employees carried out in 1969–70[20] revealed considerable radicalism among them, both on questions referring to policies of nationalization of the banks and on questions referring to perceptions of Spanish legislation as being class-biased.

(iii) The secret trade unions had great difficulties in organizing building workers, particularly because of the high proportion of recent immigrants, the scattered distribution of the sites, and because of the extended use of casual labour. About 40 per cent of building workers in Madrid were hired on a short-term basis, and many building companies considered workers who had been employed 120 days as casual (Barceló 1974). The conditions of work were dangerous: there were roughly 200,000 accidents every year, a serious injury every five hours, a death every day; accidents in the building industry represented 24.8 per cent of the total number of labour accidents in Spain. Building workers became more active after 1970. Underground organizations had been working on the sites, distributing leaflets and organizing assemblies on the spot. The first step was taken in 1970 and it consisted of the draft of a proposal for the negotiation of a collective agreement for the building industry of Madrid, which was then discussed every week in assemblies on the sites; a survey was also carried out among workers in eighty-five building companies. The results helped to produce the final proposal. Arrests were made among the leaders, many workers were sacked, and a strike was organized for September 8, 1970, when 25,000 workers stopped work[21]. Sympathy strikes both within and between sites increased very much between 1970 and 1974: for example, the building industry of Madrid was paralyzed by a strike which followed the arrest of non-official, elected representatives of the workers when they met to discuss the state of negotiations for a collective agreement, and again after the sacking of over 300 workers from the building company Comylsa. There was also an increasing use of 'plataformas reivindicativas' (platforms of demands) which in the 1970s included claims for amnesty, for the right to strike, for the right to organize assemblies in the sites, for equality for foreign immigrants, together with demands which referred to wages, the working day, holidays, retirement, social security, and vocational training. In the 1970s, the underground labour unions achieved substantial strength in the building industry of Madrid, and they were able to organize co-ordinated actions with other areas, mainly Barcelona, Sevilla, Cádiz, and Granada – where three workers were killed by the police in July 1970.

7 Conclusions

The emergence and development of a working-class movement in Spain under the Francoist regime between 1939 and 1975 were therefore based on certain working-class areas that were the main sources of working-class militancy. The importance of a few strategic centres for the organization of a working-class movement was particularly great in Spain under a repressive dictatorship which had suppressed all working-class parties and unions. The working-class movement was thus based on Asturian miners, steel and metal workers in Barcelona, the Basque Country, and Madrid. These four groups produced 62 per cent of all industrial confrontations reported by the press from 1966 to 1974. Only after the substantial gathering of strength of the movement in the 1960s, did the struggle become more diversified, involving new working-class areas in other parts of the country.

Working-class militancy was concentrated in what had been the historic centres of political radicalism in the 1930s and where, after the Civil War, political opposition to the regime was strong. In spite of massive repression, Francoism could not totally eradicate working-class organizations in these areas and they were important in re-kindling the struggle. However, this political factor was supplemented by changes in the economy. The working-class movement re-emerged in pockets of political radicalism which were also the most industrial-ized centres in Spain, with a high proletarian concentration and comparatively high rates of immigration. These enclaves were also the wealthiest parts of the country. The main course of action taken by workers was to strike, and workers mobilized mostly on the issue of solidarity. Later on in the 1970s, when, as a result of organizational success and of industrialization, the movement expanded to new centres, the main features of the struggle did not vary much. Conflict in the new centres was often associated with collective bargaining, as the underground groups took full advantage of the possibilities opened up by the system of industrial relations. But conflict was also very often openly political, both through displays of working-class solidarity and through the open challenge to official trade unions (a major issue even among bank employees).

Conflict was increasingly co-ordinated on an inter-provincial basis.

The growing use of rather complex '*plataformas reivindicativas*', articulating political and economic demands, was another important feature of conflict in the last years of Francoism. If we look at the characteristics of the struggle in the four major areas of working-class militancy, strikes were mostly used by Asturian miners, followed by steel and metal workers of Barcelona and the Basque Country, while the strike-on-the-job was more frequent in Madrid. Solidaristic and political claims were more central issues for the metal workers of the Basque Country and of Madrid, while labour accidents in the pits and wage claims were the major issues for Asturian miners and Catalan metal workers respectively. Conflict among Barcelona and Madrid metal workers had two common characteristics: first, disputes over collective bargaining were particularly important; second, dismissals of official trade-union representatives because of their active participation in the struggle were much more frequent than in the other two regions. Such variations in the characteristics of conflict between the four working-class areas were possibly associated with ecological differences (e.g. large metropolis v. concentrated industrial communities – Madrid and Barcelona against Asturias and the Basque Country) and with economic differences (a modern and competitive industry v. an obsolete industry in crisis, such as the Asturian coal mines). However, political differences seem to have been of great importance: in particular the strength or weakness of traditional and new labour unions, basically UGT in Asturias and the Basque Country and the Workers' Commissions in Barcelona and Madrid. Although the leaders of the illegal labour unions, whose interviews are studied in the next chapter, generally stressed the influence of their organizations in all these parts of Spain, they also often acknowledged variations in the distribution of their support[22], which followed the geographical lines here indicated.

4 Working-class organizations and working-class militants

The resurgence of a working-class movement under non-democratic political conditions does not depend only on the two main factors studied in the previous chapters, namely the political contradictions brought about by economic development and social change on the one hand and the presence of particular industrial communities and strong local traditions of working-class radicalism on the other. These are pre-conditions that require a third factor: the existence of working-class organizations, which have either survived underground from an earlier period of political democracy or which have been newly set up in secrecy. These organizations are decisive in mobilizing the working class and in structuring a working-class movement – their policies are influenced by the political contradictions and the community circumstances but at the same time their strategies activate conflict.

Under non-democratic regimes, political organizations are particularly important in the dynamics of working-class movements of dissent. Spontaneous confrontations are difficult and costly; preventive deterrent policies and repression hinder the overt expression of political claims. Also, working-class organizations are outlawed and persecuted and there are state-controlled unions that regiment the working class[1]. Thus, an examination of the re-emergence of secret working-class organizations is a crucial element in the study of working-class dissent.

The present chapter will focus on secret labour unions under Francoism, while the politics of political parties will only be discussed in so far as they directly impinge on trade-union developments. Working-class politics will be analysed by considering not only official documents, leaflets, pamphlets, and reports, but also the point of view of strategically situated militants, who acted as 'informants' and provided evidence both on questions referring to the organizations and on their personal experiences[2]. I shall use as evidence the main documents produced by the three major clandestine labour unions, the Workers' Commissions (*Comisiones Obreras*), the UGT (*Unión General de Trabajadores*), and the USO (*Unión Sindical Obrera*), and also tape-recorded interviews with seventeen representative leaders of the main trade unions. These sources of evidence have been discussed in Chapter 1.

1 Defeat and repression

The 1936 rebellion against the Republic and the Popular Front government had as one of its major ideological components the suppression of autonomous working-class organizations and the setting up of a corporatist system. The destruction of the two large labour unions, the socialist UGT and the anarchist CNT, was a central part of the repressive policies of the Francoist side during the war and of the new state after 1939.

The consequences of the defeat of the Republic and the Popular Front organizations are vividly illustrated by the following account that one of the interviewees gave of his personal experience:

'In the war I was the editor of a CNT newspaper in Madrid. This was until the 28th of March, 1939, when we had to leave Madrid ... We went to Valencia, in a truck, shooting our way through Madrid. Two of us were killed. In Valencia, there were a lot of people but no ships. So we followed on to Alicante, and the ships had left at four. And no other ship came into the harbour. People from all parts of the Republican front had gathered there, the fronts had crumbled. Some 30,000 people were collected in the harbour. We started to wait for ships that did not arrive, ships that the government and the Defence Council had paid for and which the International Commission for Evacuation had found. The ships didn't come, they were sailing around Alicante but they didn't get in. That was the 29th, 30th, and 31st of March. And on the 1st April there was nothing else left but to surrender to the Italians of the Littorio Division and later to the Francoists. Except those who committed suicide, and there were many who did. We spent our last night in groups, deciding whether we should commit suicide or not. Because the future was not very hopeful, of course. That was the end of the war for us. I was taken to a jail in Madrid, where I was questioned for forty-nine days, with thirty others. Five of them died by torture and seventeen were shot. I was sentenced to death the 18th January, 1940, by the same Military Tribunal that sentenced Miguel Hernández[3], and I was waiting for the execution sixteen months and three days, until I had the sentence commuted the 21st May, 1941. In this period, on 103 occasions they took groups out from prison to be shot and 517 people were killed, and this was only in the prisons of Yeserías and Santa Rita, but there were twenty-six more jails in Madrid at that time. This was the worst period, but people were shot through the whole history of Francoism, until September 1975 ... I spent nine years in prison, until 1948. Of course, this is of no importance as an isolated case, but there were thousands of people in the same situation. After that I was again arrested in 1949 because of some letters that they found when they arrested a group of guerrillas and I was tried by the *Tribunal Especial de Espionaje y otras Actividades* [Special Tribunal of Espionage and other Activities] and I was put in jail in Oviedo. Since then I have been arrested five or six times. (interview no. 16)

The extent of the destruction of working-class organizations can be glimpsed by comparing the pre-1939 membership of the UGT (1,444,474 in 1933) and the CNT (1,577,547 in 1933). It involved village-by-village, town-by-town, tracing and persecution of militants, and the massive use of a wide range of political measures – from executions to confinement and professional sanctions. It also involved the widespread use of terror. Total political domination from 1940 was based on the disintegration of working-class organization and representation, and it lasted through the 1940s and 1950s. It was reinforced by the compulsory regimentation of the working class in state-controlled unions. As has been described in Chapter 2, corporatist organization of the working class had been a central part of the programme of *Falange* (as stated in the *26 Puntos de la Falange* in 1934) and it was set up by the Francoist regime as the main pillar of the new 'organic state' as early as 1938 with the *Fuero del Trabajo* (the Labour Charter) and later fully carried out in 1940 with the *Ley de Unidad Sindical* (Trade Unions Unity Act). Some of the interviewees tried to describe those years of complete working-class organizational destruction.

'I was at the time working in a kind of shop and canteen, in a working-class quarter beyond the *Puente de Segovia*[4]. That was in the years of hunger, a tremendous hunger here in Madrid. You could see the total prostration, a prostration not only economic, with very low living standards, but also psychological and political. A fear that I have seen around for years and years, practically till very recent times. It was a frightful fear then ... There was nothing resembling an organization, you never saw two workers together, the only link was friendship or booze ... People were mostly employed in the railways, and also in building ... As my mother's family had been in the railways I got a job in the RENFE[5], first as an apprentice for two years ... I was on night shift for two years, and we got to have some kind of trust among ourselves and we got to speak with less inhibitions. And yet, never, never once did we talk about politics in all those nights, waiting for the arrival of a train, listening there to footplatemen, plate-layers, rolling-stock maintenance men, guards, signalmen, and people shutting up about politics. I met some folks there, old ones, who had been the most militant before the war, because they had a strong union in the railways, the UGT that was. But in that area of the *Estación de las Pulgas* [the Station of the 'fleas'], as they called it, of the *Estación de Santa Catalina*, and in all the railway belt of Madrid, the four or five main stations, all the leaders were liquidated. No resistance was possible. There were other factors too, the presence of a detachment of the *Guardia Civil* ['Civil Guard' – the para-military police] within the RENFE. I was once forced to stay for a whole day in a cattle wagon for nothing. Just as intimidation. There was no trace of a working-class organization, no trace...'

(interview no. 1)

The 1940s were years of widespread repression. There was no possible defence through working-class organizations or through collective action. Repression was the foundation of the new order, and private firms helped the dictatorship in the purges. The close collaboration between the state and capitalist groups in eradicating working-class organizations and militancy was described by the interviewees who survived those years.

'The firms contributed to the repression. That is, the firms produced black lists, with the names of those who had held posts in the UGT and these were sacked, you see.... And these people had to survive somehow – I've met many comrades who were selling in the streets, ties, perfumes, books ... You had to cling to whatever you could. The files that they got hold of were bad enough but then there was also the information from collaborators. In order to gain the benevolence of the regime they provided lists and made accusations. Repression was unbelievable, and nobody, absolutely nobody, not even when the war was finished – the people who had been in the *Campo de los Almendros*[6], none imagined what was going to happen. What people thought was that there would be purges of the main leaders and no more. The war should have been enough, the defeat should have been enough. A lot of people did not leave the country because they thought there was no reason for it ... Only a few dozens remained of the hundreds of thousands of UGT militants, you see, in some villages not even the tail remained of the UGT.' (interview no. 5)

Military defeat, repression, and total political control of the country made the early attempts to reorganize the unions underground extremely difficult and costly. These attempts resulted in a long series of arrests and successive crises of survival, which made the strategy of struggle from within Spain difficult to carry out at that stage. Accounts of leaders of UGT and CNT were similar. One of the leaders described repression against the UGT in the following terms:

'The truth is that from 1943 to 1954, the UGT tried to struggle within the country. But, you see, until 1954 seven Executive Committees were caught by the police. There was a great drop in 1945, when a full Executive Committee and several members of the National Committee were arrested. In 1953 the general secretary, Tomás Centeno, was tortured to death in the *Dirección General de Seguridad* [the police headquarters in Madrid]. Every time an Executive Committee fell, the whole organization crumbled, and it was extremely hard to rebuild it. And then in 1958, over two hundred were caught, with that man from Vitoria, Antonio Amat, and all those people; that was important because it reinforced the belief that the Executive Committee had to stay outside Spain, in Toulouse.'

(interview no. 13)

The descriptions of repression were always similar. This militant talks again about the same period, the decade of the 1940s and the early 1950s:

'Those years were a desert, a political desert. You see you have to remember what the repression was, what the 1950s were ... After 1947, after the strike of the 1st of May 1947 in Vizcaya, and after the strike of 1951, the surviving militants of UGT and CNT were practically exterminated. In 1951 militants of UGT and CNT were still being shot. From 1940 to 1947, seventeen national executive committees of the CNT fell – that is, one every five months.'

(interview no. 12)

The early difficulties in reorganizing a working-class movement did raise two primary considerations: on the one hand, whether to concentrate all the organizational strength on an underground struggle from within, whatever the costs, or to keep a considerable part of the membership in exile; on the other hand, whether a strategy of infiltration within official institutions was an effective strategy or whether it would reinforce the official unions rather than undermine them. These two questions will be raised later on. What must now be noted is that in the 1950s the two democratic labour unions under the Second Republic, the UGT and the CNT, withdrew a large part of their organizational apparatus from Spain. There was a less clear-cut situation in the parties of the left: the Communist Party (PCE) became increasingly committed to a mass underground activity, while the Socialist Party (PSOE) was still facing difficulties in the 1950s in adapting to the political struggle[7]. The political conditions were then most unfavourable, with the long-lasting effects of military and political collapse combining with drastic repression. A link between the politics and the economy of Spain in that period was often pointed out by the interviewees.

'The type of exploitation of the working class from the end of the war until the late fifties was plain enough. To squeeze and squeeze as much as possible. The conditions couldn't be better: a defeated working class, its organizations suppressed, total defencelessness. The militants had been eliminated, or were in jail, or had gone into exile. The organizations were defeated and routed. A mechanism of control and discipline had been set up with the state-controlled "vertical" trade unions. Exploitation took place under complete impunity. This allowed for a very strong capital accumulation. So it was; this is a very schematic description of capitalist development in those years, but this is how it was...' (interview no. 6)

2 From square one: the first attempts towards reorganization

The early stages of the political reorganization of the working class consisted of attempts by a small number of surviving militants to revive the labour associations under the Republic. Under repression and secrecy the different groups of the left struggled to survive.

'So, very slowly, the working class was reorganizing itself. The working-class struggle did not stop – what happened was ... as I've heard old communist militants say, "we struggled from within the prisons". Yes, from the prisons, this was the beginning.'

(interview no. 6)

'In 1943 a few comrades of the UGT were released from jail, and also those of us who had had some kind of representation started to meet again, to organize, you know, in a kind of tight and small brotherhood. So one could say that thenceforth there was an organized activity. Before that, yes, there were contacts between comrades who met, with due precautions, but only after 1943 was there a reorganization of the UGT as such. There were of course many who did not want to take part, who were frightened or who had changed their minds ... Of course repression was very hard.'

(interview no. 5)

Now, while there was general agreement about the history of those early years as a long series of frustrated attempts to rebuild the organizations, the union leaders did not always agree about the continuity between those attempts and the later emergence of an organized working-class movement. To what extent was the working-class movement in the 1960s and 1970s associated with these organizations during these years? To what extent was it based on new developments? It was obvious that there was a bias in the reports according to the affiliation of the leaders – they were arguing continuity *pro domo sua* in the case of UGT militants, and discontinuity in the case of USO and militants of Workers' Commissions.

Leaders from the Workers' Commissions and from USO insisted that an organizational void existed over the post-war period so that the organized movement was built on completely new foundations. These bases included the emergence of new working-class leaders whose militancy was the result of experiences within legal Catholic workers' associations[8] and also of experiences as elected shop floor representatives within the official union (the *enlaces* and *jurados de empresa*). They also included clandestine party militants (in particular from the Communist Party) within these legal institutions. Two modifications of the industrial relations system were described as having contributed to the birth of the new organized movement: the system of collective bargaining introduced in 1958, and the elective character of the official trade-union's shop-floor representatives. These two modifications are also discussed in other sections of the book. What is now relevant is that leaders from the Workers' Commissions and USO dismissed the importance of underground activity during the first twenty years of Francoism, and laid emphasis on the grass-roots movements that followed changes in the economic situation and in industrial-legal regulations. It must, of course, be noted that *Comisiones* were set up between 1962 and 1964. One of the leaders of *Comisiones* described as follows the discontinuity of the struggle and the birth of the first Workers' Commissions in the early 1960s.

'The first Workers' Commissions started to emerge from the grass-roots, from the factories, from assemblies where workers started to elect their representatives ... So far there had been no successful reorganization of the trade-union movement, you know, although UGT or CNT militants might have been struggling. But as organizations, the UGT or the CNT lacked any real weight inside the factories, they did not have a mass following. And this is only natural: under the long years of Fascism no labour union could exist, because this required contact with the workers and that was impossible in secrecy.' (interview no. 7)

The Workers' Commissions were presented as a direct emanation from the movement to elect autonomous workers' councils at the work place *and also* as the result of the use made by workers of the official elective posts within the state-controlled unions to try to promote 'authentic' representatives. This last point was also made by USO leaders as a crucial factor explaining the new strength of the working-class movement in the 1960s and also to defend the infiltrationist strategy that they shared with *Comisiones*.

USO was set up in the same period as *Comisiones*, when Spanish capitalism moved towards more liberal policies in the economic sphere and when this change was felt in the hitherto strongly repressive system of industrial relations. This new union was created by ex-militants of UGT and by active left-wing Catholic workers. It was independent of political organizations and defended a programme of self-managed socialism and a strategy of infiltration into the official trade unions. The following account by one of its leaders stresses again the changes in economic policy and in the industrial relations system, as well as the alleged break between the contemporary working-class movement and the old labour unions.

'The USO has its origins in the late 1950s, when two important factors coincided: first, changes in the political economy of the regime, economic liberalization, and the new system of collective bargaining; second, and perhaps most important, the void left by the old organizations, the UGT and the CNT, as they had been harshly repressed by the regime and were only surviving in exile, a void that had to be filled by a new generation of the working class. So, USO was born from socialist groups of the UGT, mostly in Catalonia, that broke with the leadership in exile, and also from the Catholic movements of JOC and HOAC which had been the only organizations that workers could possibly join. Both JOC and HOAC had played an important part in the first strikes of the 1950s, they were the only ones who could be known, who could act publicly. I remember selling *Juventud Obrera*[9] when I was fifteen or sixteen, at the gates of the *Bazán*[10] and it went like hot cakes. The Workers' Commissions had plenty of people coming from these religious organizations, and today the PTE, the ORT, the Communist Party, ourselves, we all have many militants with these backgrounds.' (interview no. 12)

UGT, the traditional socialist union, defended, on the other hand, a view of working-class struggle continuing under Francoism. Its leaders argued that UGT was never destroyed, that it was able to survive in particular areas – mainly in the Basque Country and Asturias – and that these surviving pockets were reorganized and revived from the late 1940s (using as examples the strikes of 1947, 1951, and 1956). UGT leaders also believed, however, that changes in the economic situation and in industrial relations contributed to the strengthening of the working-class movement in the mid-1960s, and that the 1970s saw a 'qualitative' leap with a rapid growth of the secret unions. These militants acknowledged, too, the importance of the autonomous grassroots movement to elect representative delegates. But they did not accept that this movement was concerned with infiltrating the official elective posts nor that it was embodied in any new labour union. What must now be examined are the interpretations that the union leaders offered of the changes in the economy and in the system of industrial relations and their subsequent impact on the working-class movement.

3 System contradictions and the growth of secret labour unions

Changes in the Spanish economy and in the industrial relations system have been analysed in Chapter 2. They consisted basically in a greater degree of economic liberalization, a greater openness to international economic relations, and a drive towards economic growth. New policies attempting to stimulate productivity included the replacement of the rigid instrument of the *Reglamentaciones de Trabajo* by a system of collective bargaining which introduced incentives and agreements on production and wages. At the same time, limited representation of the workers at the shop-floor level was introduced within the framework of the official trade unions. These changes were all inter-connected, and this was perceived by the union leaders as a manifestation of the transition of Spanish capitalism from economic autarchy to competition and development and, with it, to a new form of working-class control and exploitation.

The new system of collective bargaining was thus seen originally as an instrument to increase productivity. But this instrument had the unintended consequence of stimulating the organization of the workers, of mobilizing them in the defence of their interests. This created more favourable conditions for collective action and for greater influence of and activity by the secret groups.

'What happened was that these new instruments of exploitation carried an internal contradiction and the workers were able to exploit this contradiction. The working class started to mobilize, and in that situation the clandestine groups that were in a state of hibernation started to emerge and to gain in strength. They could reach thousands of workers with questions that they could understand, that they could feel, with their very own problems and interests. It was really the beginning of a new stage of the working-class movement.' (interview no. 6)

There was a fair degree of unanimity among the union leaders about the relationship between the changes in the economy and the industrial relations system on the one hand, and the new possibilities for working-class activity on the other. These changes were seen as having introduced important contradictions within the structure of the state: in particular, the contradiction between a para-Fascist corporatist control of the working class and the new requirements of the economy. These 'system contradictions'[11] opened up new objective possibilities for social and political change. More specifically, they allowed for new possibilities for reorganization of the working class and the underground groups. There are differences, however, in one respect: infiltration and the use of legal means. Leaders of the Workers' Commissions and USO tended to associate the new possibilities opened up by collective bargaining *with* the possibility of infiltration into the elective shop-floor posts within the official trade unions. Leaders of the UGT accepted the contradictory strategic importance of the new system of collective bargaining both for the economic policies of some sectors of Spanish capitalism and for the reorganization of the working class. But they viewed the political possibilities in a different way than *Comisiones Obreras* or USO: it was out of the question to use collective bargaining *from inside* the official trade unions as this would only delay the struggle for democratic unionism and would also involve some kind of collaboration with the regime.

Trade-union leaders saw the changes in the economy and in the industrial relations system since the mid-1950s as a major stepping-stone in the history of the working-class movement under Francoism and as a fundamental factor for understanding the new strength of the movement in the 1960s and 1970s. There were nevertheless differences in the strategies of the secret organizations and they will be analysed in the next section in greater detail. What were considered to be the main turning points of the re-emerging movement in its new phase? The leaders from the Workers' Commissions agreed that 1962 had been the beginning of an uninterrupted working-class movement; that 1966 and the successful infiltration into official trade-union posts in September of that year had represented the maturity of the new working-class movement; that because of a dramatic increase in repression which accentuated internal political differences, the period between 1968 and 1973 had been one of crisis; that 1973 was the beginning of a process of recovery and of increasing strength which, by the end of 1975, at the time of Franco's death, had already crystallized in a powerful underground working-class movement.

The first stage of the Workers' Commissions was one of relative political tolerance towards them as they were seen as only a somewhat unorthodox development of the official *Sindicatos* at the shop-floor level, which could increase workers' support for the official corporatist unions. This tolerance gave the militants of the Workers' Commissions three years to infiltrate and gain in strength: roughly from 1964 to 1967. The first reaction from the regime to *Comisiones* was described as follows:

'The elections of 1966 were truly a triumph. A triumph that surprised the enterprises themselves and also *Sindicatos*. *Sindicatos* was not expecting this challenge. The elections had been a farce for a long time and nobody cared, and so when *Comisiones* fought them they did not think it was important, they thought that they could control it. There was a first stage of observation and of relative tolerance towards the Workers' Commissions, with some hope that they would inject new blood into *Sindicatos* in the context of a relative political liberalization. And so we could have our meetings in premises of *Sindicatos*. Of course, the result went beyond anything they could expect.' (interview no. 6)

The second stage of the Workers' Commissions was marked by repression. The movement of reorganizing and re-mobilizing the working class had gone beyond the control of *Sindicatos* and the dangerous presence of militants who had infiltrated the groups became apparent. At the same time, *Comisiones Obreras* had begun to lead important demonstrations, particularly in Madrid where marches of several thousand workers started to take place from June, 1966. These actions produced the first arrests and mass repression quickly followed.

'Repression began towards the end of 1966, stimulated also by the mass demonstrations being staged by *Comisiones*: a chain of arrests, sackings, and dismissals. In 1968 the Supreme Court declared the Workers' Commissions illegal and subversive and there was joint repression by the police, firms, and the courts. In Pegaso[12] there were four or five collective sackings of thirty or forty workers each, there were constant preventive arrests of union leaders, sentences of up to twenty years. From 1968 to 1973 we've reckoned that we've had some 2,000 union representatives, *enlaces* and *jurados*, dismissed in Madrid alone. There were dismissals, and also mass arrests and prison sentences. The regime used a very important instrument: conditional freedom; there were never less than five hundred working-class militants arrested at any time in those years, but many more had upon them the Damocles' sword of provisional freedom. The police failed to destroy *Comisiones* inside the factories, but it smashed all the directive organs. There were three consecutive arrests of the National Commission and the moment came when it was no longer replaceable.' (interview no. 1)

'On 30th March, 1968 I was in the Interbranch of *Comisiones* in a secret meeting in Zarzalejo. The police heard about it, rounded us up and arrested 120, only ten or twelve managed to escape. The Sunday before that, the police caught an assembly of the *Comisiones* of Metal Works, in the Mariano de Cavia square here in Madrid, with over a thousand workers. That was everyday life after 1967.'
(interview no. 11)

Although the Workers' Commissions had gathered substantial strength by the late 1960s, mass repression proved very costly. It seems that the leadership had underestimated both repression and the capacity of *Sindicatos* to survive infiltration. This somewhat optimistic conception, which increased the vulnerability of *Comisiones*, was generally accepted.

'I think that the basic problem was that we believed that everything was at hand, you see. So we didn't really expect the brutal repression that was to follow, the series of states of emergency, the systematic beheading of *Comisiones*. I remember that in 1969 the Provincial Commission of the Metal Industry had only two members, while in 1967 it had sixty ... The openness of *Comisiones*, which was one of the reasons for its success, made repression easier.'

(interview no. 10)

The increase in political repression that followed the sentence of the Supreme Court that declared the Workers' Commissions illegal was a major factor in the crisis of the Workers' Commissions from 1968 to 1973. There was a second factor as well: internal ideological disputes. These disputes centred on the type of organization and the strategy of *Comisiones*: some groups criticized what they considered to be an excessive reliance on 'personalities' and individual leadership, an over-optimistic belief that a democratic 'breakthrough' was close, a lack of secrecy, and consequently an over-exposure to repression. Criticisms were mainly voiced by the *Partido del Trabajo de España* (PTE: Workers' Party of Spain) and the *Organización Revolucionaria de Trabajadores* (ORT: Workers' Revolutionary Organization), and they were directed against the Communist Party's strategy of full use of legal means and open activities. Leaders of the Workers' Commissions stressed the importance of these internal political struggles in the organization's crisis.

'In 1968, when repression started, *Comisiones* went practically into pieces in all the big factories ... It was then that the parties hostile to the use of legal platforms became more influential. We had to accept that we had believed that fascism, one way or another, would tolerate *Comisiones*, that we would occupy all the legal posts, that we were going to undermine *Sindicatos* from within. And there was a bitter struggle within *Comisiones*, against the official position of "legalism" and openness defended by the Communist Party. The return to clandestine activity was seen as an answer to repression, but also as ideologically and strategically sound.' (interview no. 3)

The third stage of the development of the Workers' Commissions under Francoism consisted of the resurgence of the organization in the 1970s, both through the protection of the underground structure of the union and through the maintainance of high visibility and openness using the legal machinery. Thus, the strategy of the Communist Party finally won the day, but the agreement between the different groups of the Workers' Commissions (an agreement that was reached in 1973 and lasted until the Autumn of 1976) also involved a greater effort in strengthening the organization. The crisis and the solution to the crisis will be discussed again in the next section; we must now turn to the situation of the UGT.

The process of development of the UGT was very different. Of the three major unions, it was the only one to have preceded Francoism. It had been a very powerful union in the 1930s and Francoism had persecuted it severely after 1939. The survival of the organization had been marked by twenty-five years of repression and secrecy, by successive waves of arrests, and it led to a decision to protect the central body of the union by moving it to France. The survival of the militants was marked by fear, imprisonment, uncertainty, and by a secluded world of personal relationships whose boundaries were those of the union. But the UGT had been relatively active in 1947, 1951, 1953, and in 1956, when it played an active part in the movement of strikes that spread in the north of Spain (in Asturian mining and Basque steel and metal industries). UGT leaders accepted that, in the mid-1960s, the situation had started to change: that the new dynamics of industrial relations had led to renewed political activities and to a strengthening of the working-class movement. However, over a period of time, the UGT suffered heavy costs by having its leadership in exile. The split between the interior groups and the external leadership became very serious in the late 1960s. It finally resulted in a reorganization of the union in 1972, in which the executive moved to Spain and a group of old leaders in exile left the organization. After that date, the UGT developed very quickly, not only in Asturias and the Basque Country (which had always been its two principal strongholds), but also in Castilla and Andalucía. The importance of the late 1960s and 1970s in the re-emergence of the union is stressed in the following quote from a member of the national executive:

'The union never stopped fighting. It did so with more or less strength depending on repression. But the truth is that by 1967 we were all aware in the interior that we had to reorganize the UGT. We started to do so, and the proof of our success are the massive police raids in 1969, mainly in the Basque Country, and the deportation of a large number of comrades when the state of emergency was declared – Nicolás Redondo was deported, as was Lalo, Enrique Múgica, Ramón Rubial, the great leaders of the north, where the union was stronger. In 1970 the union was much stronger throughout the country, thanks partly to the contribution of the people from the north, who had never stopped fighting. The fears were no longer there, our membership was now dominated by young people, who did not have the inhibitions that repression had produced, and the organization was rising up again in the whole of Spain. In 1972 the Executive Committee moved to the interior and we've had a spectacular growth since then.' (interview no. 14)

The 1970s represented, therefore, a fundamental change in the strength of the illegal trade-union movement as a whole. This change was especially significant in Madrid, where repression had been particularly intensive after 1968, but it also meant an expansion of the labour unions and of the struggle to areas where the working-class movement had been very weak since 1939, namely Andalucía (Sevilla and Granada in particular) and Galicia (El Ferrol and Vigo). The importance of these new areas has been analysed in Chapter 3. The re-organization of the movement in Madrid was described as follows:

'The Metal Industry was the branch where everything had started and where the movement re-emerged in the 1970s. It is a very modern branch in Madrid, you see. My company, Isodel, was set up twenty years ago and most of the important firms are twenty or thirty years old ... So in 1973 there was a strike in Rodamientos SKF in Madrid that lasted twenty-seven days, and there hadn't been such a long strike for a very long time. We had achieved a new organization, after the repression of the five earlier years, when 1,500 workers were dismissed in the metal industry alone because of their activities, particularly in the large firms that were the strongholds of the movement: each has had over a hundred militants dismissed in a few years, you see ... But with the strike in Rodamientos, there was a new organized solidarity, we could feel it, see it, we were able to collect a lot of money in their support. And, immediately afterwards, there was a strike in Standard, and this strike mobilized support from different areas. The vanguard movement was active again. It was then that the general strikes in Getafe, in Vallecas and in Alcalá followed, and they were very successful: I could give you an endless list of factories in strike, the main ones were Marconi, Chrysler, Tudor, Robert Ward, CASA, Noguera Hermanos, Zanussi ... A very important event was the "trial 1,001" because it produced innumerable actions of solidarity, under very difficult conditions, because it coincided with the death of Carrero Blanco[13], and this produced some withdrawal due to fear. In general we were not resorting to street actions but to strikes of solidarity. And now, this last September [1975], again under very difficult political conditions, with the five executions of militants of ETA and FRAP, well, we've shown our strength, with innumerable factories stopping, and mind you, there was an atmosphere of terror, this September, I can tell you because I've felt it right in my factory ... Then, after Franco's death, a rapid strengthening of the movement was possible because the bases were there. And in January and February we've only seen the beginning. In a month, more than double the number of strikes of any previous year. Now we shall not have any more set-backs.' (interview no. 8)

The crisis in the regime, which was accelerated by the death of the Prime Minister, Carrero Blanco, and the political success of the working-class organizations in gathering increasingly wide support, very rapidly changed the conditions of the working-class struggle from 1973. The Workers' Commissions had re-emerged from their crisis with a much greater strength and UGT was growing extremely fast (apparently doubling its size every year until 1976). These two organizations and USO had two important things in common: first and foremost, opposition to the regime, but also common socialist principles. These common elements had made a temporary coalition possible in the summer of 1976: the COS (Co-ordination of Trade-Union Organizations). But there were also important differences between them. It is to the common features and the differences in programmes and strategies that we must turn now.

4 The secret labour unions: their programmes

The programmes of the three major trade unions, which in the 1960s and 1970s had been leading the struggle and which in the summer of 1976 created COS as a unitary platform, will now be analysed more closely, using as information interviews with leaders of the UGT, USO, and the Workers' Commissions, as well as manifestoes, leaflets, and declarations of the three unions. It must, however, be noted that the Workers' Commissions were in the 1970s a coalition of two main groups, whose political views were notably different, and that this difference led to a split in the Autumn of 1976 between what was known as the 'majoritarian trend' (represented by twenty out of twenty-seven posts in the national executive) and the 'minoritarian trend' (represented by the other seven posts). The first trend was mostly influenced by the Communist Party, while the second was supported by the two Maoist groups, PTE and ORT. The confrontation between the two groups involved: (a) the combination of a legal and a revolutionary struggle; (b) the strategies 'of inter-class alliances in the struggle for democracy; (c) the imposition of a single working-class trade union, avoiding the risk of pluralism and fragmentation.

The Communist Party had been the main political force behind the Workers' Commissions. After the defeat of guerrilla 'resistance inside the country, the PCE turned to a dual strategy: infiltration of legal institutions and clandestine struggle. The *Oposición Sindical Obrera* (OSO) as an underground 'mass' organization that was intended to lead the working-class struggle. Political repression and isolation within the working class meant that the OSO was only a small appendage of the PCE. Meanwhile, the party was defending a pro-gramme of 'national reconciliation' that was intended to be the basis for an alliance of all the anti-Fascist groups. Two important policies for reaching this goal were the increase of limited struggles defending democratic non-revolutionary claims, and also the creation of unitarian platforms. The emergent Workers' Commissions appeared to be a particularly well suited organization to carry out this strategy within the working-class movement. Thus, the Communist Party dropped OSO and joined the bandwagon of shop-floor workers' councils from its very early stage, trying to steer it through the organization of the Workers' Commissions and attempting to make of these a single democratic labour union absorbing other organized working-class groups[14]. At the same time, the Communist Party was trying to put into practice the strategic objective proposed by Dimitrov in the Seventh Congress of the Comintern in 1935: infiltration within the 'mass fascist organizations', for 'it is here that the masses are', turning these organizations into 'the legal or semi-legal starting point for the defence of the everyday interests of the masses'. The PCE had started doing so in 1957 and had achieved considerable success through the participation of the Workers' Commissions in the 1966 elections within the official trade unions.

Other political groups also joined *Comisiones*. They included a small populist-Falangist group: the UTS (*Unión de Trabajadores Sindical-istas*), the socialist trade union USO, and two Catholic groups: FST and AST. The Falangist group left in the late 1960s because of the Communist preponderance within the Workers' Commissions; and USO also broke away in 1967 because of the contradiction of being a trade union within a trade union, and also because of disputes with the Communist Party. After 1968 the Workers' Commissions involved the Communist Party, different splits from this party (the most important of which was to be the PTE – the Workers' Party of Spain, a Maoist splinter-group that grew very much in strength and influence in the 1970s), and also groups of Catholic workers. Of these the most relevant was the AST: it was of Jesuit origins (two Jesuit priests, Granda and Castiñeiras, were founders of the group), it attracted numerous workers from Marianist Congregations, and then it went through a rapid and intense radicalization which culminated in a change of name to ORT (Workers' Revolutionary Organization). This political transformation was partly due to the close collaboration with the PCE, and at the same time to the need to develop a distinct strategy within the militant working class. The distinct strategy ultimately was a rather curious mixture of anarchism and Maoism, and in the mid-1970s many early members of Marianist origins were leading the left minoritarian trend within *Comisiones*. This had two consequences: on the one hand, the new ORT absorbed part of the anarchist tradition of the Spanish working-class movement; on the other, it came closer to the PTE so that they converged in the left minoritarian trend. Also, the ORT became rather powerful, particularly in some areas of the Basque Country (such as Navarra) and in Madrid.

The Workers' Commissions were, however, unsuccessful in attracting the socialist working-class groups. USO had been an organization within *Comisiones* from 1965 to 1967 but then it broke away, and the UGT never accepted being absorbed. The leaders of the Workers' Commissions tried strenuously to integrate the socialists.

'The third force was missing, the socialists that is, in that re-organization of the working-class movement. They were missing and I could tell you about Camacho and myself searching for socialists in Madrid. In search of socialists! We had to enlarge *Comisiones*, but the socialist problem was a difficult one. You see, they were the great victims of the civil war. Mind you, it is not that they were hit more harshly, it is that there was more of them. There were few Communist union leaders, you see: the majority of the Communists grew out of the war. And those who could not go into exile, because they did not have the means, were the little officials of the local unions. The large mass, the million members of the UGT could not get away. So many of them were caught, all in the net; what happened was that the *Casas del Pueblo*[15] were ransacked and very often there were lists of members and officials, there, on top of the tables. "Let's see, Union of Railwaymen, president: you; vocals: you, you and you. Union of Building Workers ...", and there was a complete liquidation. They cleaned it up. It's not that they shot everybody, but in those years you could stay in jail for over a year, without trial, and they had you in a cell of the General Direction of Security for months, easily. So, the whole organization was dismantled, and this has lasted for years. But the UGT was not extinct, and I think that a lot of people, particularly in the Communist Party, had got it wrong. It was there, in a state of latency. Because, yes, all this had happened but at the same time it had created a tremendous potential force: everybody has a father, an uncle, a brother, who has been a member or perhaps a very little local leader, and who produced an image of sacrifice and duty. And this potential force is now emerging. The growth of UGT is difficult to understand otherwise.'

(interview no. 1)

There were, then, two socialist trade unions: the UGT and the USO. Unity was not possible: the COS, a joint platform of these two unions and the Workers' Commissions, which was agreed upon in the summer of 1976 and which was intended to be an important step in a long process of unification, was only a fragile temporary co-ordinating agency, due to the differences between UGT and *Comisiones*[16]. The programmes of the UGT, the USO, and the Workers' Commissions, the three unions involved in COS, will now be analysed.

(i) The UGT had a programme which contained a rather carefully elaborated presentation of the union's ideology[17]. It described the socialist struggle of the union towards 'the substitution of capitalist society by a socialist society where man's exploitation by man will disappear' and which would involve extensive collectivization of the means of production (sources of energy, basic manufactures, banks, and insurance companies), socialist planning (as the instrument determining production priorities) *and* workers' control (after collectivization and after the possession of political power by the working class). It also presented an economic programme of agrarian reform, and policies in relation to taxation, education, justice, health, and the environment. The programme contained a violent attack on the regime: it called for 'the disintegration of the dictatorship of the bourgeoisie', for 'a struggle against the fascist regime and the capitalist system that sustains it'. The following quotation is illustrative:

'When a constant characteristic of the regime is violence, when crimes and tortures are happening everyday, when the population is living in an atmosphere of daily terror, when the working class and the democratic sectors are being repressed for exerting their legitimate rights and fill the prisons: let us all move together to end the oppressive and murderous dictatorship.'

(UGT Bulletin No. 357, March 1975)

The union, then, presented a 'platform of demands', involving democratic rights, amnesty, specific legal reforms (that included legal abortion and divorce) and concrete industrial claims (referring to wages, stability of employment, retirement, pensions and benefits, length of the working week, etc.). This platform referred to a transition, first towards democracy, and, in a second stage, to a programme for the transition towards socialism.

Although the demands for the transition towards democracy were fairly precise, the UGT was less explicit about strategic and tactical questions. As has already been described, the union had been strongly opposed to infiltration and to the use of legal means (basically the elections inside the official, state-controlled trade unions). A representative of the executive committee defended this position on the following grounds:

'We've fought for the boycott of the official elections and, believe me, we haven't done it for sentimental reasons or because we had been one of the great defeated of the war, with the CNT and the PSOE. Our repulsion has been due to the belief that *Sindicatos* was a fundamental pillar of the regime, an instrument of control and repression of the working-class movement. Infiltration and "entryism" strengthened the vertical union and therefore the regime ... Our position has been to empty *Sindicatos*, to leave only the shell, and at the same time to set up factory committees that would become the true representatives of the workers.'

(interview no. 14)

The UGT indeed defended in its publications the organization of three non-legal representative platforms: factory workers' councils, factory assemblies (as the 'sovereign organ of workers' democracy'), and area workers' councils (to be composed of representatives of factory councils). The union saw these platforms not only as a tactical instrument, but also as 'the voice of proletarian democracy and the germ of an authentic socialist self-management of the economy'.

Finally, the UGT was much more clandestine than either USO or the Workers' Commissions. This was partly a result of the Civil War and of mass repression, but it was also associated with this union's rejection of the use of legal means in its struggle. It seemed, however, to be the case that the sharp growth of UGT after 1972 and its new strength led to a relative erosion of the requirements of secrecy.

(ii) The ideology of the USO was defined in the official literature of the union as self-managed socialism. The final objective of the union was the suppression of 'capitalist exploitation' and of the domination of 'those who own the means of production', because 'trade unionism expresses the interests of the workers in the transformation of capitalist society and in the implementation of socialism'[18]. The political goals of the union seemed, however, significantly less radical than those of the UGT, and they included many references to a 'humanitarian' socialism, possibly related to the union's origins both in left-wing Catholicism and socialism. But besides this possible persistence of socialism *cum* Catholicism, the programme of USO stressed self-management and also the rejection of political parties: this is in line with the opinion of a member of the national executive that USO had taken up important elements of the old anarcho-syndicalist tradition in Spain. The total separation between the USO and political parties is presented in the following terms:

> 'USO will oppose any plan to turn workers' councils or assemblies into organisms dependent on an external agency, for instance a party. This is the reason why USO ... got out of the Workers' Commissions. The effort of USO to be independent forced it to leave the Workers' Commissions ... when the Workers' Commissions started to become a seedbed of political organizations, PCE and ORT.' (USO Internal Document)

Besides the total political autonomy of the union and workers' self-management in the enterprises, the transition to socialist democracy would involve the socialization of basic industries and the banks, agrarian reform, democratic planning, political pluralism, and self-determination for Catalonia, the Basque Country, and Galicia.

In the fight against the dictatorship, USO, together with the Workers' Commissions, accepted the use of legal means and participation in official trade-union elections. This strategic point was repeatedly defended in the publications of USO. It was, however, presented as compatible with a struggle to create non-official workers' councils and assemblies within the factories, following a dual strategy. At the same time USO leaders insisted on the importance of both visibility – necessary for mobilizational purposes – and secrecy – necessary for the survival of the organization. The leaders had to be visible, so as to attract supporters; the organization had to be kept underground in order to avoid repression.

'The militants have never been very clandestine. In the sense that the leaders cannot be secret. The "apparatus" is a totally different thing ... All the propaganda machine, the organization, yes, this had to be kept underground, but the men, the militants, had to be known. As they mobilized people, as they were a factor of agitation, they have suffered repression. Our militants have paid with heavy costs.' (interview no. 12)

Finally, USO was described in its publications as being bound to have a temporary existence, eventually disappearing within a unified labour organization. These publications made clear, however, that USO would only move in that direction when the time was ripe and through its willing participation in the process of unification, but that it would never accept the external imposition of a single and compulsory union. This was a deep source of friction and suspicion in USO's relations with the Workers' Commissions.

(iii) The Workers' Commissions also situated their struggle within the context of capitalism[19]. In one of its earliest and most important documents, it is stated that 'the capitalist system generates and conditions the class struggle. In a capitalist socio-economic system there is no possibility of harmonizing the interests of the two sides' (*Ante el Futuro del Sindicalismo*, March 1966). It must, however, be noted that in no document was it possible to find a statement referring to specific features of the alternative society defended by the Workers' Commissions: there is no reference in their publications to planning, nationalization, self-management, nor to demands for wide economic reforms. The whole thrust of the claims of the Workers' Commissions is on immediate trade-union demands, which were occasionally placed within the context of a strong attack against the regime[20].

The Workers' Commissions stressed the need to present 'a democratic alternative to the country', which would include 'the right to strike, a true workers' union, and a change of regime' (*Declaración de la Séptima Reunión General*, October 1971). Besides democratic rights and freedoms, the documents of this union mentioned agrarian reform (with the non-socialist PCE slogan 'the land for those who work it'), the extension of free education, and housing policies. But it was in the sphere of industrial relations that the Workers' Commissions, although being politically more limited in their programme, were more specific than the other two trade unions: their claims covered sex and age discriminations; wage increases; the working week and holidays; sickness, unemployment, and retirement benefits, etc. Also, the Workers' Commissions put a very strong emphasis (from 1967) on political amnesty and on job reinstatement for all those workers dismissed for their union activities. In fact it appears that amnesty and a democratic trade union were the two main pillars of the Workers' Commissions programme from the late 1960s.

The *Comisiones'* conception of this democratic trade union was possibly the greatest source of friction between the Workers' Commissions, UGT, and USO, and also within the Workers' Commissions themselves. There was disagreement over a very long period, apparently until the summer of 1976, over (a) the conception of a single and possibly compulsory trade union, internally democratic, created in an open constituent process involving workers' assemblies in every factory[21], and which would allegedly avoid the risks of trade-union pluralism; and (b) another conception of free trade unionism, which would hopefully evolve towards unity through a process of convergence in strategies and programmes, and which would avoid the danger of forceful and compulsory regimentation of the working class in a single union. The latter view was shared by UGT and USO, while the former conception was that of *Comisiones* until 1976, when the dominant sector led by the Communist Party moved towards a more flexible position, producing an internal split with the sector led by the Maoist parties ORT and PTE.

UGT and USO contested the kind of trade unionism defended by *Comisiones* on the grounds that it would forcefully abduct the workers into a compulsory organization; an organization that was, furthermore, of a diffuse character. The vague outlines of the Workers' Commissions contributed to the friction, as their self-description was in terms of a broad socio-political movement rather than a trade union. This was indeed the case both in the documents and in the declarations of the leaders of *Comisiones*: the membership was defined as being the whole of the working class.

'The Workers' Commissions were born at the shop floor level and all workers belong to them' (*Declaración de la Tercera Reunión General*, July 1968).

'In the union elections we had the candidatures openly promoted by the Workers' Commissions, and then we had other candidatures promoted by workers. We know that these workers today, subjectively, do not consider themselves to be members of *Comisiones*, but we believe that objectively they are part of this movement of *Comisiones*, and this is not because we have any wish to absorb anybody but because we are deeply convinced that these men have been following strategies of struggle which are those of *Comisiones* ... Where else would you situate these people?' (interview no. 2)

'The Workers' Commissions are a socio-political movement, not an organization but an organized movement, and this is our form of struggle. The tactics of the Workers' Commissions have been assimilated by the whole of the working class ... 80 per cent of the workers have joined the last strike in the building industry; what is clear is that these men have followed the direction of the Workers' Commissions, that they are also Workers' Commissions men. Because obviously the Workers' Commissions are not only the organized vanguard, but all the workers that organize themselves in order to struggle.' (interview no. 9)

The crucial distinction between, on the one hand, the UGT and, on the other, the Workers' Commissions and USO was, as it has been repeatedly said, the use of legal platforms of struggle – basically elections within the official *Sindicatos* – and of infiltration. This side of the Workers' Commissions' strategy was systematically emphasized and strongly defended in the documents and the interviews. It was presented as a major source of strength of the union, as its revolutionary contribution to the struggle against Fascism, and as the means whereby the working-class movement gathered support in factories pits, and building sites. The legal level of action made it possible to work overtly and to contact and mobilize the workers, even though *Comisiones* would pay the price of a greater vulnerability to repression. It was indeed the case that due to the combination of a legal and an illegal struggle, the Workers' Commissions worked under vaguely defined conditions of security. In fact, its documents frequently rejected strictly underground activities:

'We reject the clandestine status ... We refuse to be considered as an "illegal association" and we shall continue to work in the open and declare who and what we are' (*Qué son las Comisiones Obreras*, June 1966).

'We must break this clandestinity daily by coming out more into the open inside the factories, turning these into real fortresses of the workers' movement' (*Declaración de la Tercera Reunión General*, July 1968).

In the interviews, however, the leaders of the Workers' Commissions indicated that there was greater care and considerable secrecy in the internal organization of *Comisiones*, beyond the openness of the factory assemblies and the public nature of the leaders *qua* factory leaders.

'What would have happened? Who would have addressed the assemblies? Because it was obvious that the assemblies were a very good thing to educate the workers, that they were essential for mass actions. A factory assembly couldn't be secret! And what about the lads who were the leaders, who were involved in everything? How could they be secret? The workers could more or less know the members of the factory commission, but of course the representatives for the area co-ordinating commission, for the branch and the inter-branch commissions, for a national co-ordinating commission or a national secretariat, they were not known. We had to be careful at these levels: protect the head but work openly at the base.' (interview no. 10)

There appears, then, to have been some significant differences between the three major unions under Francoism. These differences related to: (i) the political alternatives (the ideological programmes), which were comparatively more explicit in the UGT and less so in the Workers' Commissions; (ii) the kind of organization achieved and the type of trade unionism that they wanted to set up. The Workers' Commissions had a loose organization with ill-defined limits between members and non-members, and sought to establish a single union by way of a constituent congress encompassing the whole working class; (iii) the conception of factory assemblies and workers' councils, which UGT and USO promoted as institutions of the working class as a whole, while the Workers' Commissions considered them as part of their own organization; (iv) the use of legal means and of infiltration, which set USO and the Workers' Commissions in opposition to UGT; (v) conditions of secrecy, which seemed more stringent in the case of UGT, less so in the case of USO, and of a dual character in the case of the Workers' Commissions (apparently associated with the vague organizational structure of this union). All three unions worked within the system of collective bargaining and tried to take the fullest possible advantage of the opportunities which this system had opened up for a strengthening of the working-class movement. A final characteristic of the underground unions will now be considered: the policies of recruitment and the typical workers who joined them.

5 The policies of recruitment and the recruited militants

The policies of recruitment of the three unions were developed in the context of political repression: efforts to expand and strengthen the movement had to adapt to the requirements of secrecy and underground work in order to protect the organization. These requirements principally involved cautious approaches to and contacts with the potential recruit, and careful screening. Differences between the unions and also changes over time appear to have some correspondence with the distinction between 'exclusive' and 'inclusive' organizations drawn up by Zald and Ash (1966): a distinction mainly based on the presence or absence of restrictive criteria regarding who is eligible for membership and of a period of indoctrination of the new militants. As it could be expected from their particular insistence on secrecy, militants of the UGT came closer to the 'exclusive' organization's strategies of recruitment.

'Obviously, you needed certain guarantees that the lad was reliable. To belong to the UGT could mean many years in jail. You must understand that in those years, because of repression, the UGT was concentrating on the recruitment of officials, not of masses. The place to recruit members was the factory, of course. As you worked with your mates, you started talking to them, and in conflicts, etc., you could see how they were behaving and you could start leaving them leaflets, you know; at first they wouldn't know who was leaving that in their locker. You had to take precautions. It was all too slow, you see, talking with a lad about a leaflet, pretending that you had nothing to do with it. And then you had to find out whether he already was in another organization. And then, "well, fuck it, we are a group of friends and we have meetings. If you're interested . . ." And then the seminars on trade unionism and on the UGT. The UGT was very careful in selecting people, in keeping control on who was wanting to join. Recruitment was not spectacular, we were very prudent.' (interview no. 13)

Recruitment within the USO seems to have also been a secretive and slow process, with careful attention to the individual, potential militant. The factory, and also the neighbourhood, were again the centres for recruitment, and the crucial agency was the secret factory committee of the union.

'We did the classic thing: look at who was active, start passing propaganda, our press, the bulletins of our organization, and so on ... We had a period of probation for every possible militant, followed by seminars. We've always been very concerned with the trade-union education of our members. With ideological education too: you need a good dose of ideology if you want to survive, in secret that's the truth.' (interview no. 15)

The Workers' Commissions appeared to be the union closer to the type of the 'inclusive' organization, being less restrictive in their definition of the potential militant and more open in their approaches. Here, assemblies within the factories are described as the relevant occasions for contacting people.

'People were recruited in assemblies ... Assemblies started due to the need to negotiate with the management. A few men would stand at the gate or they would talk in the canteen or in breaks: "look, comrades, we've got these problems, we must do something, see?, there's this negotiation. We should think of something, we should meet to talk about what to do. What do you say? The comrades in the machine shop, what have they got to say?" That sort of stuff. Then, there are lads whom you notice in the assemblies, they are our bread and butter: they are the ones you start talking to, you start involving them. But all the workers take part in the assemblies ... It is the contact with the parties which is slower. With seminars on trade unionism, on socialism...' (interview no. 11)

What were the characteristics of the militants of the three secret trade unions? What were their political backgrounds? Sociologists have only too often assumed that militancy (or contrarywise, lack of militancy) among the workers is the natural product of objective circumstances – deprivation, community factors, the sale of labour power, their disposal as a commodity, etc[22]. In a repressive context, the inadequacies of this view are quite apparent: militancy also implies costs and the risk of very heavy penalties. Also, today's militants have families: their parents – and indirectly themselves – must have lived through the Civil War and repression in a particular way. To what extent is this relevant?

The union leaders did not give a consistent answer to the question of the importance of the family. The leaders of the Workers' Commissions and the UGT were split among themselves and only the leaders of USO agreed that the parents had been a relevant influence in militancy and that most of the militants, at least in the early stages, came from families that had been active in workers' organizations under the Second Republic. Those militants of *Comisiones* and UGT who stressed the politically heterogeneous backgrounds of today's militants thought that this was due to the attraction of today's unions to the working class as a whole (assuming that parental involvement in the pre-civil war trade-union movement was an experience of only a part of this class).

'The militants were not particularly the children of old militants. You didn't inherit that, being a revolutionary is not something that you inherit. Of course, the vanguard assumes the historical experiences, the tradition, but that's another thing ... No, no, you don't transmit it from parents to children ... You see, very often the old militants have totally withdrawn, they were concerned with their survival, with bringing up their children, with forgetting about politics. The new militants had very different origins, for example, social Catholics were important in the 1950s and 1960s. People were turned to militancy by the hardship of the working-class condition, by exploitation, by the proselytism of the organizations.'

(interview no. 1)

Half of the leaders declared, however, that, mostly in the early stages but also more generally, there was in the leadership of the unions a predominance of militants with a parental history of activism.

'If you go and look at the personal life of most of the people, well, their families have been anti-Francoist. I can't say whether they were in the UGT, the Communist Party, or the Socialist Party, but the majority of the people, their families, they were fighting on the other side. That's for the majority. I can tell you from my experience in Standard and at the provincial level through all these years. Most of the people, as soon as you get them to talk, tell you "well, yes, my family was on the other side" and so on ... Although people are still very reticent about talking, even today. But very often their parents were "reds", often they had been in prison. Just look at the leaders in transport, in the building industry, in the metal industry ... True that very often the families, well, they hide their histories: I know of cases where the parents, who were active before the dictatorship, well, they were hiding it from their children and they tried to frighten them off so that they wouldn't be involved.' (interview no. 3)

It is difficult to assess the accuracy of these conflicting reports. It would, however, appear that the 'founding fathers' of the re-emergent working-class movement in the 1950s had a history of militancy, which often involved not only the families but themselves, and that they 'converted' many people. In the 1960s, although militants were not drawn only from a limited sector of the working class, individuals with backgrounds of parental militancy were predominant in the leadership of the organizations. Thus, if the seventeen interviewees are considered, eleven of them have such backgrounds (let it be remembered, though, that they are not a representative sample). These backgrounds must now be considered, as they provide information about the 'life histories' of working-class leaders under Francoism.

All the trade-union leaders reported experiencing strong ideological control in their youth. This was shared by those whose parents had been involved in working-class organizations and also by those whose parents had not. It was the general experience of Spanish youth after 1939, and it must be compared with the reported experiences of student leaders in Chapter 6. These ideological controls were directly experienced within the schools:

'I was a member of the *Legión de María* ['Legion of Mary'] when I was ten, for a couple of years ... We visited hospitals. I was going to the Menéndez Pelayo school, in Atocha, and in the breaks we had to stand in rank order, singing the *Cara al Sol* [the Phalangist anthem]. Five hundred kids singing the *Cara al Sol* day after day after day, that was crazy, that was bloody stupid, we were raising the flag and all that shit ... I remember that one day propaganda had been distributed, it was a working-class area, and the director of the school said that he would punish anyone who looked at it.' (interview no. 8)

The political repression and ideological controls that had existed and were existing in Spanish society often brought fear and secrecy into family life: parents who had been politically active tried to conceal from their children their past affiliation and, furthermore, attempted to turn them away from politics or from involvement in trade-unionist activities.

'What I've always felt in my family was that they desperately tried to keep me away from any kind of political activity. You see, I've always been aware of that great terror, a terror which existed amongst the people as a consequence of the war – the only ideology that I got in my family was fear: "don't get involved in anything", that's what they always said.' (interview no. 2)

'My grandfather was killed in the war. But even that I didn't know. They were hiding all these things from us. It's simply that they were people who were frightened, they have been living with a lot of fear. In Toledo, you see, repression was very harsh. It was mainly fear...' (interview no. 11)

There was sometimes an explicit opposition between the activities of the parents, when they were maintained after the war, and the activities of their children.

'My father was a Communist and he fought for the Republic. He is a metal worker, he works in a factory with three hundred workers. We've always lived in Madrid. My father was on conditional freedom until 1966. He was working in that factory where he had also been sanctioned and he could get no promotion, you see. And at night he worked in a garage. My mother was a servant. And yet we had to go to get American milk, you know, charity, etc. This made me sick. I thought that with both of them working as beasts we shouldn't have to live on credit.... We lived first in the house of my grandparents, there was a real crowd living there. Later with an uncle who was handicapped and had got a job as a porter, we were living in the porter's house ... At home nobody ever talked about politics. They wouldn't let me go to demonstrations, and what happened was that sometimes I met my father. We lived in an atmosphere of fear, you see ... Well, as an example, I remember that when I was at school and the nuns were telling me about the "reds", this was something that terrified me. I came home one day and I asked my mother: "listen, mom, who are the 'reds'?" And the poor woman, she became half-hysterical, she started to cry and said: "the men who've got tails and horns like your father, can't you see how red he is?" ... You had an education, well, totally anti-communist at schools. This all affected my mother very much, and I had to leave home when I was twenty-five, she was saying that I was putting my father at risk.' (interview no. 3)

The fear of political activity is described in more general terms in the following quote:

'There was all the repression and the exile, and the people who stayed in, well, they were frightened because of their children. This fear increased after 1945, when it was hoped that Spain would be liberated, and when it didn't happen people realized that this was going to last for quite a while and that to bring their children in contact with the organizations would be a grave danger, many years of jail that many of them had already experienced in the flesh.' (interview no. 14)

Only in three of the cases does there appear to have been an open communication between parents and children, which also involved telling the children about trade-union or political activities. Thus, one of the leaders said that his father, a militant of the anarchist union CNT, used to take him to meetings of the Federation of Post Office and Telegraph Workers. The other two were children of a socialist and of a communist militant who did not conceal their ideological convictions nor their active political commitments.

For trade-union leaders political activity had been quickly followed by repression. The seventeen leaders were arrested by the police 119 times, an average of seven apiece. Some of these leaders had accumulated long prison sentences (one of them fourteen years, another twelve), and nine-month sentences were considered to be light. But besides arrests, they experienced much repression within firms: they were often sacked and put on black lists. They had also been the object of different forms of persecution and occasionally they had been tortured. Persecution and harassment are reported in the following quotes:

'I survived six years in John Deere and then I was sacked with two other members of the *Jurado de Empresa*. Since then I've been looking for a job. There is a police report on me and I am followed by members of the *Brigada Político-Social* [the secret police] who work as private detectives for the firms. I have tried endless firms in Madrid: Chrysler, Pegaso, Iberia, SKF, Erikson, Intelsa, I don't know how many. But there is no way ... You know, don't you, that if the sacking is considered to be justified you don't get unemployment benefits.' (interview no. 15)

'I've had the lock of the door of my house broken, so that I can't use it, in a co-operative in Zarzaquemada. The police were there. They broke the lock, they forced the door. But they can't find me that easy: I change house at least four or five times every year, if not more.' (interview no. 3)

Torture is reported in the following case:

'One day, a Sunday it was, in Vitoria, when I was out with some friends, as I was walking down the street I was suddenly pushed, dragged into a building, where they pulled their guns, and asked for my documentation. I gave it to them, and then a car arrived, a blue Renault 4, I shall never forget it. They took me in and I started to protest, to claim that I didn't understand what that was all about. They drove me to the Civil Guard post: there, as soon as I got in, they started to kick me, to hit me. Later, I think it was a Lieutenant-Colonel who arrived and he said that I was one of the leaders of the organization and that they wanted to know the names of the militants. Then I said that I was simply a socialist, that I would not deny this, that I sympathized with the UGT, and that that was all. The interrogation started, they were asking about comrades ... I refused to talk and then they started to torture me with thumbscrews. I don't know if you know ... They put little pieces of wood between your fingers while you're handcuffed, they put these pieces of wood and then with a kind of clamp they start to press until they break your finger bones. This lasted twelve hours. In a week they also broke my lip, they left me with this scar. I was so bad that when I had to go for a pee I had to be carried by two of them and they had to unbutton my trousers because I was unable to move. But I did not talk, I could never give up a comrade, and they got tired. They took me to a judge, and the first thing I said to the judge was that I had been tortured, but he said that the Spanish police did not torture and he sent me to jail.' (interview no. 13)

The second half of the 1970s appeared to these trade-union leaders as the end of a long and dramatic phase of the struggle for democracy in Spain. The struggle was going on, hardship was far from over, but the conditions had improved – the unions were much stronger, there was less repression. Indeed a stage of the history of the trade-union movement and of Spanish politics was being transcended. It seems adequate to conclude with the remark by one of the 'founding fathers' of Spanish post-civil war trade unionism, still a very prominent leader in the 1970s:

'In Europe the son of a building worker finds everything ready, for him the union is the normal thing. This is not our case. Because, my friend, the years and years of struggle, the price we've had to pay for it! So ... And this is gonna count. You see, when I hear that this is going to be like in Portugal, like in here or in there, well, no, no, believe me, it's going to be something else. We're having our own process, which, yes, has some similarities with others, a few things, but no more. The Spanish working class set an example once and it's gonna do it again. There are lads who've got their own views: "here this is gonna happen, like in there." Balls! We're gonna do plenty of new things over here. I may be wrong, but so far that's how I see it. And of course, that what is my evidence? Well, my own experience, what I am seeing, this and that, and that's what counts for me more than ... But as this hasn't been written by Lenin or by Mao or by any clever guy around, but that we ourselves are building it, it remains to be seen, but we shall see it.' (interview no. 4)

After 1973 there was a rapid growth in the strength of the underground trade unions and a more intensive struggle for the working-class movement. In the last year of the dictatorship the wave of strikes reached a new peak. It is, however, a futile exercise to speculate about what might have happened if Franco had not died. His death was followed by a crisis in the dictatorship which ended in the elections held in June 1977; the underground unions became legal and a new chapter started for the Spanish working class.

5 Universities and politics: the development of the Spanish student movement*

The reorganization of Spanish universities after 1939 and the end of the civil war was congruent with the main traits of the new state: it was directed by a combination of Fascist ideology and traditional clericalism. A year and a half before the end of the war, in November 1937, Franco had declared in a statement through the NGW News Service: 'No Catholic university will be needed because all our universities will be Catholic and a religious higher education will be provided by them' (Franco 1943: 434). In 1943 a new *Ley de Ordenación Universitaria* (Law of University Organization) was promulgated, which established the joint control of the Catholic Church and the *Movimiento* on the universities. The law declared that teaching was to be in accordance with 'Catholic dogma and morals' (article 3) and with the programme of the Falange (article 4); that the recruitment and the activities of the academic staff was to be guided by the 'political spirit' and the 'watchwords' of the Falange (article 33); that the Rectors of the universities were to be appointed by the government among university professors 'militants of Falange' (article 40); that

* The evidence used in this chapter and in Chapters 6 and 7 consists of intensive interview material with 50 student leaders and 564 pamphlets. These sources have been described in the Introduction.

a single and state-controlled student union, the *Sindicato Español Universitario* (SEU) was to be in charge of the indoctrination of the students into the 'spirit' of the Falange (article 34). The SEU had been a pre-war Falangist student union, and from 1939 it was organized on the same pattern as the official state-controlled trade unions (the *sindicatos*): that is, it followed the lines of the *corporazioni* of Fascist Italy; indeed, the Law of University Organization of 1943 defined universities as 'state corporations of teachers and students'. The major national pre-war student union, the FUE (*Federación Universitaria Española*), which had been staunchly pro-Republican, had been abolished and many of its leaders had been killed in the war[1]. The organization of political control within the universities also included dramatic modifications in the composition of the academic staff. Between 1939 and 1944, 155 professors were appointed – 56 per cent of all professors in Spanish universities in 1944[2], whereas exile and the Law on Repression of Communism and Free Masonry had eliminated a large number of Republican university teachers.

However, the heterogenous political coalition of the Francoist regime, resulted in a contradiction between Fascist rhetorical populism and traditional clerical conservatism, which was manifest in the political organization of Spanish universities. The SEU was for a long period committed to the pseudo-revolutionary demagogy of the Falange. And this populistic ideology, in which slogans on nationalization of the Banks, on agrarian reform, and 'the pending revolution' in Spain were central, produced a number of crises. In the early post-war years some members of the SEU felt betrayed by what they thought was a sell-out by the regime to a conservative-clerical-monarchist coalition. This feeling was expressed very militantly in the National Congress of the SEU in 1940 and even led to a frustrated bomb attack on General Varela in August 1942 as a consequence of which a member of the SEU was sentenced to death. The SEU came progressively under direct control of the state as the political decay of the Falange was accelerated after 1945.

The influence of nationalistic Catholicism was perhaps more systematic: it had to do less with the direct political organization of the students than with an ideological control at the level of teaching. The Law of University Organization of 1943 had made the following declaration: 'the University is the theological army to fight heresy and the creator of the missionary phalanx that must affirm Catholic unity.' It also stipulated that all university activities 'should have as supreme guidance Christian dogma and morals'. Ibañez Martín, the Minister of Education, had declared in the *Cortes* (the Spanish

Parliament) in his speech introducing the law:

> 'What is indeed important from a political point of view ... is to
> eradicate from teaching and from scientific creation ideological
> neutrality and to banish laicism, to train a new youth imbued with
> that Augustinian principle that science does not bring one any closer
> to the Supreme being.'

A concordat between the Spanish regime and the Vatican in 1953
established a Catholic monopoly over Spanish education. The state
assured the teaching of Catholic religion as a general and compulsory
part of the syllabus in every educational centre of the country, as well
as the conformity of teaching to the principles of the Catholic church.
The Catholic church was to be in charge of 'purity of faith, good
manners and religious education'. It was also entitled to prohibit and
to withdraw books, publications, and teaching material that was
contrary to Catholic dogma and morals. The *Instituto Secular de la
Santa Cruz y del Opus Dei* (Secular Institute of the Holy Cross and
the Opus Dei), founded in 1928, began from 1939 an attempt to control
the educational system, particularly higher education, as a strategic
ground to carry out a Catholic worldly calling through control,
indoctrination, and recruitment.

1 Beginnings

The origins of the Spanish student movement are located in the
mid-1950s. Before that date the general factors that prevented the
existence of an underground organized opposition in Spain were also
present in university life: the civil war massacre, the post-war purges,
repression, and fear. However, in the first half of the 1950s, four
main trends in the evolution of Spanish politics converged, which
facilitated the re-emergence of political dissent. These four trends
were:

(i) Attempts towards improving the international acceptance of the
regime. These attempts were quite successful in the context of the
Cold War and led to the admission of Spain as a member of the United
Nations, UNESCO, OEEC, and the International Monetary Fund.
The attempts included some very limited steps towards political
liberalization which, in university education, were, for example, the
appointment of a then moderate Christian Democrat (Ruiz Giménez)
as Minister of Education, of other moderates as Rectors (Laín in
the University of Madrid, Tovar in Salamanca). Non-orthodox

literature circulated with less restrictions. Writers like Unamuno, Ortega y Gasset, Baroja, Machado, were no longer considered as subversive. The universities slowly began to become arenas of discussion, and university magazines such as *Alcalá* or *Revista* were sometimes used as platforms of non-orthodox or reformist political and cultural views.

(ii) Groups of non-exiled or newly-converted liberals and republicans also became more active. They were encouraged by the timid liberalization; moreover, the fear of reprisals and the shock of the war had somewhat receded. People like Aranguren, Tierno Galván, Ridruejo – the 'alegal opposition', using Linz's (1973) terminology – began to express their views more openly. Film societies and theatre societies (the TEU); discussion meetings called '*Revistas orales*' (Oral Reviews), such as '*Nuevo Criterio*' (New Criterion) in the Faculty of Philosophy of Madrid or '*Tierra*' in the Faculty of Economics; student publications such as *Aldebarán, Cuadernos de Arte y Pensamiento, Libra, Arista*; homages paid to anti-Fascist writers (García Lorca, Hernández, Alberti, Machado) – all these flourished in the universities in that period, were organized by anti-Francoist students, and served as popular platforms for the diffusion of dissenting political views. Two homages to Ortega and to Baroja were used as occasions for the gathering of democratic opposition to the regime in the universities, and for the public expression of claims of liberalization and democratization.

(iii) Groups of populist Falangists were excluded in those years from the inner circles of the regime – from the coalition in power (Linz 1970; Payne 1962). This was particularly so after the Cabinet reshuffle of February 1957 and the passing of the Constitutional Law on the Principles of the Movement of May 1958, but that trend in the evolution of the regime dated from an earlier period – particularly from the victory of the Allies in 1945. In 1951 Falangists had joined demonstrations in Barcelona against the cost of living and in 1954 a Falangist demonstration calling for the return of Gibraltar to Spain turned into a demonstration against the regime. These groups of populist Falangists felt more and more estranged from and marginal to the regime. Their social demagogy – to which they were deeply committed – often led them to forms of political opposition and sometimes to leftist conversions. The magazine *Marzo* was particularly committed to an anti-capitalist rhetoric which superficially seemed to adopt leftist ideas. That rhetoric however pushed some of its members towards socialism.

(iv) In this period of the mid-1950s attempts at reorganizing leftist parties under clandestine conditions were intensified and eventually produced some results. This was particularly so in the case of the Communist Party. After 1955 Jorge Semprún and Simón Sánchez-Montero started to rebuild the party, with some success. The socialists were slowly rebuilding two groups, the Socialist Youth (JS) and the University Socialist Group (ASU), and a third socialist organization existed in Barcelona: the Catalan Socialist Movement (MSC). A new left-wing socialist party was founded at that time – the Popular Liberation Front (FLP), with an affiliated student organization, the University New Left (NIU).

The situation within the universities at the beginning of the 1950s is described as follows:

'There were three or four students who were socialist and there was only one affiliated to the Communist Party ... But, you see, the situation was then so difficult, that he was behaving like a mild liberal. The most daring thing one could do was to comment on an occasional article – by Tierno-Galván, by Ridruejo – which could have faint liberal overtones. Even in 1956, student politics were the product of no more than 20 persons. It was an archaeological world, and I very much doubt that you can describe it other than through literature.' (interview no. 1)

The first underground burgeoning of political activity and its survival in secrecy were reported by one of the early student leaders:

'The SEU, the regime, had the university really in their hands. They controlled it and you had to stay in the shadow, aware that you could be arrested any time, at the slightest negligence. Then what started in 1954 and 1955 was a slow re-organization of the socialist and communist parties, a slow infiltration in student magazines, in theatre and film societies, and then in the SEU itself. We also started to distribute pamphlets.' (interview no. 9)

The first stage of the student movement started at the end of 1955. In October 1955 Ortega y Gasset died, and his funeral was the occasion for a show of liberal dissent. The public expression of radical ideas on the occasion of Ortega's death led to the prohibition of a National Congress of Young Writers that was going to be held in November of that same year and to police arrests among its organizers, which increased the cultural unrest. Two months later, in February 1956, a manifesto signed by hundreds of students was handed to the president of the SEU, demanding the democratization of the SEU and a National Congress of Students. The president of the university district of Madrid, Jesús Gay, accepted free elections for representatives of the student body at Faculty level. The government invalidated the elections and the students protested by occupying the premises of the SEU in the Faculties of Law, Economics, and Political Science. Falangist groups invaded the Faculties (the *'Centurias de la Guardia de Franco'*, *'Primera Linea'*, and *'Escuela de Mandos José Antonio'*) and violent confrontations took place, which were repeated in a student demonstration in front of the Ministry of Education and also during the commemoration of the anniversary of the death, under the Republic, of a Falangist student. In the clash that resulted on this latter occasion, a Falangist was shot and the Falange threatened to execute one hundred intellectuals. The universities were closed for two weeks, many arrests were made, and both the Minister of Education (Ruiz Giménez) and the Minister of the National Movement (the *Movimiento Nacional*) were dismissed.

A summary of these first events, whose climax was the demonstrations of 1956, is provided by this account of one of the leaders:

'We organized the *Encuentros de la Poesía con la Universidad* [Encounters of Poetry and University], with recitals of anti-Fascist poets. Then there was the forbidden National Congress of Young Writers, when we wrote a manifesto calling for democracy for which we collected signatures. There was also the solemn burial of Ortega y Gasset, and memorial notices appeared which said "Spanish liberal philosopher", which seemed a very daring thing to say at that time. Baroja died shortly afterwards and his burial became again a sort of anti-Francoist meeting. Funerals were in those years a safety valve for political expression. These were the antecedents of 1956. The 1956 confrontations started because of the union elections within the Faculties, that the government tried to stop. There were serious clashes and Miguel Alvarez was shot. A national state of emergency was declared, and I was arrested.' (interview no. 3)

New student demonstrations took place in the following year. Then, in October 1958, the SEU was reorganized by the government: democratic representation of the students at Faculty level, based on elections for a Faculty Chamber of Delegates, was introduced. The national president of the SEU and the presidents of the districts were still appointed by the Government, but the Chamber of Delegates of each Faculty was now composed of elected representatives. Elections led to a politicization of university life. Cultural associations contributed indirectly to that politicization – particularly the Spanish University Theatre (TEU) and the University Labour Service (SUT), through which students participated in educational programmes in working-class suburbs or in isolated rural communities. The still timid but growing cultural dissent was also reflected in the politically-committed literature that flourished in the late 1950s: the main names were Celaya and Blas de Otero in poetry, Sastre and Buero-Vallejo in the theatre, Sánchez-Ferlosio and Goytisolo in the novel, as well as in a new critical cinema (Bardem and Berlanga and a new wave of film-makers influenced by Buñuel).

In January 1957 the Minister of the National Movement, Arrese, who had been appointed after the student revolt of February 1956, resigned as a consequence of lack of support for a Falangist project of constitutional reform, which had been presented in December 1956. A reshuffle of the Cabinet in February 1957 brought the *Opus Dei* into the government. A new phase in Spanish post-Civil War politics started. It was during 1956–57 that the first age group born after the Civil War reached university. Outside the university the series of strikes that took place in March and April 1958 in Asturias, Catalonia, and the Basque Country had important political repercussions. They led to a state of emergency and four articles of the *Fuero de los Españoles* (Spaniards' Bill of Rights) were suspended for four months. After fifteen years of total domination, dissent, although limited, was coming into the open.

The three main political groups in this first stage of development of the student movement were the ECM (a student organization of the Communist Party), the NIU (the student organization of the *Frente de Liberación Popular*, FLP), and the ASU (a socialist group which later merged in the Socialist Youth of the Socialist Party). These three organizations established a university co-ordination committee (*Comité de Coordinación Universitaria*) in 1958, and took active part in the attempt to organize a general strike in 1959, which failed. This frustrated attempt led to many arrests among militants in the three groups, which were considerably weakened. As a consequence, from 1958 to 1960 there was little organized political dissent in the universities and the secret political groups which survived were isolated and minuscule.

Until the end of the 1950s, political activities within the universities were scarce and the political mobilization of the students was very limited. Political and ideological controls were efficient and kept anti-Francoist militant students isolated within the student population. Political radicalism was often the result of non-orthodox family backgrounds, of rather exceptional personal experiences, and was some-times the outcome of individuals becoming politically interested in a context that was forcefully demobilized and depoliticized. The 'founding members' of the student movement often had links with dissident intellectuals. These comparatively privileged channels of contact with politics reinforced the peculiarity of radical students and their isolation within the general student population. Secret organizations were small, tightly-knit, and strictly selective in their recruitment.

These secret political organizations led a shadowy existence in the first stage of the student movement. Only when a student had reached an advanced stage of political involvement was he able to perceive the political groups more clearly.

'I had only a faint vision of secret political organizations. A few individuals were said to be communists ... communists acted in special conditions of secrecy. And then people who were "democrats", who were more visible because they were only arrested if they did something, whereas if you were a communist you were arrested for being so. But it was a world of hearsays and rumours, even among politicized students. After 1956 and my arrest, well, yes, I could perceive the groups much better. Although in those years the number of politically involved students was so limited that it was more important to be a member of the opposition to the regime than being a socialist or a communist.' (interview no. 12)

The accounts of the slow process of increasing perception of the secret political organizations do not differ between political groups, but they vary strongly according to the type of political background of the students. These backgrounds will be discussed in Chapter 6. What must now be noted is that whereas the political perception of students from democratic families and backgrounds was dependent on networks of friendship (friends who were already affiliated to organizations), students from populist Falangist backgrounds gained more political information about secret groups only after intensive political activity and repeated expressions of political dissent. The difference between both types is reflected in the following two reports. The first is from a student leader whose background was anti-Francoist; he easily contacted the political groups and was soon involved in the first political activities which consisted of using the state-controlled union and cultural platforms:

'When I entered Law I quickly got in touch with some people

that I knew from school. These contacts were my first link. We started a magazine, which we made in multicopy, and which had five pages. This magazine served as a reference in the context of these years, people could come to us. There were also the politics within the SEU: infiltration into the Faculties' Chambers of Delegates was very effective, and the students could see you, they could perceive the hints of dissenting ideas. The cultural activities were also important: the public reading of poems of Miguel Hernández or Alberti, a homage to Picasso...' (interview no. 7)

The second report is from a populist Falangist turned anti-Francoist and converted to socialism, who joined the student movement and eventually, through a slow process, was able to contact the secret groups:

'I had a very important post in the Falange at the university just before 1956. But I had lost almost any hope that the Falange could lead any revolutionary reform in Spain. Then, the events of 1956 brought an end to these few hopes. I wanted a democratic reform of the SEU, a democratic political representation. So I broke with the Falange, together with five other leaders. And in the clashes I fought on the side of the students preventing the Falangist assault on the university. There was still a short-lived attempt to reform the student representation, by a few SEU delegates and a group of the 'Frente de Juventudes' [Youth Front – an organization of the Falange], most of whose members later joined the Communist Party. I started to meet some of the student leaders, but of course I did not then have a clear idea of the political identities of the individuals. That was the beginning of a chain. I started to study Marxism.'

(interview no. 2)

2 Consolidation

The second period of the student movement started after 1960 with a more cautious strategy following the arrests of the previous stage. Underground organizations in Spanish universities tried to shift their politics to unionist activities and to the professional problems of the students. The goal was to make full use of the new legal platforms of elective representation (the Chambers of Delegates), to gain electoral support, and then to mobilize the students against the control of the legal student union by the state. Simultaneously, underground re-organization of the political parties was slowly carried out.

This strategy was very skilfully carried out by careful steps. In

1960 and 1961 the students were successfully mobilized on the issues of the increasing control of the *Opus Dei* over higher education and the dramatic unemployment which affected particular branches of study (e.g. law and philosophy). Strikes and sit-ins led to sanctions (arrests and loss of matriculation fees), and this stimulated solidarity, in a spiral of conflict. At the same time Chambers of Delegates were gathering support from the students: they appeared as the 'true' representatives of the students, who had been elected and given a mandate, and who should therefore be backed against the SEU and the government. The Chambers of Delegates' capacity to mobilize developed considerably. A strongly politicized atmosphere started to develop within the Faculties. Elections for the Chambers of Delegates became a crucial event in university life – and they indeed had an important impact on Spanish political life.

In the autumn of 1961 a secret student union, the FUDE (*Federación Universitaria Democrática Española*), was set up in Madrid by the FLP, the Communist Party (PCE) and the Socialist Party (PSOE). It was intended to become a 'mass' organization: a democratic alternative to the corporatist state-controlled SEU which would attract both party militants and independent democrats. The statute and programme of FUDE were drawn up in the academic year 1961–62. Its original self-definition in the statute was as a 'democratic and free student union which attempts to group the students opposed to the compulsory state-controlled union'. A similar organization was set up in Barcelona, and FUDE was quickly established in Valencia, Bilbao, Zaragoza, and Oviedo. In February 1962, four students in Madrid were imprisoned for being founding members of FUDE. In that same year a wave of strikes took place in the mines of Asturias, in the iron and steel works and machine tool industries of the Basque Country, Madrid, Catalonia, Valencia, and Andalucía[3]. These strikes had a profound impact within the universities, and the political parties, FUDE, and the Chambers of Delegates mobilized the students in support of the workers. There were three large demonstrations in Madrid (under the slogan '*Asturias sí, Opus no*' – 'Asturias in, Opus out') and a long sit-in (called Free Assembly of Students). The challenge to the regime from the universities was to be uninterrupted until the end of the dictatorship.

FUDE was used as a 'transmission belt' in a strategy which was shared by the PCE, the FLP, and the PSOE. In 1962 secret FUDE candidates were very successful in the official elections for representative posts in the Chambers of Delegates. At this stage political strategies consisted of the combined use of three levels of action: first, the legal level of the Chambers of Delegates; second, the underground level of FUDE as a 'mass organization'; finally, the underground level of the political parties as 'vanguard organizations'. Again political sanctions were used against three alleged members of FUDE in Madrid in the academic year 1962–63, but FUDE was able to expand its support both in elections and in confrontations (such as the strikes in support of a Professor of the Faculty of Law of the University of Madrid who had been threatened with dismissal after attending a meeting in Munich of the democratic opposition to the regime).

In December 1963, the secret union covered nine out of the twelve university districts: Madrid, Barcelona, Bilbao, Granada, Oviedo, Sevilla, Valencia, Valladolid, and Zaragoza. In March 1964 a 'week of university reform' was organized in Madrid, Barcelona, and Bilbao. After two lectures in Madrid by Ruiz Giménez and Aranguren, which were critical of the regime, a third lecture by Tierno Galván was banned and the whole 'week of university reform' was prohibited by the government. This resulted in a. violent confrontation between the government and the student movement: in five days there were four massive student demonstrations, a sit-in, and the establishment of a new Free Assembly of Students, the government closed the University of Madrid, and ninety-six students were expelled from all Spanish universities. The skilful management of the 'week of university reform' by FUDE and the enforcement of limitations to free speech and political repression by the regime produced a sharp politicization within the universities and a greater radicalism of the struggle.

The collapse of the SEU was the next step in the strategy of the student movement. The goal was to impose a democratic union and to convert the universities into 'liberated territories' or platforms of anti-Francoist struggle. According to the political strategies, the corporate organization of both the workers' unions and the student union was a central feature of the Francoist regime. This should give a political character to the struggle and should result in similarities and contacts between the working-class and the student movements.

The abolition of the SEU was achieved in 1965. That year saw a long political confrontation, which started with student demonstrations against increases in transport fares. Confrontations with the police, sanctions, and solidarity again started the spiral of conflict. A great number of political pamphlets and leaflets were distributed in the universities at the three levels of political activity: the Chambers of Delegates, FUDE, and the political parties. Two main types of claim were put forward in them: on the one hand, independence of student representation from the SEU; on the other, political demands

– freedom of association and freedom of expression. A new series of lectures under the topic 'the True Peace' were organized in the University of Madrid in February 1965. They were prohibited as soon as they had started. As a protest, a new Free Assembly of Students was set up, demanding freedom of association and expression, political amnesty, and declaring its solidarity with the working-class movement. On the fourth day of the Assembly, a peaceful demonstration was organized and three university professors (Aranguren, García Calvo, and García Vercher) joined it; three other professors joined student meetings (Tierno Galván, Montero Díaz, and Aguilar Navarro) and others declared their solidarity with the demands of the student movement. Meetings and demonstrations were constantly held, many arrests took place, and the professors were dismissed from their chairs (the first three and Tierno Galván permanently, the other two for two years). All but one of the university districts left the SEU and the elected students' representatives established themselves as an embryonic democratic student union. In March a first national meeting of student representatives took place in Barcelona. In April the government abolished the SEU and tried to establish a plurality of student associations, devoid of any political content and with a strict control upon them. A second national meeting of students' representatives rejected the government's project and established the skeleton of what was to become the SDE – *Sindicato Democrático de Estudiantes* (Democratic Union of Students). The underground parties believed that FUDE appeared to be a leftist organization controlled by secret political parties and the SDE was planned as a wider organization covering the whole political spectrum of non-Fascist students.

The period 1960–65 was characterized by skilful deployment of strength, rational political strategy, and by an accurate presentation of issues. For the country as a whole, it was a period of rapid economic growth, of changes in the political coalition within the regime, of alleged 'europeanization'. The cultural climate for the dissenting intelligentsia and for university students was very different from that of the previous two decades: translations and imports of foreign books increased, the press provided more information. It was also a period of dramatic intensification of working-class protest: it was then that the first 'workers' commissions' were organized and they followed a strategy similar to FUDE's – developing public/legal action at the elective levels of the corporatist union, complementary to underground subversive action.

The growth of the student movement also meant an increase in sectarianism. The old debate that opposed Lenin to Martov and the Mensheviks in the 2nd Congress of the Russian Social Democrats in 1903 rose again, on questions of organization as a political vanguard and the requirements of discipline, centralization, exclusiveness, and ideological purity[4]. This debate, together with strategic differences concerning, first, political alliances, second, the intermediate phases before the revolution and, third, the relevance of a general strike in the struggle against the dictatorship caused two very serious splits within the Communist Party between Maoist and Togliattist factions[5]. The three-level strategy was, however, systematically followed by all groups.

The change from the first to the second stage of the student movement (1960–65) consisted basically of increased support for the radical student movement by the student population. The setting up of the secret 'mass organization', FUDE, was the main step in the mobilization of students. Professional claims were used to conceal long-term political subversion. Infiltration into the state-controlled student union, the SEU, was successfully carried out and most of the Faculties' Chambers of Delegates came to be controlled by members of FUDE and of secret political parties.

The change between the first and the second stage was described as follows by one leader of the first stage of the student movement who lived through the period of transition:

'At the beginning there was a total lack of support among students. The best reaction you could expect was a certain admiration with little comprehension. That was the situation when I went to prison. There I had very serious doubts about the meaning of my activities, about whether they were of any value, whether they were leading anywhere ... That was the feeling, based on what I had left behind me ... There really was almost nothing. And then, through the news that was reaching us in prison we saw that everything was starting to change. There was a qualitative change. All those plans and strategies, which had looked so artificial, well, all that crystallized into something real ... I had taken part in the creation of the FUDE; it was an agreement between the communists, the FLP and ourselves, the socialists. That was in 1961, in the autumn. It was the first "mass organization" to be set up and it turned out to be one of the greatest achievements of the opposition to the regime.'

(interview no. 10)

The political perceptions of radical students who were not affiliated to an underground party were still considerably limited in the second stage of the student movement. The conditions of secrecy were still such that these students did not have a clear perception of the political organizations, even though they would belong to friendship networks that included militants. The following account describes this misty world of the underground student movement that required a novitiate period even for students who had contacts with active militants:

'From the very moment I entered university I decided to be politically active. Political activity came by way of the elections to the Faculty's Chamber of Delegates. It was the natural place to go, it was the main platform of political action and I had plenty of friends there. At the beginning, of course, I had no idea of where the political organizations could be, I was totally lost. I knew there were political parties around, but I was unable to identify militants among the people I knew. I was aware that they were anti-regime, democrats, leftists, but not more than that. For instance, I was startled every time I heard that somebody was a member of the Communist Party. That ignorance quickly disappeared once I was in FUDE...' (interview no. 25)

The slow period of apprenticeship is again described as a series of stages in which affiliation to FUDE was a crucial threshold:

'I entered on a FUDE ticket for the elections to the Faculty's Chamber of Delegates. I suspected it was a FUDE ticket, but most of them were friends of mine. I knew they were politically radical, but I wasn't quite clear about what their involvement was. Even FUDE was at the time taking secrecy very seriously. My ignorance about political parties was still greater. I had certain myths and certain fears, particularly of communism. But after a period of political activity as a student delegate I became more familiar with political organizations.' (interview no. 26)

3 Maturity

The third stage of the student movement was a phase of open political claims, general political participation, and greater radicalism. From 1965 to 1967 the immediate issue was opposition by the students to the associations that the government tried to impose as replacements to the SEU. The confrontations were often very violent. The three strategic levels of the student movement that have been described for the second period were still important characteristics of student politics. There was, however, a difference in that the once-legal electoral platform of the Chambers of Delegates had now become independent from the SEU and was being used as a skeleton of a democratic national student union. To indicate their independence, elections to the Chambers of Delegates were held in the autumn of 1965, in anticipation of the official elections for the new associations. When the latter were held shortly afterwards, abstentions amounted to 80 per cent of the vote, although voting was compulsory. A new Free Assembly of Students was organized in Madrid in December 1965 in order to demand freedom of association and expression, the end of repression, and political amnesty. These demands were supported by demonstrations, by a massive sit-in, as a result of which 341 students were sanctioned, by a written declaration of solidarity drawn up by over one hundred Spanish intellectuals, and by a message sent to the Permanent Commission of Human Rights of the United Nations. In March 1966, some 500 students and a large number of intellectuals and academics held a secret meeting in a convent in Sarriá (Barcelona). The convent was surrounded by police, all the participants were arrested, and sixty members of the staff of the University of Barcelona were dismissed for two years. As a consequence a large number of demonstrations were held in Barcelona and in other university districts, in solidarity with the students arrested in Sarriá, and declarations of support were made by intellectuals and academics. A National Day Against Repression was organized in the University of Madrid, also in March, in which well-known intellectuals participated. Demonstrations were then held from March to May. The links between the working-class movement and the student movement were also starting to crystallize in joint actions. Then, in July 1966, the government changed some aspects of the legal regulation of student associations and tried unsuccessfully to impose them in the following academic year 1966–67. However, the attempt was abandoned in April 1967, after the resignation of the associations' national delegates.

The period between the abolition of the SEU in April 1965 and the collapse of the state-led associations in April 1967 had four main features. First, there was continuous confrontation, taking the form of demonstrations, sit-ins, Free Assemblies, etc., in which the participation of the students was widespread. Second, an embryonic democratic student union was set up, on the basis of the Chambers of Delegates, with autonomous elections and national co-ordinatory meetings. Third, the conflict was extended to all Spanish universities, with joint strategies being carried out in all of them (such as a national strike in February 1967). Finally, stronger links between the student movement and the working-class movement developed: for example, a number of demonstrations of solidarity with industrial strikes in Madrid, Barcelona, Asturias, and the Basque Country took place in the universities of Madrid and Barcelona in the summer of 1966 and later, between December 1966 and May 1967, in support of a long strike in the steelyards of Echevarri in Bilbao. On January 27, 1967 students of the University of Madrid joined a demonstration of over 30,000 workers, organized by the 'workers' commissions'. Joint demonstrations by workers and students were frequent after that date.

In the academic year 1967–68 the illegal democratic student union, the *Sindicato Democrático de Estudiantes*, was operating in all Spanish universities. The SDE distributed a declaration of principles which was again a combination of claims referring, on the one hand, to students' rights and, on the other, to democratic freedoms. The structure of the SDE consisted, first, of a representation within each Faculty; second, of a representation for the university district, on the basis of a Chamber of the District and an executive *Junta* of the District; and, third, of the national co-ordinatory meetings which articulated the different SDEs of the twelve university districts.

Within the Faculties, union activities were intensive and extended to many areas. It must be pointed out that many Faculties in Madrid and Barcelona had more than 5,000 students. The SDE collected financial contributions, provided grants, organized seminars, established shops and bookshops, edited magazines, etc. The success in setting up the SDE fostered much political participation among students. As it was reported in the interviews, 'there was a feeling of having won, of having achieved freedom. We had "our" union, we had to build it and protect it, every one of us with his own personal contribution' (interview no. 41). A complex intellectual and political subculture developed within the Faculties: activities included seminars on Lautréamont, Surrealism and Trotsky, public discussions on nationalization of the banks, the organization of anti-imperialist, pro-Vietnam committees, etc. Life within the Faculties is described as follows:

'It was a period of permanent assemblies and sit-ins against repression. The claims were for a democratic student union and for general freedoms, of association, reunion, and expression. These freedoms were established within the Faculties, which became "liberated territories", and we had to defend them day by day. Support from the students quickly increased through the struggle. There was a fantastic life within the Faculties, with plays, film exhibitions, student bookshops, conferences and lectures, seminars, posters, wall magazines which were now openly anti-regime, denouncing repression and the dictatorship.' (interview no. 42)

As this subculture emerged, political activities were increasingly carried out in the open: secrecy diminished, individual political identities became more visible. The organizations were more public, proselytism and recruitment were more transparent and less discriminating. Contacts were established with groups of students in secondary education and political information started to circulate within schools. Generalized involvement in political activities went with an increasing radicalism. Limited demands for the legalization of the SDE, for a democratic university, were articulated in a global attack against the regime and this was in its turn integrated within a socialist alternative against monopoly capitalism. The link with the working-class movement was still central, but after 1968 the working-class movement was seen as 'rezagado' (lagging behind), 'frenando' (putting on the brakes), as wage-orientated. A theory of 'political substitution' began to circulate, according to which the students would have to carry on in a situation of 'proletarian retreatism'.

This was part of a more general problem. The Communist Party had controlled the SDE, sometimes sharing this control with the FLP, which had grown substantially since 1967. But whereas the CP considered that FUDE had completed its strategic goal and should now be replaced by the SDE as a more widely-based 'mass organization', some groups within the FLP believed that FUDE could be used as a revolutionary organization. FUDE therefore lost its previous orientation, which had been based on unionism/democracy/socialism (with a strong emphasis on the first two dimensions), and became an instrument of attack against the 'reformist' policies that the CP was allegedly trying to carry out within the SDE. As an example, FUDE distributed a pamphlet on March 4, 1968 attacking 'the bureaucrats and the reactionary elements of the SDE' and another pamphlet in February 1968 in which it said 'we must adopt an anticapitalist programme and revolutionary methods of struggle ... [We must defend] the functioning of universities under the control of workers and students.' At the same time, Trotskyist and anarchist groups (the *Partido Obrero Revolucionario* – POR; the *Fuerzas Armadas Revolucionarias* – FAR) started to gain some influence outside the representative machinery of the SDE.

The ideological sophistication that had developed within the cultural and political ghetto that the universities had become since 1967 facilitated the growth of a large number of political groups which seldom had more than a few members, as well as constant splits and sub-groups. These groups were extremely radical and there was an increase in political violence and repression, which came to a head with the deaths in January 1967 of Rafael Guijarro and in January 1969 of Enrique Ruano. Both deaths took place in suspicious circumstances, while they were being arrested by the police, and the events had a strong impact on the student movement. Commandos were organized within the universities and lightning attacks, using Molotov cocktails, were frequently made against banks, business offices, etc., and at the same time strikes in different parts of Madrid took place. Spontaneous meetings were organized in the underground transport system or in small squares and they were seen as attempts to increase public information and 'raise consciousness'. Some groups of the left criticized these strategies as 'funambulesque', 'mystical', and 'fanatical', claiming that they were the result of political pessimism and that the ultra-radicalism and violence was only compensation for their lack of a substantive ideological basis[6]. The groups defending strategies of violent confrontation and armed struggle were totally opposed to the SDE and to the organizations that had led the student movement until then.

'On the one hand were the SDE and the CP, and on the other hand FUDE. It was a period of bitter clashes between the SDE and FUDE, between the CP and the Maoists. There were also the people of the FLP, who were very influential. Within FUDE itself the Maoists and the Trotskyists had deep quarrels. Then, in the Basque Country, there was this split in the ETA[7] when the ETA-Berri was set up. These people had members at the University of Madrid, even though they were not very active in the student movement; they created the "*Círculo de Estudiantes Vascos*" ["Circle of Basque Students"], in which both groups of ETA participated. ETA-Berri later organized an affiliated political group in Madrid: the "*Grupo Lenin*" [Lenin Group]. I collaborated in it. In the autumn of 1968 there was a wave of arrests at the university, and we had to make a decision about the usefulness of a public student union. The FLP was against it whereas the CP supported it on the grounds that we had to adapt the union to that difficult period, but not abandon it for direct revolutionary action. I supported that strategy of the CP, and I was subsequently accused of "unionist errors" by the "*Grupo Lenin*", the FLP, etc. So I joined the CP. The political struggle became more intensive and radical. Police repression was massive. This is when Enrique Ruano was killed, the state of emergency was declared and the Faculties were occupied. The state of emergency was extremely brutal and we returned to strictly underground activities. Militancy in that period was intense, with day and night meetings, you see, day and night. I spent the whole year sleeping each night in a different place.' (interview no. 45)

Police repression increased as the leaders became more visible and secrecy decreased and because of the greater radicalism and violence of confrontations. Between August 1968 and December 1970 three states of emergency were declared by the government and the police occupied the Faculties. The representative members of the SDE were systematically rounded up and arrested. The FLP, which had been one of the main organizations of the Spanish left in general, and of the student movement in particular, broke down in 1969 as a result of the opposing views that had grown within it. A new influential group was eventually set up by a Trotskyist fraction of the FLP, the *Liga Comunista*. The withdrawal of the support of the FLP, the attacks from the *'groupuscules'*, and repression created a major crisis within the SDE: the role of a 'mass organization' in these political conditions was questioned and after 1969 the end of the SDE was decided on.

The intense and open political action, the increasingly radical aspect of the struggle, the presence of many revolutionary groups and the general participation of students in political activities, together with the intensity of repression, are further stressed in the following interview:

'We had made a fantastic effort to organize and to protect the SDE based on a day-by-day, hour-by-hour struggle. We were challenging Fascism and the leaders came to face a brutal repression. We had also tried to co-ordinate the student and the working-class movements. This was very successful after the autumn of 1967, when students joined working-class strikes and demonstrations. In 1967 and 1968 the university was a fortress. The vanguard of the student movement was able to carry out thousands of initiatives. It looked like the Nevski Palace in 1917. We started an anti-imperialist campaign, we organized massive actions, immense assemblies. Then May 1968 happened in France and people thought "this is it!". People fled to Paris and many of those arrested were Spanish students. In the autumn of 1968 the revolutionary *momentum* was still on. Repression was very wide, and then Enrique was killed[8]. The state of emergency was declared, and repression was fantastic. We tried to adapt the organization of the student movement to the new conditions, our activity was political agitation, propaganda, demonstrations, and commando group activity all over Madrid. Four or five groups of commandos a day. I was a professional revolutionary organizer, twenty-four hours out of twenty-four. The police then occupied the Faculties and had to remain there for three years. Arrests were endless. It took a long time to re-organize the movement after this, but after some hard underground work the struggle started again in 1974.' (interview no. 47)

The main characteristic of the third stage[9], from 1965 onwards, was that the student movement as a whole, and the secret organizations in particular, had achieved a rapport with a highly mobilized student population. Organizations now had a defined public image and their leaders and militants had a high degree of public visibility, which finally resulted in a transparent political world. The universities gradually became a subcultural ghetto within Spanish society and, in these enclaves, the dominant ideas were the ideas of the student movement. Claims and issues were openly political and eventually openly subversive. Political repression was very intensive and the universities were frequently closed by the government. In the last years of the regime the democratic student organizations – first the FUDE and later the SDE – lost importance until they finally disappeared. The secret political parties had global political strategies which did not include the presence of a student union and which conceived the university as an instrumental platform for anti-Fascist struggle. Student politics were the result of a highly mobilized student population and subversive political organizations, without the mediation of a union.

6 The background of militancy

The main problem to be discussed in this chapter is that of the political socialization of leftist student leaders. I intend to analyse two aspects of this problem: first of all, the typical social processes and experiences through which certain groups of middle-class adolescents turned towards political radicalism and eventually towards militancy; second, the relationship between processes of political socialization and the emergence and development of an underground student movement. The questions to be answered are therefore: who were the students who, in the context of the changes in Spanish political conditions, set up a secret movement of dissent? Who were the students who were recruited in the successive stages of the movement? What were the shared characteristic backgrounds that differentiated these students from the rest of the student population? It is the 'life histories' of the militants themselves that will be used as the main evidence.

Three conditions in the process of becoming a dissenter have to be considered: the availability of radical ideologies, the commitment to such ideologies, and the conversion of this ideological commitment into political action. These three sequential steps in the process of political radicalization are determined by the existing political conditions, which act as restrictions on radicalism. These restrictions may be normative and non-normative, preventive and repressive. From this perspective, becoming a political dissident within a non-democratic context can be interpreted as a process similar to that of becoming deviant[1]. The availability of deviant alternatives is a first element in the genesis of deviance or political radicalism. When a certain margin of availability is provided by families, schools, or universities, a succession of events can render sanctions ineffective, lead to a neutralization of political controls and sanctions, and to an acceleration of the process of becoming a dissenter. Exceptional opportunities for political contact would then make the enactment of political commitments possible, in the form of political affiliation to a secret organization.

Because of the constraints that non-democratic political conditions present, student radicalism often has a minoritarian, elitist origin. In these circumstances, access to available ideological alternatives is restricted and becomes the privilege of a few. The restrictions imposed upon dissenting ideas are less effective in certain milieux. The militant has, then, very distinctive features which make him non-representative of the student population as a whole. In its first stages, a secret political movement is very much the product of a few politicized individuals with rather exceptional backgrounds and who converge and create the movement. But from the moment when a minoritarian group of politicized and dissident students emerges and an embryonic organization is set up, the group itself starts to create conditions for radicalism and for its own development. These conditions are that the radical movement itself becomes a new agency of political socialization, that it carries out recruitment policies, and, therefore, that the movement contributes to the 'making' of dissenters. When the political support of the movement widens, a political subculture emerges which provides a new context for political radicalism[2]. An antagonistic and consistent student subculture allows for better conditions for proselytism and for an increase in solidarity. This subculture is a fertile ground for the processes of political radicalization, recruitment, and affiliation[3]: radical ideas circulate within its boundaries and ideological conversion is an easier process. As a consequence, whereas in the first stages of the movement the militants have very distinctive traits, which make them non-representative of the student population as a whole, in the last stages the group of radical militants tends to become increasingly representative (again in sociological, non-political terms). It was therefore assumed that in the early stages, the militants of the student movement did not come at random from the student population, but were a particular group of students who had been subject to atypical processes of socialization.

The main questions, then, are, what were the factors related to political radicalism among students, how did these factors combine in typical paths leading to a deviant political identity, and what changes were brought about by the evolution of the student movement. Two types of experiences in the political socialization of Spanish radical students will now be analysed: namely, experiences of ideological political deviance within the family, and adolescent experiences of cultural non-orthodoxy related to the type of school attended, to influential literature, to religious beliefs, and to the impact of travelling abroad.

1 Family experiences

The theory of political socialization has stressed the importance of the family in the configuration of political attitudes. Family-based experiences, family structures, socialization patterns within the family would provide crucial clues for interpreting the genesis of political beliefs and commitments. The influence of the family in the formation of political beliefs would have as a result a certain ideological consistency over generations; political discontinuity would be the exception. This explanation of political learning via ideological inheritance has been presented by Lane (1959) as the 'Mendelian law of politics'. Most of the sociological evidence for the influence of the family in the crystallization of political orientations refers to voting patterns[4], but there is also evidence for an intergenerational transmission of political deviance[5] and for an ideological continuity between generations in the case of radical students[6]. Although the cumulative character of the findings is somewhat doubtful, they seem to indicate that radical students tend to come from liberal-leftist families and that, more than a result of reaction-formation processes, the radical student learns the basic elements of his radicalism within his family, through processes of socialization that may be deviant in terms of the dominant values of society but are orthodox in terms of parental values.

(A) In the Spanish case, becoming radical represented a series of breaches of the preventive and repressive rules set up against political deviance[7]. Radicalization was a result of overcoming, to a certain degree, these preventive and repressive rules. This was particularly possible when compensatory factors were provided by the family. The family acted as a first subcultural enclave against the control of political deviance. Radical students tended to come from family backgrounds that were ideologically deviant: this was the case for 58 per cent of my sample of radical militants (see *Table 1*).

Table 1 Family backgrounds of radical students (in percentages)

	political orientations of the parents		
	democratic	non-democratic	totals
A Cultural orientations of the parents			
(i) religion*			
non-Catholics	86	43	68
Catholics	14	57	32
	100%	100%	100%
	(N=29)	(N=21)	(N=50)
(ii) pattern of parental-filial relationship†			
permissive-democratic	69	62	66
authoritarian	31	38	34
	100%	100%	100%
	(N=29)	(N=21)	(N=50)
B Social status of the family§ upper and upper-middle			
status categories	76	48	64
lower status categories	24	52	36
	100%	100%	100%
	(N=29)	(N=21)	(N=50)
totals	58%	42%	100%
	(N=29)	(N=21)	(N=50)

* t = 3.61; p < 0.01
† t = 0.51; p > 0.05
§ t = 2.13; p < 0.05 (status was here considered to be the independent variable)

There is no available comparative information on parental political attitudes for the population of university students. However, two national opinion polls carried out in 1966 and 1968 provide indirect indications. In both surveys interviewees were asked to point out, from a list of closed choices, which were the main political problems that had to be solved in Spain in the future, and three of the possible choices may be considered as rough indicators of ideological deviance: 'political freedom', 'political democracy', and 'legalization of political parties'. Parents of university students would generally be included in two of the socio-economic categories of the sample: that of 'higher education' and of 'high social status' respondents. And yet in both surveys these two categories provided percentages of 'democratic' political answers that were considerably smaller than the proportion of democratic parents of my sample. The highest percentage provided by either of the two categories for any of the three indicators was 25 per cent[8]. Political deviance seems to have been much more frequent among parents of radical students than among individuals of similar education and status.

Student radicalism was, then, associated with ideologically deviant families. And yet, this association was also more complex than a simple intergenerational continuity or a straightforward ideological reproduction, and an important intergenerational distance seems to have existed. This was so in two respects: first, the political orientations of the students were much to the left of their parents, even when these were politically deviant (the core of the deviant type of family background was provided by left-of-centre 'liberal-republican' families); second, there was no relevant association between the political affiliations of the radical students and the parental political orientations (that is to say, students affiliated to the Socialist or Communist parties did not come in higher proportion from socialist or communist families). Thus, families may have provided the basis for 'neutralization' of orthodox political indoctrination as well as crucial facilities for the 'availability' of, and the access to, alternative ideologies; but the transmission of ideas appears to have been implicit and indirect, and always very loose.

The *democratic deviant family background* was characterized by the following traits: (i) conversations on politics between parents and children were reported to have taken place in four out of every five cases; (ii) parents were reported to have been associated with republican organizations or institutions, also in four out of every five cases; (iii) parents were reported to have friendship networks with other dissenters (whether friends from past times of militancy or present dissenting intellectuals or politicians), with whom the children often talked, in slightly over half of the cases; (iv) parents were reported to have suffered sanctions after the war (ranging from professional discrimination or harassment to prison) in slightly under half of the cases; (v) political fear on the part of the parents was reported to have been perceived by the children in two out of every five cases. The sum of this sub-population of deviant parents was characterized by its disallegiance and opposition towards the dominant ideological values and the political regime, and the children had a comparatively reduced experience of political restrictions to deviant ideologies. These were the conditions of 'affinity' (Matza) in the family experiences of radical students from such backgrounds. The following report illustrates the feeling of marginality and the persistence of the civil war in family life:

'There was, then, an awareness of isolation. Not of persecution, because it wasn't exactly that any more, the majority of the families had a good standard of life, they had a good professional and economic position. But you knew that you did not belong to the "official" life of the country. You knew that there were people with whom you shouldn't mix, because they had done terrible things, because terrible things had happened. The awareness of isolation was tangible. There was a double sensation of difference: a difference of being something better – an island in the middle of barbarism – and a difference because of political isolation.' (interview no. 29)

Isolation and fear are again brought up by the following student leader, whose father had been a member of the Spanish Socialist Party (PSOE) and had spent three years in prison after the Republican defeat:

'He later told me that he had been very worried about talking politics with me because that could have been a very serious handicap, a trauma of a lost war. My father employed the instrument of irony. He spoke with us, or rather he spoke to the walls, as if he were trapped, with bitter irony. Of course I was fully aware that he had been with the Republic, that he had fought in the war, and that he had lost the war.' (interview no. 46)

As another report on the perception of political alienation:

'We lived a number of years outside Spain, you see ... when I was a child. The impression that I had of Spain, as I have kept remembering it, was rather dark, there was even a grim sensation of something rather sinister, rather menacing. Franco was something bad; I felt clearly that it was not a country to love – of course, I had difficulty in distinguishing the regime and the country as a whole. But I also had a lot of love for it. I remember that some Spanish songs used to make me sentimental ... Later, the experience of politics was an everyday experience; it was in the conversations within the family, everywhere ... My father got more and more bitter about the political situation, everything seemed to hurt him deeply, until he came to be a sort of exile within the country ... Of course there was a lot of political information at home. That's how things were ...' (interview no. 15)

Fear and repression had been the general experience of politics on the part of democratic parents, and the students seemed to have felt the political position of the parents in post-war Spain. There were, of course, differences in the experiences of repression and in the adaptation to Francoism, according to ideology, to the kind of political involvement, and also according to socio-economic status – within this group of non-exiled anti-Francoists. As has been said, only a small proportion of anti-Francoist parents were leftist militants, and repression was much harsher for those parents. The following quote refers to the consequences of the defeat of the Republic for a civil servant in Murcia who was a militant socialist and to the difficulties that the family found in surviving under the dictatorship:

'My father got eight death sentences when the *Nacionales* entered Murcia[9]. They took him away from Murcia and kept him in a prison for a very long time. My mother declared her solidarity with him and joined him. They had two daughters, who were born before me, and my mother took them with her into prison. My mother was a very strong, very proud character, and she didn't accept any sort of help. When my father finally got out of prison they left those lands and emigrated to Andalucía. In one week the two small girls died, because they had caught something in prison ... That is, they suffered deeply the reprisals of the war, and that in a certain way destroyed their lives. I was the next son ... But you see, I cannot remember having a clear ideological picture of all that. I was particularly puzzled by small things, you know – for example, that being four children, the family didn't have the *Carnet de Familia Numerosa*[10]. You know, that kind of problem ... The familial setting was very precarious. My father worked as a salesman, a commercial agent. He worked like a madman, I came to hate that profession. The circumstances were very difficult.'

(interview no. 32)

The hardship and the precarious conditions for survival faced by leftist families are illustrated again in the following two reports:

'My father had been an anarchist. He was hiding after the war but got caught because of a denunciation. He spent two years in prison. Afterwards life was an odyssey, my father could never get stable employment. He was able twice to get a job in one of those old retail-shop-bars, you remember them? He died when I was quite young and I went to live with an aunt in Madrid. I started working ... Obviously I had come to have very deep political opinions. I had problems in school because of that, I remember the scandal that I once caused in school when I told a girl that Franco was a swine!' (interview no. 19)

'We lived in a small village in Asturias. My mother was a school-teacher and we had some livestock. My father died in the Civil

War, shortly after my birth in 1938. My mother and my uncle were the reds of the village. She was very leftist and after the war she was totally isolated. We had very little money. So much so that, because there was no other opportunity left, my mother took the desperate decision of sending me to a convent, because she thought it was the only possibility open to me to have a way out.'

(interview no. 20)

This last report points to what seems to have been an important consideration in parental strategies for survival: the relevance of religion for adaptation and ideological concealment. Self-protection and protection of the children often involved disguising non-religious beliefs and also sending the children to religious institutions. Thus religious practices were often symbolically manipulated to simulate political conformity and to avoid reprisals.

'My father was on the left of Azaña. He took part in the organization of the elections of the Popular Front[11] and he was purged for a number of years after the war ended. The Civil War broke him up ... He was not religious, even though he had his doubts. He was basically very anti-clerical. But my mother made him go to mass from time to time, out of fear of him losing his job.'

(interview no. 6)

Religious beliefs were also concealed from the children, in order to maximize the children's integration in society:

'My father was teaching at the University of Barcelona before the war. After it, he was purged and dismissed ... Both he and my mother were non-religious but they tried to conceal it from their children.' (interview no. 3)

'I knew that my mother was an agnostic, but I was then going to a school which was run by priests, and she began showing an apparent interest in religion. And then one day she told me that she wanted to learn to say one's rosary and that of course upset me very much. It made me very much ashamed that my mother should want to learn the rosary.' (interview no. 14)

It has already been pointed out that, although student leaders and their parents had shared democratic and anti-Francoist values, there was a considerable political distance between them. Somehow the two generations seemed to live in two separate worlds: the parental world was described as one of long-time abandoned political activities and of verbal anti-Francoist expressions. The long time lag in middle-class radicalism, ranging roughly from 1939 to 1956, appears to be reflected in the political differences between leftist student leaders and their parents.

The *non-democratic orthodox family background* had by definition one basic component: parental support for the political regime established in Spain in 1939. There were three main types of orthodoxy: first, the Francoists, whose political support for the regime did not limit itself to the military uprising of 1936 and the new state of 1939, but extended to developments of the regime up to its end; second, the Conservatives, whose support for the regime was of an instrumental kind and was compatible with an attitude of political distance from the cruder aspects of the dictatorship; and third, the Falangists, whose support for the military uprising and the first phase of the regime later turned into opposition to subsequent developments in the State. However, the degree of political involvement and of politicization of these non-democratic parents appears to have generally been minimal in accordance with Linz's description of authoritarian regimes in general, and Spain in particular, in terms of political demobilization and a passive, non-participatory political culture (Linz 1964). Political and ideological allegiance to the regime was compatible with a fear of politics, with politics as a family taboo. The Civil War and the Francoist regime were seen as a reaction and a safeguard against the abysmal dangers of politics. The children's experiences of 'exposure to politics' and of explicit political indoctrination, then, were declared to have been minimal in three out of every four cases.

The exception were the Falangists. The populist Falangist parents kept alive the ideological demagogy of the old Falange. This strong ideological commitment was incongruent with the more relaxed political culture which was promoted by the regime after the 1950s, and this showed itself in the loss of influence of Falange within the regime[12]. Radical students with Falangist backgrounds represented 14 per cent of the sample. These students had believed in the Falangist rhetoric of social reform and a 'pending revolution' requiring the mobilization of youth against injustice. They saw themselves as against the 'rich', the 'privileged', and as defenders of the 'people', the 'underprivileged'. Nationalization of the Banks, agrarian reform, redistribution of wealth through tax reforms, and the expansion of education and the social services, had been incorporated in a populist Falangist programme which excluded class struggle and a working-class direction to the 'revolution', as well as parliamentary democracy, freedom of association, and freedom of expression. This populist Falangist programme, which had been influential in the years of the

Civil War, still had some influence in the early 1950s, when the first generation of radical student leaders was finishing secondary education. 1956 was probably the turning point in the long crisis for these ideas, a crisis due to the orientation of the regime towards liberal capitalist societies and the subsequent loss of importance of the Falange as a main political force within the regime. Disappointment over the Falangist programme, because of its ambiguities and contradictions, sometimes led to political radicalism. Two student leaders from the first period of the movement described their Falangist backgrounds. The first indicates the ideological influences and the contradiction between these influences and the evolution of the Francoist regime:

'I believe that in the passionate political life of the *"Frente de Juventudes"*[13], the two real influences were José Antonio Primo de Rivera and Ramiro Ledesma Ramos[14]. The atmosphere in the *"Frente de Juventudes"* was highly critical ... There were populistic components, and a very strong "syndicalist" orientation. I became very influenced by Pestaña[15]. But really the anti-Francoists of the *"Frente de Juventudes"* were Fascists. They opposed Franco because he had betrayed Fascism. The internal opposition of the Falange was organized around the ideas of Ramiro Ledesma Ramos, the most purely Fascist of the three[16] and probably the most intelligent too ... These ideas were in full contradiction with a regime that wanted to set up a clerical conservative Monarchy. This contradiction produced a political collapse among groups of Falangists.'

(interview no. 2)

The second stressed the Falangist conception of social reforms to be implemented by an elite in control of a non-democratic state:

'We were a very amusing species of the early 1950s: the dissident Falangists, we were pure *"Joseantonianos"* or *"Ledesmistas"*, you see. We believed that Franco was a traitor, that he had betrayed the National-Syndicalist Revolution[17], that he had not nationalized the Banks, things of the sort. If you remember, there was a group in the Italian Communist Party with similar origins, for example Alicata. We believed in the State as a dynamic, rational, reformist factor, opposing an inert, bland society. I mean, in that period one was really a Fascist, seriously, in the sense that one opted for an interpretation of History. And curiously enough the contact with Marxism took place because of Fascist stimuli. We thought that we had something in common. Particularly with the Soviets. Stalin had just died ... And that, you see, was the starting point of an inversion of Fascist ideology.' (interview no. 1)

The Falangist view of the state and the populist ideas suffered a mutation whenever politics came to be conceived in terms of class. A student leader described his experience of ideological transformation as a Falangist adolescent in Oviedo in the Asturian region:

'My first political activities were as a pure Falangist. Fifteen years ago that was a frequent case. Because, you see, in those years there was no other ideology in circulation and there was also the ambiguity of the radical social demagogy of some sectors of Falangism, the revolutionary verbosity of National-Syndicalism, populism, agrarian reform, nationalization of the Banks, etc. ... Some groups of Falangists had secret meetings, that I attended, where people spoke about the working class, about the miners, and so on and so forth, you see ... So there was in me a combination of social Catholicism and a Falangist verbal radicalism. And this together with a strong influence of Latin-American and Third-World revolutions, of Algeria and Cuba ... Radicalization was a process that took its time. You see, in those years, there was nothing, one was a pioneer. You discovered the poor, and later the working class. Then you had general ideas that society had to be transformed, that one had to go beyond individual solutions. So the moment came in which you asked yourself, "well, how the hell can one overturn that?". And you came to realize that organizations had to exist somewhere out there. Then in 1956, there were the big miners' strikes which left me flabbergasted and I thought that I was seeing the agent of historic change in action. You began to hear rumours that some organizations had been active: that the Communist Party, that the "*Frente de Liberación Popular*" ... This information came to me mainly from the Catholic working-class movement. You idealized all that. But you see, one was alone. When I entered university, I was standing alone as a palm-tree, I spoke of strange things: miners, agrarian reform, change, revolution, Algeria...' (interview no. 16)

For highly politicized adolescents who became increasingly aware of the incongruences of the Falangist programme of social reforms, a view of society in terms of class inequality and class struggle provided the crucial step in the conversion to Marxism. A Marxist ideology and political commitments were not the outcome here of a process which started as political alienation from the regime due to the inheritance of democratic principles from the parents; they were, on the contrary, the result of an inversion of populist Fascist ideas of a revolution from above. This experience of conversion was rather frequent in the first period of the student movement, but the increasingly limited influence of Falange resulted in the progressive decline in the proportion of radical students from populist Falangist backgrounds.

(B) The ideological and political characteristics of the family backgrounds of radical students are further illuminated if we examine cultural experiences within the family that had indirect political connotations. Religious beliefs and practices would appear to have been a relevant experience in processes of socialization within the families. The assumption that non-Catholicism can be considered as a form of socio-cultural deviance in Spanish society since 1939 seems reasonable. The *Fuero de los Españoles* (a constitutional law promulgated on July 7, 1945) and the Concordat of August 27, 1953 between Spain and the Holy See declared that Catholicism was the official religion of the state. Most of the students came from families that were non-orthodox from this point of view. Two thirds of the radical students reported that their parents were non-Catholic and this is a much higher percentage than that of reported non-Catholics in several national surveys[18].

Within this overall religious deviance, there was an association between religious beliefs and political orientations of the parents (see *Table* 1). Thus, the democratic families represented 58 per cent of the sample but 74 per cent of the total number of non-Catholic parents, whereas the politically orthodox families provided 42 per cent of the sample but 75 per cent of the total number of Catholic parents. A substantial proportion of radical students were therefore socialized within families that deviated from what was the official cultural pattern: the parents were non-Catholic and tolerant of the religious beliefs of the children.

> 'My father and my mother were atheists. However, when I got a kind of religious fever in my early adolescence, my father forbade the smallest irony. He chatted with me, without imposing anything, with a lot of respect towards me.' (interview no. 46)

The experience of religious non-orthodoxy within the family often had political overtones: the discovery of the restrictions to religious and to cultural deviance, the exploration of the consequences of such forms of deviation, were often part of a process whereby religion and religious deviance became politicized.

A second type of cultural experience, which is generally assumed to be relevant in the process of political socialization, is the pattern of parent–child relationship. A democratic pattern within the family has been often associated with leftist political attitudes in the children[19]. Radical students would tend to come from families in which child-rearing practices are permissive and parent–child relationships are non-authoritarian. At the same time, permissive rearing and democratic relations within the family would be associated with parental political orientations of the progressive kind. These hypotheses were accepted in the present research: I expected to find a strong proportion of students who had good relations with their parents, and I also expected that this pattern of parental-filial relationship would be associated with the political orientation of the parents. In fact, two thirds of the interviewees defined their education within their family as permissive, and their relations within the family as non-authoritarian (see *Table* 1). This appears to give support to the hypothesis that a permissive family education is associated with an eventual political radicalism on the part of the children. This type of relationship within the family is well illustrated in this declaration by one of the student leaders:

'There was a very intensive ongoing dialogue, both between parents and children and between brothers. My political activities had a rather strong impact upon family relationships, but family relationships also affected my political involvement. Because on the one hand family relations were enriched: a new communication developed in the family on the grounds of political criticism and political activities. And on the other hand the openmindedness of my parents was important, because they accepted my experience as an independent experience and as a positive one. Instead of censoring it, they strove to understand it, to assimilate it. There were tensions, of course...' (interview no. 25)

(C) The final aspect of political socialization within the family that will be examined here refers to the influence of social position. An association between high social status of the parents and radical political orientations of the children has often been reported in analyses of student radicalism[20]. Radical students tend to have radical parents from upper-middle social strata; right-wing students tend to have conservative parents from a lower-middle strata or from the working-class, and these students often have a compulsive orientation towards upward social mobility and individualism. These assumptions have been criticized on the grounds of alleged cultural limitations, and contrary evidence has been produced for a number of countries[21].

However, political conditions such as those existing in Spain under Francoism must have reinforced the association between upper-middle-class status and student radicalism. Because of the characteristics of universities and of the student body, students coming from working-class backgrounds would experience particular social isolation; in their university life they would be cut off from working-class subcultures, and their social isolation would keep them apart from political organizations and student politics. Political constraints could better be overcome when families provided a secure milieu and material means of access to unorthodox ideas. Radicalism would have a minority character: its availability would be restricted to the offspring of well-placed families with democratic views. This would be a limited number of people not only having opportunities to learn ideological deviance, but also the possibility of turning deviance into open dissent.

A secondary analysis of the questionnaires used in a survey of students from the University of Madrid, which was carried out in 1969[22], indicated a strong association between leftist political views (a declared potential vote for socialist and communist parties) and upper-middle-class status. Seventy-two per cent of students with a leftist potential vote located themselves in the upper-middle status category, whereas the rightist potential vote was located mainly in lower and lower-middle class (85 per cent). The distribution of my own sample of radical students is similar: roughly two-thirds were located in upper and upper-middle status categories. The following quotation illustrates the combination of parental democratic political orientations and high social status. Here the parents and their group of anti-Francoist friends seem to have been able to build up an intimate community of 'internal exiles' in which a high social status goes counter to political marginality.

'My parents had been members of the "Republican Left" (*Izquierda Republicana*). They used to gather with friends at home. They had had important positions in the party and they were always talking about the years of the Republic and the war. But it was a recollection of the past, they had since stopped being militants. What still remained in these people was a dreadful fear ... Well, every one of them had been in prison, and some had received death sentences, which had been commuted. Then, well, they lived with these reminiscences. The atmosphere was obviously very anti-Francoist ... They were also members of the bourgeoisie, they now lived very well, they were no longer threatened ... They were radical bourgeois, and they had a bourgeois view of politics. Of course we talked politics. More than anything else they tried to compensate for the external context, to counter external influences. So they sent me to a liberal school, which the children of their friends also attended. And I spent my life between home and school.'

(interview no. 42)

Democratic families appear to have been particularly concentrated in the upper and upper-middle status categories (three-quarters of the cases), whereas over four-fifths of the non-democratic families were located in the lower status categories. These social differences between the two types of family background are again underlined if we consider the educational levels. Whereas three out of every four 'politically deviant' fathers had a university degree, this was so for only half of the 'orthodox' fathers.

A sketch of the family backgrounds of radical students, considering parental political and cultural orientations (i.e. religion and parental-filial relationships) as well as the social status of the family is provided in *Table* 1.

The combination of the different variables indicates the importance of a consistent type of democratic, agnostic, tolerant, and permissive family, with a university education and upper-middle social status[23]. For roughly half the sample of radical student leaders, the democratic/deviant type of family provided an avenue of socialization into dissenting ideas. In this type of family, children lived in relative isolation from the dominant political norms. These children also enjoyed privileged conditions of access to deviant ideologies, whereby they could develop alternative political outlooks. In fact, a number of the conditions that Lofland and Stark (1965) have singled out in a different sort of commitment seemed to be present; namely, 'encountering the doctrine', 'an affective bond with other converts', 'an exposure to intensive interaction'. Also, the availability of political information, the intensive exposure to politics, and the security resulting from high social positions, were associated with a propensity to translate ideas into actions.

2 Adolescent experiences

Adolescent cultural experiences of socialization that were, to a certain extent, external to the family played a significant part in the radicalization of students. These experiences included the type of school attended, religious beliefs and activities, and travels abroad. Schools, books, religion, and travelling provided experiences whereby certain groups of adolescents were able to come into contact with deviant cultural/political ideas and develop an attraction towards them.

(A) The school attended was in general determined by the politics of the family. Thus, three out of every four radical students from democratic family backgrounds attended a secular school, whereas this was so for only one out of ten of the radical students from non-democratic families. Liberal-radical families of upper and upper-middle status could also afford an elite education for their children and they tended to send them to elite-secular schools: they compensated for their ideological stigma by selective education for their children.

The combination of two dichotomies – elite versus non-elite and secular versus religious – gives the basis for a four-fold typology of schools of secondary education. The cultural experiences that radical student leaders described varied considerably in each of the four types.

The *elite-secular school* was attended by 34 per cent of the sample of radical students. These students came mainly from liberal-radical families of upper-middle status, and the schools were strongholds of well-to-do, non-exiled Republicanism. With only one exception the experience of political deviance within the family was prolonged by educational privilege and cultural unorthodoxy at school (see *Table* 2). The following report may be illustrative of this experience.

> 'The school was a kind of shelter for the offspring of what had been the pre-war intellectual elite, and a refuge for people who didn't want to send their children to religious or fascist schools. It was a place were nobody used to sing the *"Cara al Sol"*[24] with his arm raised and no one was forced into religious activities. The parents of the majority of the students knew each other. They had, somehow, a past that was akin. People from a liberal, republican tradition. Professionals, mostly: university teachers, doctors, architects, and so on; that's what they were. We talked politics at school; well, the whole school talked politics and there was a clear awareness that it was, politically speaking, exceptional.' (interview no. 29)

The school provided an early exposure to unorthodox political ideas. The elite-secular school was often a source of political information and of early contacts with dissident political groups. Political identities were developed and enacted; the process of political affiliation started.

> 'There was a constant flow of information within the school about the activity of ex-students in university politics. They were people we had known, and we followed eagerly their experiences as student leaders. When we came to meet them we talked about student politics. There was a constant link with the student movement.'
> (interview no. 43)

'When I was in *"sexto"*[25] the Socialist Youth was re-organized. I had contacts through ex-students from my school who were already at university. I was asked to join the group but I refused at that time. I joined the following year.' (interview no. 13)

The *non-elite secular school* was attended by 14 per cent of the sample. This institution was represented by the State-owned *Institutos*, where the teaching staff was often of high quality but where student numbers and lack of supervision posed serious problems. The staff of the *Institutos*, paradoxically, included a number of ideologically unorthodox staff, and displayed a relative openness to political discussions. All but one of the students attending this type of institution were from democratic family backgrounds (see *Table* 2), and their social status was lower than that of students attending the elite-secular type of school. Although the *Institutos* may have allowed for cultural experiences that were relatively liberal in the context of Spanish secondary education, they seem to have been less of a sanctuary against a hostile political environment than the elite secular school:

'I went to an *Instituto*: it was my parents' decision, the alternative was the *Marianistas*. My friends, of course, were the sons of other republicans, who had also sent their children there. We had an intensive intellectual life, we discussed every conceivable subject. We circulated books among ourselves – Neruda, Camus, Unamuno – some of us were atheists. We had a number of liberal, republican teachers. But, you see, we were conscious of our singularity, even within the *Instituto*. Singularity that manifested itself in many ways, but particularly in a certain inhibition on some issues, a certain fear of saying on which side our fathers had fought in the war. I have a clear memory of those years. Of course, it was a time of hardship. One could talk about almost nothing. It was in the years between 1946 and 1956, bad years.' (interview no. 26)

The remaining two types (the *elite religious school* and the *non-elite religious school*) were fully orthodox. Francoist parents sent their children to orthodox religious schools: nine out of ten of the radical students from such family backgrounds attended these institutions, whereas this was the case for only one quarter of students from democratic families. In these institutions, a cultural censorship was enforced, particularly of books, and there was strong religious pressure.

'You had to attend mass every morning, with collective prayers and lots of religious symbolism, ecstasies, and so on. We also had Rosary in the evenings. Not to have daily Communion was very badly considered – you would face problems. I was very religious. Very religious and very "top of the class", the darling boy of the priests. You also had to have the right looks to become the archangelic boy – that was an important factor, you see, you had to have not only intellectual or moral, but also physical grace. The hand of God showed itself also in that.' I was also a very good student – that was part of the image, and of course I fully shared it.'

(interview no. 34)

'There was strict censorship of our reading. You see, the Index of Prohibited Books was taken very seriously. I remember having burned certain books ... I never read anything without advice ... This lasted until I was fifteen or so. I enjoyed reading, so I read all the Catholic authors, but when I came across a Pérez-Galdós or a Unamuno, well, then, all this was forbidden.' (interview no. 23)

The distinction between these two types of religious institutions lies in differences in their academic style and in differences in the family status of the students. Both types were attended by a similar proportion of the sample – 26 per cent – but whereas all but one of the students who attended the elite-religious type were from upper or upper-middle status families, all but two of the students having attended the non-elite religious type were from lower status categories.

A substantial proportion of the sample of radical students had comparatively favourable ideological conditions, in the family and the school, which created a certain margin of independence. In 62 per cent of the cases this comparatively privileged situation was provided by either the family alone (14 per cent) or the school alone (4 per cent), or most often by both agencies (44 per cent). The dominant pattern was that deviant parents sent their children to non-orthodox schools, which had a reinforcing effect on deviant socialization. Whatever the limitations, the precautions, and the fears, these students could hear, learn, have access to, become familiar with ideas and experiences whose diffusion in Spain was strongly restricted by the regime. As for the remaining group of students who were subject to similar experiences neither in their families nor at school, another type of event brought disruptive consequences: namely, an indirect 'encounter with the doctrine' (to use Lofland and Stark's terminology), in which religion, reading, and travel were crucial factors.

(B) The information on adolescent religiosity and the influence of 'forbidden' books on radical students refers here to their last three years at school (generally between the age of fifteen and seventeen).

These were considered to be the crucial years in the development of political ideas before entrance to university. In these years the perception of political authority appears to become separate from family images and independent political attitudes begin to emerge[26].

Religiosity is again considered as a dichotomy: orthodoxy *versus* non-orthodoxy, orthodoxy referring to Catholicism. Twenty-nine out of the fifty radical students (58 per cent) declared that they were not Catholic at the end of their secondary education. The proportion of religious deviance seems to have been very high when compared with national surveys corresponding to the period of the research[27]. This unorthodoxy also varied sharply according to (i) the political orientations of the parents: over four out of every five radical students from democratic families were non-Catholic, whereas this was so for less than a quarter of the radical students from politically orthodox families; (ii) the elite character of the school: two-thirds of the radicals from elite schools were non-Catholic, but less than half the radicals from non-elite schools were; (iii) the religious character of the schools: four out of every five radicals from secular schools were non-Catholic in their late school years, whereas the proportion was only slightly over one-third for radical students from religious schools. It seems, however, that the political orientation of the parents was the main explanatory factor in the religiosity of the children. When these orientations are held constant, the effect of the type of school on the religious beliefs of adolescents is significantly reduced.

A pattern of unorthodox reading, as defined by the context of the cultural restrictions of the 1950s and early 1960s was reported by thirty-four out of the fifty cases (68 per cent). It included, on the one hand, authors who had a reformist democratic image in Spanish culture and had been involved in the Second Republic (especially writers like Machado, Lorca, Unamuno, Baroja). On the other hand, it included authors who were unorthodox from a rigidly Catholic point of view (such as Nietzsche or Gide), and who sometimes displayed rather explicit political attitudes (as Pavese or Sartre). The influence of Sartre and Unamuno appears to have been particularly deep.

To a large extent, radical students had been able to overcome the cultural restrictions of a non-democratic society in their adolescence. This was particularly so when the families and/or the schools provided favourable subcultural conditions. The relationship between these factors can be detected in the following report of one of the students whose father was a liberal republican of upper-middle status:

'You see, my father had a very impressive library. He was the one who introduced me to it, who talked to me about novelists, poets, essayists. Thus I entered a world inhabited by Conrad, Dostoievski, Machado, at first, and then by Gide, Camus, Hemingway, Miller, Ortega, Unamuno, and later by Sartre, Malraux, Nietszche. Well, a world without limits that absorbed me ... I had the feeling of living in an exceptional world, well above the mediocrity and brutality of the "normal" world. This, of course, had an obvious political potential. I was quite aware of it. Everything was coming together, the political position of the family, the religious problems of adolescence, the intellectual discoveries – mainly through literature – the general scarcity and cultural obscurantism, the sensation of cultural privilege. All this contributed to an exciting feeling of political dissent, and I was sharing it with a group of friends at school.' (interview no. 15)

Although politically deviant families, non-orthodox schools, and adolescent cultural experiences (manifested in religion and reading) were associated, the latter played a relatively independent role. Thus, if we consider those students from orthodox families who had attended orthodox schools, 18 per cent were deeply influenced by 'forbidden' literature and 10 per cent were non-Catholic. Cultural restrictions made it clear to adolescents that there was in Spain a relationship between culture, religion, ideology, and politics, an interdependence that was underlined by the students' experience of censorship. Cultural deviance, then, was perceived as political deviance: Gide was as subversive as Lenin. Whereas non-orthodox schools had very little independent effect and were basically dependent on family orientations – reinforcing the socializing impact of the family – cultural non-orthodoxy in reading or religious beliefs, although associated with family ideological deviance, had a somewhat more independent margin of influence. Reading and religion were thus important in the turn towards political dissent of those students who had a politically orthodox family background and had studied in orthodox religious schools.

(C) Travelling abroad added new opportunities for exposure to and contact with deviant ideologies. A large majority (70 per cent) of the students had travelled abroad before entering university and, of these, three out of every four declared that this experience had been relevant in their process of radicalization. Variations according to family background were not significant, and the impact of travelling had, therefore, either a cumulative or an independent impact on the adolescents that were to become militants in the secret Spanish student movement. In particular, 21 per cent of radical students from orthodox families reported to have been deeply affected by their experiences in other countries. The following quotations may be illustrative of the effect that ideological discoveries through books and personal encounters abroad had on adolescents who had been living in the closed and restricted cultural world of the dictatorship:

'I went to Paris with a friend. I was then sixteen. I remember that I bought *The Communist Manifesto*. Catholicism had cracked up and there was a great attraction towards sin ... The discovery of the Civil War, of Marxism, after the Catholic collapse, made a lot of sense; one could reconstruct the world. You see, whenever one went to Paris, one came back loaded with books ... One entered *Maspero*, *Le Globe*, every Paris bookshop, full of enthusiasm.'

(interview no. 22)

'It is amazing to remember what the journey to Paris meant to a lot of people ... walking into bookshops ... later *Maspero* would become a meeting place ... Encountering a Spanish anarchist while having breakfast in a cafe in the *Place de la Contrescarpe*, for example, and the man telling you as a start that you were an arse-licker of Franco's dictatorship, and this of course was a hell of a shake-up. Or somebody starting to ask you about the execution of Grimau[28]. This shattered the blissful ignorance of your adolescence.'

(interview no. 31)

The table (overleaf), then, gives an account of the distribution of the sample of radical students according to the main influences leading to political dissent.

3 Deviant socialization and the stages of the student movement

The development of the underground student movement brought changes to the social characteristics of the militants and modifications to the typical experiences through which these students became involved in politics[29]. The movement went through its first expansion around 1960, consisting in recruitment based on similarities between recruiters and recruits (affinities of family backgrounds and common cultural experiences). As a consequence, the singularity of the population of militants was particularly noticeable. Then a second pattern of expansion took place around 1965 when the movement achieved considerable support from the student population, succeeded in a series of tactical struggles, and provided a new socializing sub-

Table 2 Adolescent socialization of radical students (in percentages)

| | political orientations of the parents | | |
	democratic	non-democratic	total
A Type of school attended*			
elite – secular	55	5	34
non-elite – secular	21	5	14
elite – religious	14	43	26
non-elite – religious	10	47	26
	100%	100%	100%
	(N=29)	(N=21)	(N=50)
B Adolescent cultural non-orthodoxy			
religion†			
non-Catholics	83	24	58
Catholics	17	76	42
	100%	100%	100%
	(N=29)	(N=21)	(N=50)
influential reading‡			
non-orthodox	86	43	68
orthodox	14	57	32
	100%	100%	100%
	(N=29)	(N=21)	(N=50)
C Influence of travel abroad§			
travelled	76	62	70
influenced	(77)	(69)	(74)
not influenced	(23)	(31)	(26)
did not travel	24	38	30
	100%	100%	100%
	(N=29)	(N=21)	(N=50)

*t = 5.74; p < 0.01.
†t = 5.12; p < 0.01.
‡t = 3.61; p < 0.01.
§t = 1.11; p > 0.05 (this t-test refers to the influence of travelling abroad for the two subsamples. A t-test referring to the differences in travelling abroad, whether influential or not, produced t = 1.14 between the two subsamples, therefore p > 0.05; another t-test on the influence of travelling abroad only for those who travelled produced t = 0.53, and hence p > 0.05.)

culture. In this new stage (1965 onwards) the movement expanded from the initial group of family-bred radicals and became more representative of the whole student population. The three periods that have been described in Chapter 5 correspond to these changes in recruitment: 1955–60 as the period of organization; 1960–65 as a period of consolidation; 1965 onwards as a period of mass mobilization. The changes in the social background of militant students included the following:

(i) The importance of parental politics as a factor in the development of radical commitments was very great when the political movement became organized, but decreased when the movement reached its maturity. The social backgrounds of the militants became more representative: family backgrounds were more similar to that of the whole student population, and the proportion of those from politically orthodox families correspondingly increased.

(ii) This went hand in hand with a decrease in the proportion of students from upper and upper-middle class homes. The distribution of the population of militants according to the status of the family became, in the last stage of the student movement, more similar to the distribution of the student population as a whole.

(iii) The relevance of non-orthodox schools in the process of developing radical commitments also tended to decrease in the last stage of the student movement. The combination of secularity and elitism characterized a smaller proportion of the schools that had been attended by the radical students. The types of school that had been attended by militants and by the student population were more similar.

(iv) Cultural experiences in the adolescent socialization of militants were of less importance. Intellectual concerns diminished, non-orthodox religious beliefs, and reading as well as travelling abroad, were also less influential.

(v) Channels of access to politics changed. In the first stage the main channels of political information were democratic families, reading, and travel abroad. However, in the last stage, the movement itself became a main source of political information. This was so in a direct way, as the clandestine organizations established contacts with students in institutions of secondary education, distributed propaganda, and widened their policies on information and recruitment; it was also so in an indirect way, as information on student politics was provided by the press and circulated in conversations. Political commitments, therefore, were not so much associated with particular family experiences and influences or with exceptional circumstances in adolescence, but resulted very much from the existence of the student movement.

The founders and early members of the student movement appear to have had deep affinities as a result of their family backgrounds and the schools that they had attended. Family and school provided the first elements of trust, the first symbols of a common political outlook. Recruitment of new members was made on the basis of these affinities: militants were attentive to students from their own school entering university and/or coming from well-known democratic families[30]. Access to the clandestine organizations in the absence of such common features was possible only after lengthy observation and evaluation of the candidates, on the grounds of political activities and/or ideological-cultural expressions. The enlargement of the original group of militants and the success of the student movement between 1962 and 1965 led to a more ambitious policy of recruitment and wider political activities. The creation of FUDE as a clandestine student union, which was intended to lead to mass-mobilization of the students, was the main step in that direction at the beginning of the 1960s. The changes in the policies of recruitment of the secret organizations and in the social characteristics of the militants were described as follows by one of the student leaders:

'From 1965 or 1966 the forms of recruitment and the origins of the militants changed completely. Before that date, the organizations were only attentive to those students who had shown themselves as already politicized, wishing to have a role in the vanguard. It was the Communist Party that made the switch, starting an avalanche, giving admission into the party to every chap who simply didn't like Carrero Blanco's face[31]. That was considered to be enough. It started massive recruitment, careless, unselective. People entered without any ideological training. At the beginning, every organization, and the Communist Party in particular, set up seminars for theoretical discussions, for political training, they worried a lot about conditions of secrecy, they were only interested in individuals who would lead a role in the vanguard. But after 1965–66 the "vanguard organizations" became "mass organizations", there was no difference. They became public, known to everybody. This meant a jump forwards, but secrecy was given up. There was an obvious cost in the quality of the militants. Their origins were different too. They came from the mass of students. This was very clear, you know, this was absolutely clear. Before that, the majority of the militants were the children of republican families, or else people who had turned to the left after being passionate fascists in their adolescence – you know, deeply believing in the "revolutionary" fascist rhetoric. In any case they had very distinct origins. Later, militants came from the obscurity, from "nothing" families. Individuals started to come close to the movement and eventually joined it once they were at university, without the family having any importance whatsoever.' (interview no. 46)

Table 3 shows the impact of the successive stages of the student movement upon the different non-orthodox experiences in the political socialization of radical students.

Table 3   Changes in socializing influences by stages of the movement

| | stages of the student movement | | | |
	a *first* *stage* %	b *second* *stage* %	c *third* *stage* %	*total* (*100*% = *50*)
*Socializing experiences**				
unorthodox families	62	76	40	58
secular schools	46	53	45	48
elite schools	62	65	55	60
adolescent religious un- orthodoxy	54	65	54	58
unorthodox pattern of reading	77	71	60	68
travel abroad	31	53	65	52
	(N = 13)	(N = 17)	(N = 20)	

* $F = 2.44$; $p > 0.05$
  $t(a\,v\,b) = 0.91$; $p > 0.05$
  $t(b\,v\,c) = 2.30$; $p < 0.05$
  $t(a + b\,v\,c) = 2.05$; $p < 0.05$

The F-ratio and the t-test were calculated on the basis of an index composed of the added numerical values attributed to the different possibilities of each of four variables (family, school, reading, and religion). The range of the numerical values attributed to the variable 'family' was equal to that attributed to the other three variables together (and which were considered three dimensions of 'adolescent cultural experiences').

These unorthodox socializing experiences were very influential among the founding militants and early members, and this influence persisted in the first expansion: the movement recruited mostly (and the movement was mostly joined by) those individuals who had developed a deviant political orientation through adolescent cultural experiences as well as through their families. The transition to the phase of 'mass mobilization' took place under different circumstances: from political action in terms of clandestine organizations, the student movement entered a new period of action in terms of an inclusive political subculture. This political subculture had a ghetto-like character within the wider context of the dictatorship but it was a necessary protective milieu for the growth and development of the movement. The population of militants later became more diversified; radicalization and recruitment were less dependent on familial and school background than on entrance into an absorbing world of student politics offering totally new experiences of political life.

7 Recruitment and political militancy

Militancy in secret political organizations can be studied from two different perspectives. The first has been that of Chapter 6, which has studied deviant political socialization and the process of becoming a political dissenter and a radical. The second will now focus on the strategies of recruitment developed by secret political organizations, and I shall try to provide an interpretation of militancy in terms of organizational policies. The complementary character of both approaches lies in the fact that membership of secret organizations is the result of a convergence of an individual propensity to radicalization and an organizational policy of proselytism. There is a mutual approach between a political movement and typical individuals who eventually become affiliated members.

The development of a political movement is very much dependent on these convergent mutual approaches. That is, affiliation is a crucial question in the dynamics of a political movement, in the same way as affiliation is an equally crucial question in the career of the militant: it represents the threshold of active militancy. As John Wilson puts it:

'The process of affiliation is begun by conversion to the beliefs espoused by the movement. An individual who has been thus converted does not necessarily align himself with a specific organization.

This is followed by an act of recruitment in which the individual is persuaded to join forces with those with similar aspirations. He is, at this stage, merely "raw material" which must be processed by the movement for its own uses.' (Wilson 1973: 309)

If we want to study the membership of the Spanish student movement we must, therefore, consider the policies of recruitment developed by the political movement, together with the personal experiences of radical individuals in the process of being recruited[1]. The policies of recruitment involve two sets of related questions: the first refers to the openness of the movement, that is the degree of selectivity and the criteria of selection of potential recruits. The second refers to the management of proselytism, that is, what types of personal contact were deployed and what was the degree of ideological education required before affiliation took place. Experiences of being recruited are connected with the impact of the policies of recruitment of the political organizations. Analysis of these points is based on interviews with the sample of radical militants considered both as 'individual interviewees', providing information on their recruitment experiences, and as 'informants', providing information on the policies of recruitment, of which they had knowledge and which they helped to carry out.

The policies of recruitment were dependent on the changing requirements of secrecy of the political movement; so indirectly were the experiences of being recruited. The requirements of secrecy were themselves linked with changes in the political situation. These changes have been described for the three successive stages of development of the Spanish student movement that were studied in Chapter 5. These stages consist of a first phase of organization (1955–60), a second phase of consolidation (1960–65), and a third phase of mass mobilization (1965 onwards). If political militancy is the outcome of the confluence of individual political orientations and the policies of proselytism of a political movement, then it seems plausible to think that the different stages of the movement affected the comparative importance of these two factors. The importance of personal political predispositions was indeed highest at the stage of the 'founding members' and lowest at the stage of 'mass mobilization'. As has been shown in Chapter 6, the proportion of 'consistent radicals', (that is, those student leaders whose political commitments had a certain continuity with their family backgrounds) decreased in the final stage of the student movement, while there was a relative increase in 'converted radicals' (that is, students without family or adolescent experiences of political deviance, who were converted by the underground political organizations after entering university).

Table 1　Distribution of the sample of radical students by predominant types of recruitment and by periods of time

types of recruitment	1st stage %	2nd stage %	3rd stage %	total (100% = 50)
(a) Selectivity based on affinity and friendship*	85	88	10	56 (28)
(b) Careful and intensive proselytism†	77	82	5	50 (25)
(c) Quick conversion and open proselytism‡	—	18	65	32 (16)
	(N = 13)	(N = 17)	(N = 20)	

* F = 23.03;　p < 0.01
† F = 27.62;　p < 0.01
‡ F = 12.93;　p < 0.01
(The independent variable is obviously the stages of the student movement, and the null hypothesis is that these stages did not vary in the policies of recruitment.)

Table 1 provides information on the predominant types of recruitment in the successive stages of the student movement. It must be noted that only types (b) and (c) are mutually exclusive, although they do not cover all the sample, whereas type (a) may be compatible with either of the other two. Type (a) refers to particular criteria of selectivity (affinity of family backgrounds and friendship networks) that were used by the political organizations to define the population of 'eligibles'. Types (b) and (c) refer to the characteristics of recruitment once the potential recruits had been defined, and these characteristics include the type of approach carried out to contact the recruit, as well as checks on political safety and ideological purity of the recruit, which were used in the process of proselytism.

A significant change in the predominant mode of recruitment appears to have taken place after the student movement ended its phases of 'organization' and 'consolidation' and started its third phase of 'mass mobilization'. Over a decade (1955–65) the organizations carried out selective recruitment which was restricted to a population of 'eligibles' and which presented characteristics of a *gemeinshaft*: recruitment followed strong lines of inter-personal affinity based on a similarity of family origins, of adolescent cultural experiences, and school ties. But in the last stage the organizations turned to non-selective recruitment, while the population of 'eligibles' became undifferentiated from the total population of students. While the dominant pattern of proselytism was, at first, attentive to considerations of ideological consistency and political safety, this became far less important in the last phase.

The two distinct patterns of recruitment were assumed to be associated not only with stages of the student movement, but also with types of political background (the 'consistent radicals', the 'populist Falangists', and the 'converted radicals'). It was indeed the case that selective recruitment based on personal affinities and networks was reported mainly by the 'consistent radicals': three out of every four of them did so, but less than half of the 'populist Falangist' militants and slightly over one-fifth of the 'converted radicals'. However, these differences resulted mainly from the varying importance of each of the three types of political background in the successive stages of the student movement. Hence, if we consider only the first two stages, not only every 'consistent radical' but also every 'converted radical' reported a pattern of selective recruitment based on affinity and friendship. If the last stage is considered instead, a similar pattern of recruitment is reported by only one of the eight 'consistent radicals' and by one of the twelve 'converted radicals' of the period. This is indicated in *Table 2* which includes, in parentheses, the total number of cases for each type of political background and each stage.

There were some differences between political groups in their use of affinity and friendship as criteria of selectivity. These differences are shown in *Table 3*. Members of the Socialist Party (PSOE) and the group of independent militants underlined these criteria more frequently, whereas the members of the Trotskyist *groupuscules* reported the pattern of unselective recruitment. But again these differences were only the result of the varying weight of these groups within the student movement over time. The political groups did not significantly differ in other aspects of the policies of recruitment, and patterns of recruitment appear to have crosscut organizational lines. A typical policy was simultaneously put into practice by the different organizations and varied over time. These variations over time resulted from changes in the political situation that were experienced equally by the political organizations that co-existed in each of the three stages. What is clear is that the political organizations always displayed those patterns of recruitment that were typical of the period as a whole. The policy of selective recruitment and strict adherence to requirements of secrecy, which was predominant in the first two stages, produced a strong homogeneity in the population of militants

Table 2 Predominant types of recruitment by periods of time and types of political background

types of recruitment		types of political background			
	stages	consistent radicals	populist falangists	converted radicals	totals
(a) Selectivity based on affinity and friendship*	1	8 (8)	2 (4)	1 (1)	11 (13)
	2	13 (13)	1 (3)	1 (1)	15 (17)
	3	1 (8)	– (–)	1 (12)	2 (20)
	totals	22 (29)	3 (7)	3 (14)	28 (50)
(b) Careful and intensive proselytism†	1	4 (8)	4 (4)	1 (1)	9 (13)
	2	8 (13)	3 (3)	1 (1)	12 (17)
	3	1 (8)	– (–)	3 (12)	4 (20)
	totals	13 (29)	7 (7)	5 (14)	25 (50)
(c) Quick conversion and open proselytism‡	1	– (8)	– (4)	– (1)	– (13)
	2	– (13)`	– (3)	– (1)	– (17)
	3	7 (8)	– (–)	9 (12)	16 (20)
	totals	7 (29)	– (7)	9 (14)	16 (50)

*F = 7.37; p < 0.01
†F = 4.81; p < 0.05
‡F = 10.79; p < 0.01

Table 3 Predominant types of recruitment and political backgrounds of recruits by political groups

types of recruitment	socialists	communists	left-wing socialists	left-wing communists	left-wing groupuscules	independent militants	totals
(a) Selectivity based on affinity and friendship*	5	11	4	3	—	5	28
(b) Careful and intensive proselytism†	4	10	5	3	—	3	25
(c) Quick conversion and open proselytism‡	1	7	4	1	2	1	16
Political backgrounds§							
consistent radicals	4	11	5	3	1	5	29
populist Falangists	2	3	2	—	—	—	7
converted radicals	—	7	4	2	1	—	14
totals	6	21	11	5	2	5	50

*$F = 3.12$; $p < 0.05$ †$F = 0.61$; $p > 0.05$; ‡$F = 0.68$; $p > 0.05$; §$F = 1.07$; $p > 0.05$
(Of the three types of recruitment only (b) and (c) are mutually exclusive and the three cannot therefore add to the total number of cases within each political group. The number in each of the cells should be compared with the total for the political group.)

based on the 'consistent radical' type. Changes in the political situation in the third stage made possible the transition to a policy of quick ideological conversion and open proselytism among 'converted radicals' (these students were the main group of militants of the third stage). This uneven distribution of types of militant in the different stages of the student movement is thus associated with the variations in the patterns of recruitment over time. Different political organizations seemed to draw militants from a similar type of background.

Variations in the policies of recruitment over time will now be analysed as fitting the two main patterns typical of 'exclusive' and 'inclusive' political organizations. Whereas the 'exclusive' organization corresponds to the first two stages of the student movement (the stages of 'organization' and 'consolidation'), the 'inclusive' organization is found in the third stage (the stage of 'mass mobilization'). Zald and Ash (1966) describe the 'exclusive' political organization as one which '[holds] the new recruit in a long "novitiate" period, [requires] the recruit to subject himself to organization, discipline and orders, and [draws] from those having the heaviest initial commitments'; on the other hand, the 'inclusive' political organization 'requires minimum levels of initial commitment – a pledge of general support without specific duties, a short indoctrination period or none at all'. These variations in the conception of potential militants and in the types of recruitment have also been described by Wilson (1973: 175–76): we would have on the one hand, a situation where:

'a restrictive definition of the constituency (the pool of people likely to be open to membership) demands a well-modulated campaign in which techniques which enable the recruiter to distinguish a potentially "eligible" listener are used. An emphasis on inter-personal contacts, the use of facilities known to be segregated ... is customary under these circumstances.'

On the other hand we would have a situation where: 'movements make a broad, undifferentiated appeal and have an unrestricted conception of their constituency – anybody who will help is welcome.'

In its third stage, the Spanish student movement came close to the type of 'inclusive' organization. There was little restriction on membership, every student could be a potential member; affiliation did not require a careful and intensive political training, nor was it based on long-held and consistent political beliefs. The situation was totally different to that of the first and second stages, when restrictions on potential membership existed, recruitment was selective, contacts were dependent on carefully checked pre-existing political orientations, and militancy was the final step in a long process of ideological training[2].

1 The first stages of the student movement: recruitment in 'exclusive' political organizations

Selectivity of recruitment was very much a requirement in a political situation where secrecy was necessary for survival. Proselytism was restricted to those potential recruits who, because of their families or because of their personal connections with militants, presented no risk to the organizations from the point of view of secrecy. The offspring of families whose political orientations were known to be democratic were the target of recruitment. The secret political life and the shadowy contours of the political organizations were frequently alluded to in the interviews:

'When I entered university in 1962 I had very little information on political groups. I considered myself a socialist: I remember that I had just finished reading "*Les Chemins de la Liberté*" and I was very obsessed with the need for political commitment. But the student movement was totally underground at this time, and the militants were very careful. Immense precautions were taken.'

(interview no. 15)

The political organizations concentrated on those new students whose origins were known, either through families or schools. The pattern of recruitment followed lines of friendship.

'Recruitment was very restrictive, very selective. Its bases were the groups of friends and it was developed through personal relations of friendship. The organizations tended to recruit acquaintances, there was a clear overlapping of political relations and relations of friendship. Friendship provided the main political guarantee in those years of secret struggle. And then you were all day together, in seminars and all that ... That is how contacts were established. When you didn't have friends and you couldn't provide initial guarantees because of your family or whatever, then you spent more time out there in the cold, being scrutinized ... We were behaving like true "*Cristianos Viejos*"[3]. It was this group of friends, most of them from school, who attracted me into the ASU [University Socialist Group] and I was very active from 1956 onwards.'

(interview no. 5)

Recruitment was not only highly selective; it also involved slow and careful indoctrination, a period of apprenticeship, lengthy training through seminars of ideological and political initiation. The approaches were veiled, and infinite precautions were taken in each of the successive steps:

> 'Political recruitment used to start with seminars for proselytism, organized by FUDE and by the political parties. These seminars were very good instruments. The political affiliation of the organizers was not known – only that they were somewhat "critical", that some individuals with loose "leftist" ideas attended it. And the seminars were intended for individuals that the organizations perceived as "strange", you understand? Well, they came from families that were known to be democratic, or a militant had known them at school. Also people who used to go to film societies, to theatre societies, who read critical literature, who had been speaking publicly in a certain way, they could be invited to the seminars. Somebody, normally a student with intellectual prestige and with a certain leftist aura, would contact these potential sympathisers, telling them that a seminar was to be organized, on a question that would have political connotations ... Brecht, imperialism, Sartre, the Cuban revolution, the poetry of Neruda or Miguel Hernández. It could even be pointed out, sometimes, that a Marxist perspective or some socialist arguments would be discussed. The student would be asked whether he would be interested in joining in, and so on. Of course, no political organizations were mentioned. Then, when the seminar was well under way and when there was a better knowledge of the individuals, some of them would be contacted by one or two militants – of course initially they wouldn't say their party affiliation.'
>
> (interview no. 9)

Unorthodox cultural interests and participation in cultural activities were generally considered to be signs of deviant ideological views and they were also used as symbols of self-presentation in the interaction between potential recruits and recruiters. This connection between unorthodox culture and subversive underground political activities was the main characteristic of the processes of recruitment and, more generally, of student politics in the stages of 'organization' and 'consolidation' of the student movement:

> 'Recruitment focused on people who were showing particular cultural interests. They were reading journals like *The New Left Review*, *Le Nouvel Observateur*, even *L'Express* in those years, French existentialism, and most often the poetry of Machado, Lorca, Miguel Hernández, Neruda. These were considered to be ex-

pressions of dissent. The organizations were attentive to individuals who showed themselves to be familiar with these writers. And if you wanted to show your political leanings, you would take a symbolic book to the university. To attend the activities of cultural societies, such as poetry readings, film exhibitions, etc., was also important. That was the first main procedure for political contacts.'

(interview no. 17)

Cultural activities and discussions seem to have fulfilled a dual purpose: on the one hand, they provided a technique for contacting potential recruits under conditions of secrecy; on the other, they provided a guarantee of ideological purity in 'exclusive' organizations. This second role of ideological discussion seems to have been somewhat similar to initiation processes, probationary periods, and *rites de passage* of revolutionary eschatological sects. As Bryan Wilson writes 'only those who have been acquainted with the essential truths as Christadelphians understand them, are eligible for resurrection' (1961: 225; 1971; 1967). The cultural intensity of the underground Spanish student movement in this phase was not limited to the practices of recruitment but was extended to the internal life of the organizations:

'The intellectual component was always very strong. It didn't stop with recruitment, it went on once you were inside. The cultural atmosphere of the group was very heavy, there was a fantastic cultural and ideological effervescence. This was a main component of militancy. There is no doubt that within the subversion, within FUDE, the CP, etc., you would read much more. There was no comparison: whatever the limits, the scarcity, whatever the absurdity of the discussions, you would read much more, learn much more, discuss much more; you would find more stimulation, more encouragement than anywhere else.' (interview no. 18)

Patterns of reading indicated a general knowledge of Marx and Lenin. Every one of the thirty militants of this period had read Marx, most of them had attempted to read *Capital* or to organize a seminar within the organization to read it, even though they had generally been unsuccessful. The texts that they were most familiar with were *The Eighteenth Brumaire of Louis Bonaparte*, *The Civil War in France*, *The Class Struggles in France*, *Wage Labour and Capital*, *Wages, Price and Profit*, *The Manifesto of the Communist Party*, and *Revolution in Spain*. Twenty-six out of the thirty militants of that period declared that they had read Lenin (basically *What is to be Done?* and *The State and Revolution*). Sartre was the next most widely-read author, particularly his plays, his novels, and *Situations*. Gorz seems to have been very popular, and both *La Morale de l'Histoire* and *Strategie Ouvrière et Neocapitalisme* appear to have been widely discussed. Lukács was another major reading – particularly *The Destruction of Reason* and to a certain degree *History and Class Consciousness*. Finally, Gramsci and Trotsky were also read within the student movement (many had their first contact with Trotsky through Deutscher, and the book most widely read was *The Permanent Revolution*). Other authors, such as Baran, Sweezy, Mandel, Marcuse, Fanon, were also part of the intellectual panoply of the radical students, but they had much less ideological influence. There are no relevant differences between the first stage of 'organization' and the second stage of 'consolidation' as to these influences: only a slight increase in the influence of Gorz and Lukács (which was to be expected due to the date of publication or translation of their books). There are no significant variations either among the different political groups: Lenin and Gramsci appear to have been only fractionally more influential in the Communist Party, Gorz and Lukács among the left-wing socialists (FLP).

Participation in open political activities was the second main channel of recruitment by the secret organizations. To be elected as a student representative gave access to an intensive political life. As was described in Chapter 5, many militants had three overlapping political identities: as elected student representatives (in the legal Chambers of Delegates), as members of the FUDE, and as members of a secret political party. The Chambers of Delegates came increasingly under the control of representatives who were members of a secret organization; they became eventually a main factor in the political mobilization of the students. Participation in open student politics gave exceptional opportunities for glimpses of underground politics and secret political organizations, as well as for making political contacts. This increased once a student joined FUDE and entered secret politics.

When FUDE was set up, as a secret student union, an important step was taken towards the final stage of 'mass mobilization'. But until the second half of the 1960s, the student movement continued to be highly selective. The conception of the prototypical militant bore a strong resemblance to the description that Walzer gives for a very different social movement:

'The commitment and zeal of prospective saints must be tested and proved ... The band of the chosen remains exclusive and small, each of its members highly "talented" in virtue and self-discipline.'[4]

But obviously, exclusiveness and selectivity were not so much chosen as imposed: the political constraints of repression forced the organizations to maximize security.

'The political organizations would wait in the shadow until somebody defined himself very clearly, in a very relevant way, and then they would approach him, they would make the first step. The organizations were very careful, secrecy was rather strict. You see, there was no civil jurisdiction and the lightest sentence you could get from a military court would be three years. The political organizations would wait until somebody defined himself, until they had a strong guarantee about his political ideas, and then, under maximum security, very cautiously, they would approach him.'

(interview no. 11)

Recruitment policies were, therefore, very careful and selective in the phase of the student movement as an 'exclusive' organization. They involved a particular attention to one type of potential militant: the 'consistent radical'; a strong minoritarian and elitist definition of those eligible for affiliation. The success of the underground political organizations in gathering support within the universities and in extending an anti-Francoist political subculture led to a change in these policies of recruitment in the final period of the student struggle against the dictatorship.

2 The maturity of the student movement: recruitment in 'inclusive' political organizations

In the stage of 'mass mobilization' policies of recruitment came increasingly close to those of the 'inclusive' type of political organization. Recruitment became more open and proselytism shorter. The reason for this change was the much greater strength of the student movement, which culminated in the collapse of the SEU in 1965, and the setting up of an alternative illegal democratic student union (which was to be the SDE). The radical groups had much wider support among the student population and they increased their membership, their visibility, and their capacity for mobilization. The transition from one pattern of recruitment to another is described in the following report:

'In my case I joined FUDE after a long period of personal political activity. That was the first big step. And some time later, after a new period of confirmation of more specific political ideas, I joined the Communist Party. That was the general way of enlistment in my years, from what I know as a recruit and as a recruiter. But towards 1965, a few words, a short exchange of ideas, were enough. You gave to an individual what was called *el martillazo* [the "hammer blow"] simply on that basis. People who had not had any political contact, but who had made certain insinuations, well, they were in the CP the following day.' (interview no. 12)

The last stage of the radical student movement was a period of generalized political participation. This participation was based on the activities of the illegal democratic student union, the SDE. The political successes brought a sense of exhilaration, of open political opportunities. The SDE was supported as 'the union of the students', while the SEU was considered to be 'the union of the regime'. There was continuous communication between the SDE and the students, through assemblies, wall notices, pamphlets and leaflets, magazines, cultural activities (theatre, cinema, lectures); the SDE also promoted students' shops, agencies for part-time work and for financial help. There was a constant flow of political information; left-wing intellectuals were invited to speak or simply to visit the Faculties; leaders of the underground trade-union movement were also frequently invited by the SDE.

This transition took place in 1965. After several years of political activity, the FUDE-controlled Chambers of Delegates had voted in the twelve university districts of Spain for independence from the SEU and for the organization of an alternative democratic union. This was supported by endless sit-ins, occupations, assemblies, and demonstrations. The mass mobilization of the students, first by FUDE and later by the SDE, had brought about a complete change of scenario: instead of the underground politics of minority organizations, the new situation consisted of a dominant political subculture which was openly subversive. Participation in the activities of the SDE or in demonstrations and assemblies was often a very early experience for students who started their first year at university, and this provided ample possibilities for political contact. The dominant organizations in the second half of the 1960s were the Communist Party and the left-wing socialists (FLP). However, the FLP disintegrated in 1969 as a result of its ideological confusion. It had been composed of three different groups: one had a left-wing socialist orientation close to the French PSU and to the Italian PSIUP; another was Trotskyist and close to Krivine's *Ligue Communiste Révolutionnaire*; the third comprised left-wing Christians strongly influenced by Third World revolutionary ideologies. Also at that stage leftist *groupuscules* emerged, mainly of Trotskyist ideology, which led after 1969 to the *Liga Comunista*, an influential organization which brought together different *groupuscules* and groups of the former FLP.

The change in the forms of political action and in political recruitment are described by a student leader in the following terms:

'The visibility was much greater than in former years. You see, in the previous period there was now and then a lad who was, or became, politically well known and he was recruited, but this had changed. Politics were no longer based on a sort of democratic-parliamentarian activity in the Chambers of Delegates. From 1967 to 1970, political action was in the form of violent demonstrations, commandos breaking windows, stopping the traffic, setting up barricades, hurling Molotov-cocktails. From socialist reformism to revolutionary action. We had thought the conditions were ripe. The organizations operated much more on the surface ... People were enlisted much earlier, contacts were much easier. There was a qualitative jump forwards ... And then in 1969 the SDE ended. 1968 and 1969 had been two years of intensive revolutionary work. Working-class leaders came to the university, pro-Vietnam committees were organized, commando actions were very successful. But repression was appalling, the delegates of the SDE, who acted openly, were arrested one after the other, so it was decided that a student union, with elected representatives, was no longer necessary. 1969 was the year of the national state of emergency, of the death of Enrique Ruano, and eventually of the police occupying the buildings of the Faculties – 100,000 students at the University of Madrid with the police patrolling the corridors, everything forbidden, hundreds of arrests.' (interview no. 48)

The pattern of proselytism changed when the student movement came closer to the 'inclusive' organization type. The importance of careful screening of potential recruits, the long and intensive novitiate periods, ideological training, decreased due to the new importance of sheer numbers. Somehow, in a period of more intensive and more radical political action, Menshevik organizational criteria seemed to prevail.

'Everything changed a lot. After 1965 any chap who was seen as somewhat active was recruited. If you entered the university and became involved in the SDE, then, without preparation, without careful precautions and training, you could be a member of the

Spanish Communist Party in two weeks. And of course members of the Communist Party who were arrested and convicted were getting five-years sentences. But political recruitment was much quicker, less cautious. People who were very reactionary before entering university became leftist radicals in one week and militants of a revolutionary organization in another week.' (interview no. 43)

The change in the policies of recruitment is again described in the following personal experience of being enlisted:

'One day "D" came along and asked me, well, if I would help him in distributing pamphlets. I had met him a few times, he was around, in assemblies and so on, but I didn't really know him. The pamphlets were signed by the CP. I said OK and we wrapped the whole university in paper. That must have been judged favourably, because two weeks later he came again and asked me, well, why didn't I join. What I really wanted was to do a job, to carry out some work, I thought that I should have plenty of time later to mature, to learn. And so I found myself, all of a sudden, stark naked, in the middle of it all.' (interview no. 31)

The importance of literature decreased, both as an instrument in the period of screening the eligible, as an element in the stage of initiation, and as part of the ideological activity being carried out within the organizations. Marx's shorter and minor texts were still widely read, but less so than in the first two stages, as was also the case with Lukács, Sartre, and Gorz; Lenin and Trotsky were, on the other hand, slightly more influential. It is perhaps significant that while in the first stages of the student movement Lenin was read after Marx – and as consequence of a previous thorough ideological preparation – in the last stage Lenin was usually read before Marx. His writings were used as a compendium for political *praxis* while Marx, as the main body of 'theoretical' knowledge, was left for later. As one of the militants put it:

'I always saw Lenin as an author of booklets that I had to read in order to find the formula for a particular political manoeuvre. Always with a strictly tactical interest, because his work was supposed to be immediately applicable.' (interview no. 46)

But the switch towards a greater heterogeneity in the types of militants as well as the different patterns of recruitment is particularly under-lined in the two following reports:

'I never read anything that did not have a direct political corollary.

I discarded everything that dealt with cultural questions.'

(interview no. 38)

'I read nothing at all, apart from text-books. In my last two years at university my own readings outside the syllabus were the periodical publications of the FLP. Basically pamphlets.' (interview no. 32)

This lack of ideological training co-existed, however, with reported experiences of intensive cultural and ideological discussion within the political organizations. This pattern was still largely present, and the main difference in ideological training between the first stages of the student movement and its last stage appears to have been the variation in the types of militants, channels of recruitment, and of political experiences. These changes resulted from the lessening importance of secrecy, from a greater visibility of the political organizations, and from open political programmes and actions.

3 Before the revolution: militancy and the management of commitment

Differences between political expectations and political events after affiliation may obviously have an impact on political commitments and militancy. Under Francoism, militancy in subversive groups could and often enough did result in heavy personal costs through repression. On the other side, the rewards – in the struggle for democracy and the struggle for socialism – were not quick to come. Bittner in particular has discussed the personal management of the cognitive dissonance which results from the gap between political expectations and 'common-sense' assessments of the 'real situation'[5]. In this last section, I would like to examine, first, the political expectations of the militants; second, the sanctions that they experienced; third, their personal crises and the outcome of militancy.

The level of political expectations tended to be very high. The regime was conceived as cornered and worn out, and the militants viewed their struggle as a decisive battle. The very successes of the student movement in mobilizing the student population to actions of ever-increasing radicalism helped to produce a belief that revolutionary conditions were maturing. These expectations were already present in 1962, as soon as the first important strikes started:

'The student strikes and demonstrations in Madrid in 1962 were at the same time as the strikes in the mines of Asturias. One day, after taking part in a student demonstration, I took the plane to

Barcelona with two other members of the Communist Party. And there was a funny atmosphere in the plane, everybody talking about the events. It seemed that it could be the final showdown. We landed in Barcelona and there was a cut in the electricity supply, the whole airport was in darkness. So, you know, we immediately thought that a revolutionary strike was taking place, that even the airport had had its electricity supply cut off. We were ecstatic. Somebody was waiting for us, to get information of what had happened in Madrid. I didn't go to bed until 4 a.m.; you know, from conspiratorial meeting to conspiratorial meeting. And then we covered Barcelona with leaflets, summoning a general strike. We succeeded in organizing a demonstration in the University of Barcelona. But elsewhere, you know, there was no answer...' (interview no. 6)

In the 1970s the militants still had revolutionary expectations. After four decades of dictatorship and repression, hope was stronger than ever:

'All that time, political activity was my only life. I thought that revolution was imminent. I was living in a large flat with other "pro-chinese" militants. I was utterly absorbed by politics, involved in conspiratorial activities, with political meetings the whole fucking day. I did nothing else – just a bit of work to earn some money. A lot of people were doing the same thing.' (interview no. 44)

Exhilaration with political activities was associated with the belief in imminent political results. That political feeling shared some similarity with the excitement derived from risk-taking as described by Goffman: it resulted from an objective external danger, an intentional exposure of oneself, and the hope that it would turn out well. As Goffman puts it, living in challenge,

'looking for where the action is, one arrives at a romantic division of the world. On one side are the safe and silent places, the home, the well-regulated role in business, industry and the professions; on the other are all those activities that generate expression, requiring the individual to lay himself on the line and place himself in jeopardy.' (Goffman 1969: 204–205)

As one of the student leaders said, 'militancy meant secrecy and danger but also finding a reason for living, with things that you deeply believed in, and also the enjoyment of risk' (interview no. 12). Often enough the secret organizations stimulated these expectations and this romantic conception, for they presented themselves as the vanguard of the proletariat and riding the irresistible wave of historical change:

'Militancy within the Communist Party produced the effect that you saw the organization as a crucial product of History, as a superior entity. All other leftist organizations were seen as groups of nice people, you know, in a very paternalistic way, as not knowing what was really going on. And, of course, they lacked a serious working-class base, so where did they think they were going, without workers? We were the political vanguard, the bearers of the future ... I am convinced that all the militants shared this view of militancy as gratifying, with Christian residuals, with a feeling of historical destiny.' (interview no. 26)

Militancy also required an intensive personal dedication. This was often seen as an important personal cost, the other side of the balance. Militancy created personal difficulties and private problems, which were often dramatic. The personal strains brought about by the requirements of intensive political commitment and militancy have been pointed out by Almond in the context of radical politics in the US[6]. These strains were intensified by the fact that, in many cases, young student militants had the responsibility of reorganizing the underground parties: this was the case for the Socialist Party, the Communist Party, and the FLP.

'I found myself in a bloody situation. Without any serious political experience, without sufficient ideological training, there I was, in the middle of it all. When I entered the FLP there weren't more than five or six militants in the University of Madrid. The sensation of having been cheated was very grave, it was bloody. You felt unable to deal with the problems you had to solve. But I had a very militant commitment, I thought "well, I'm burning myself out. I am destroying myself, but this is necessary". I did not have a personal life, I studied less than I wanted. But I felt that I was doing it for something. You see, one gave oneself up in a rather sublime way. It was a permanent frustration, that one could only overcome idealizing, sublimating one's own political activity.' (interview no. 16)

Faced with this situation, the militants reacted by hardening their ideological commitments and discussing personal difficulties on ideological grounds:

'The personal problem of solving one's own biography became secondary. The political activity was feverish, hectic. After 1964 and the Claudín split, which had been so serious, well, the Communist Party remained a rigid, closed organization. I felt ill at ease but it seemed to me that it was the truly important party of the left. Then, well, I liked to read some of Sartre's writings, *Les Mains Sales* in particular, and think that I was a bourgeois and therefore with personal difficulties within a working-class organization.

(interview no. 23)

Two facts seem to have been particularly costly. The first one was political sanctions and it was independent from 'bourgeois subjectivism'; the second one was the adjustment of militancy to post-university life. *Table* 4 gives an indication of police arrests of the militants.

Table 4 Police arrests by stages of the student movement

	1st stage	2nd stage	3rd stage	totals
none	1	4	3	8
one	8	6	2	16
more than one	4	7	15	26
totals	13	17	20	50

$F = 2.10$; $p > 0.05$

Five out of every six militants had been to prison and more than half had been more than once. There did not seem to be significant variations between political parties independent of their relative importance in the different stages. Although the differences between stages are not statistically significant, less than one-third of the militants of the first stage had been arrested more than once but the proportion rose to two-fifths in the second stage and to three-quarters in the third stage. These data refer only to repression against the sample of militant leaders and not upon the student movement in general. Also, they refer only to arrests, but many other sanctions were used against militants: deportation and confinement, exile (up to seven years in one of the cases), expulsion from the university, fines, withdrawal of passports, police searches of a house (eleven times in another case). The range of repressive measures used by the regime increased over time and many student militants had dramatic histories of persecution. For example, one of the leaders was arrested twelve times, expelled from the university four times; another was arrested seven times, went through a military trial and was expelled twice from the university; another was arrested eight times, expelled from the university three times, and fined four times.

After leaving university radical students were faced with new problems. The university provided a good milieu for individual political action: there was an ongoing conflict, permanent political activities. Leaving the university was seen as bringing a return to political isolation and inertia.

'I had a serious problem of readaptation because, well, I had been one of those who had tried to organize the first national strike. I felt fulfilled, respected, I had my world of political relations, a lot of experience in mass actions, I was able to address gatherings of over five thousand, and then suddenly all this had to be readjusted.'
(interview no. 22)

Although the difficulty of a post-university adjustment was generally mentioned, the militants of non-student political organizations offered an image of greater continuity in their political activity.

'My affiliation to a political party made it possible to continue political militancy after the university. I could keep my links, keep my contacts. And then there were other areas of struggle: professional associations, large corporations with a strong presence of the Workers' Commissions: although nowadays large corporations have a department which investigates the records of the employees.'
(interview no. 42)

Whatever the degree of original political expectations, the personal costs, the sanctions, and the passing of time, all the leaders had maintained consistent leftist ideological positions. Some of them had, however, moved from 'active' political militancy to 'passive' ideological beliefs. This leftist ideology did, then, persist over time, and the main changes took place at the level of political activism within secret parties. Three possible variations in militancy then occurred: (i) total withdrawal from party politics, although remaining ideologically on the left; (ii) latent militancy, temporarily suspended because of dissatisfaction with the present political orientation of the parties, although contacts were maintained and a return to active militancy was seen as very likely in the near future; (iii) active militancy, that is, continuing involvement in party politics including the cases of switched party affiliation.

Overall, almost three out of every four militants between 1955 and 1970 were still in touch with political parties – as latent or active militants. There appears to be a clear increase in political 'withdrawals' in the second stage, which seems to be associated with political crises around 1964–65, that were due to frustrated expectations about the working-class movement and to the Togliattist and Maoist splinters within the Communist Party in 1963–64. In the first and third stages, only between one-sixth and one-seventh of the militants had withdrawn from party politics. The increase in the proportion of 'active militants' in the third stage may be simply a result of a more recent personal involvement in politics (see *Table* 5). Variations between political parties indicate a relatively higher persistence of militancy among militants of the Communist Party (thirteen 'active' out of twenty-one), although not substantial.

Table 5   Current militancy by stages of the student movement

	1st stage	2nd stage	3rd stage	totals
withdrawal	2	9	3	14
latent militancy	7	3	6	16
active militancy	4	5	11	20
totals	13	17	20	50

$F = 5.38$; $p < 0.05$

What is relevant is both the general persistence of ideological orientations and the maintenance of political involvement. This indicates that the qualification of student radicalism as being transient is not easily applicable to the Spanish movement, considering either the continuity and increasing strength of the student movement as a whole over time, or the individual commitments and the involvement in politics of this particular group of leaders after leaving the university. These leaders were *'non-récuperables'* to use a term which had been very influential among them, and at the very least, they were 'privatized dissenters'. As one of them put it 'What do you think my life is, but a perpetual internal exile?'. None of them drifted into conformity. But what seems to be the main point is that it was not uncommon for former student leaders to take up important posts in the secret leftist parties. Thus five out of the fifty were elected to national executives, eleven to provincial committees. It is this central importance of the political parties within the Spanish student movement which helps to explain the political consistency over time and the strong link between the student and the working-class movements that was forged.

8 Conclusions

Spain is an exceptionally important case for the study of political dissent under dictatorship. For nearly four decades, from 1939 to 1975, and after a destructive civil war that lasted three years, a regime that had abolished democratic representation and working-class unions tried to eradicate political opposition by repressive means. And yet movements of dissent emerged and grew within Spanish society, making substantial ground in the 1960s. These movements were particularly important among workers and students. Which factors were most relevant in the persistence and growth of political dissent?

Three issues appear to be particularly important in answering this question. First of all, it seems that changes in the Spanish economy tended to reverberate through society, producing system contradictions that fostered conflict. The transition from an autarchic capitalism towards a more competitive economy in the late 1950s, under the economic predominance of finance capital, introduced new productivity requirements that, in turn, accelerated the crisis of the corporatist institutions set up in the 1940s. These political contradictions had very important consequences for the organization of the working class, helping to strengthen labour unions which had survived in secrecy (UGT in particular) and also leading to the birth of a new trade union

(*Comisiones Obreras*) which was a direct result of the new system of industrial relations (that included collective bargaining and some shop-floor representation).

Second, political dissent survived in some communities that presented a high degree of resistance to the dictatorship and remained unconquered after 1939. In the case of the working class, organized actions were possible in areas that had a tradition of proletarian militancy, that were highly industrialized and had large concentrations of workers. These areas could be particularly found in Asturias, the Basque Country, and Barcelona. They were the backbone of the revived working-class movement, which later spread to new areas. In the case of the student movement, families and friendship networks provided subcultural protection for radical students but, from the mid-1960s, the universities themselves became strongholds of political dissent.

Finally, political organizations played a crucial role in the long and difficult reorganization of opposition to the dictatorship. The Communist and the Socialist parties in particular, but also other minor political groups such as the FLP, the ORT, and the PTE, were the pillars of the illegal workers' and students' unions, of the Workers' Commissions, the UGT, the FUDE, the SDE. The emergence of the working-class and the student movements was dependent on the underground survival of the parties of the left. These parties provided the strategies and the leaders, and it was the capacity of these parties to survive that kept the workers' and the students' resistance alive in the long and difficult period of the 1940s and 1950s, and that later rekindled the struggle.

The relationship between community factors and political parties in the generation of political discontent has been a classic problem of political sociology. To what extent can political radicalism spread in a coherent and tightly-knit proletarian community if political organizations are absent? And contrariwise, to what extent can political organizations attract support for radical programmes if there is no back-up in a solidaristic community? The argument of the book has been that *both factors must be interconnected in the genesis of political dissent under a dictatorship*: the underground groups were successful in those areas that were strong proletarian communities or in the protective milieu of universities, but at the same time the cultivation of the struggle was only possible where secret political organizations were active.

A brief explanation of political dissent under Francoism would be, first of all, that it resulted from the survival of political groups that could not be totally eradicated by repression. Second, that institutional contradictions which stemmed from a process of rapid capitalist development under a rigid dictatorship facilitated the organization of dissent. And, finally, that these contradictions led to organized movements of dissent when two additional circumstances were present. First, political enclaves represented by proletarian communities and universities where repression and control could not eliminate socialist traditions and militancy; second, political socialization within families which contributed to the persistence and transmission of radical political ideas. These factors made it possible for the underground political organizations to gain in strength, to mobilize, and recruit. Institutional contradictions, enclaves of militancy, deviant political socialization, and underground political organizations are the inter-related dimensions of a theoretical explanation of how political struggle was generated and sustained under the dictatorship. These four dimensions provide the framework of the former chapters and they are common to the analyses of the working–class and the student movements. It may now be convenient analytically to take up a few questions that reappear in the study of both movements.

To what extent can it be said that the working–class and the student movements of opposition to the dictatorship were the product of traditional left-wing forces that had survived persecution? Or alternatively, to what extent can these two movements be interpreted as a new development reflecting the changing social and economic conditions of the country? Obviously the answer is that it was a mixture of both processes, but it must be remembered that political groups had argued over a long period that the relative strength of the different groups of the left had dramatically changed since the defeat of the Republic in 1939. This argument was particularly defended by the Workers' Commissions and the Communist Party: the argument implied that the predominance of the PSOE, the socialist party, as the main party of the left, and the influence of the UGT, the socialist trade union, had withered away under the dictatorship. From this point of view, the working–class and the student movements under Francoism were fundamentally disconnected from the traditional forces of the left. Until the summer of 1976, the Workers' Commissions and the Communist Party (which had been a comparatively small organization until the civil war), together with the diverse new socialist groups, adhered strongly to this 'discontinuity thesis'. Obviously, the PSOE and the UGT were the main defendants of the continuity thesis. Their argument was that both organizations had survived repression, that they had led the struggle in the first fifteen years of the dictatorship under conditions of severe repression, and that they experienced a period of weakness in the 1960s, but re-emerged gradually by the end of the decade to become powerful organizations again.

It seems that the Workers' Commissions and the PCE did under-estimate the militant capacity and the strength of the socialist organ-izations in the Basque Country and in Asturias, as well as in Madrid, Andalucía, and Catalonia. They did not anticipate the influence of UGT and PSOE in the country as a whole nor their rapid growth when the dictatorship began to crumble. As to *Comisiones* and the Communist Party, they seemed to be stronger in Madrid and Catalonia. There is, therefore, support for the continuity thesis – *a fortiori* – if one considers that the influence of the Communist Party itself within the more militant nuclei of the working class and within the universities does not exactly provide support to the discontinuity thesis. However, it is also true that the economic and social transformation of the country had a deep impact on the political forces and on the develop-ment of the struggle against the dictatorship. Only in the light of these changes is it possible to understand the new vigour of the working-class movement in the 1960s and the birth of *Comisiones*, which became such a powerful union. But, simultaneously, one must not forget the fact that PCE politics and *Comisiones* cannot be divorced. It is from the perspective of this *association between the traditional forces of the left and the new possibilities introduced by economic and social changes*, which I have tried to present, that the working-class movement and, to a lesser extent, the student movement should be understood.

Clearly, all opposition groups under dictatorial regimes have to make a major strategic decision: whether to work through legal institutions in a relatively open way or to carry out resistance underground. The open/legal strategy has the advantage of maintaining contact with social groups which can be mobilized in political action, and support can be attracted more easily. The political presence of a subversive organ-ization is more visible and the organization can build up strength with less difficulty. These are the reasons why Dimitrov insisted in 1935, within the Comintern, on the necessity of avoiding a retreat to the catacombs of politics and of maintaining a visible presence for the militants, whilst infiltrating the legal institutions of Fascism. Of course, the costs of this strategy can be very heavy in terms of repression. These were the tactics of the Workers' Commissions and they were connected with the changes in the strategic conception of the Com-munist Party during the mid-1950s. This strategy was very successful in rapidly attracting support to *Comisiones* in the 1960s, but the counterpart of this success was the exposure of the organization to increased repression, which led to a serious crisis in the *Comisiones* after 1968.

The polar extreme of this position was that of a strict clandestine struggle and underground protection of the organization. This strategy can be defended on political as well as on moral grounds: on the one hand, it may be said that a subversive struggle, as soon as it moves towards public/legal activity under repressive conditions, can only become less radical and may even contribute to the stability of the regime; on the other hand, it can be said that this strategy requires collaboration with institutions and individuals that are part of the dictatorship. More generally, it seems contradictory that a subversive struggle could be carried out at a public/legal level in a non-democratic repressive regime. Whatever the tactical advantages, the outcome could only be mild reformism or irresponsible exposure of the organization. But the drawbacks of an underground struggle are, obviously, greater difficulty in maintaining a presence within the population and in attracting support and mobilizing large groups of people. This strategy of always remaining on the illegal side, of never occupying legal platforms, and of not using infiltration as a means of subversion was, of course, that favoured by the UGT. It must, however, be noted that although UGT had a very strong connection with the socialist party (PSOE), this party did accept the occupation of legal elective posts as a valid strategy in the case of the student movement.

Is it possible to evaluate both strategies given the Spanish experience? A general answer to this question is clearly difficult. It seems to me that the success of each of these alternative strategies is very much dependent on the type of community within which the subversive organization operates; and on the development of institutional tensions within the dictatorship. Thus, the underground strategy of UGT was easier to carry out and more successful in proletarian areas where traditions of militancy and a homogeneous working class made penetration of the state-controlled unions more difficult. This was the case in the Asturian mines and in the Basque industrial communities, where the influence and the activity of UGT persisted through nearly four decades of Francoism. On the other hand, the strategy of *Comisiones* was more successful in those areas where the destruction of working-class organizations had been extensive and where a break had inevitably occurred between the underground forces and the working class: these were the multi-industrial centres of Madrid and Barcelona. The universities were also difficult to mobilize under the political controls of Francoism and here also a strategy of infiltration proved very fruitful.

As to the connection between strategies and institutional tensions, it seems to me that in the first period of the dictatorship the only possible strategy was an underground effort to survive and to protect the organization – as UGT did. In the second period, when there was an increasing conflict between capitalist activities and corporatist institutions, the timid reforms and the relatively greater openness of these institutions made infiltration profitable. In that sense, the strategy of *Comisiones* produced very positive results in the decade of the 1960s, although repression led to a serious weakening of the organization after 1968. It can, however, be said that the strategy of the Workers' Commissions was effective for a second stage of the working-class movement, after the underground groups had survived the first period of general repression. In the third period, once mass mobilization was achieved, as was the case after 1967, the strategy of boycotting the legal institutions seemed consistent. The intention was to avoid repression, to produce the collapse of the official unions, and to replace them by illegal factory assemblies and factory committees. This was especially possible after 1974, and assemblies and committees spread through factories, pits, and building sites. It seems to me, therefore, that the strategy of UGT was right in the first and third period, but that the infiltration and mobilization achieved by *Comisiones Obreras* were of major importance in the growth of the working-class movement and, furthermore, that they made the transition from a first period of survival to a third period of subversion possible. It is worth noting that the two opposing strategies of UGT and *Comisiones* were made compatible within the student movement: from 1958 to 1965 the underground organizations used infiltration within the state-controlled SEU while at the same time they set up an illegal union. After 1965 the students boycotted the SEU, replacing it by an alternative democratic institution. This combined strategy, as has been mentioned, was adopted by the Communist Party, the Socialist Party, and the FLP.

Finally, what was the situation in 1975, at the time of the death of Franco, and what connections exist between the resistance movements among workers and students and the gradual emergence of a quasi-democratic system in 1976–77? There is clearly a mutual relationship between these movements' struggles and the crisis of the dictatorship in the 1970s and especially after 1973. The increase in repression after 1968 was not supported by large parts of the power bloc: repression was seen as a temporary reprieve only, as displaying the incapacity of the regime to move towards a different type of political system. This different type of political system was now thought to be necessary, partly due to the demands of Spanish capitalism and partly to the strength of the movements of dissent. It must be remembered that repression did not stop the working-class struggle – the number of strikes was higher than ever in 1970 – nor did repression put an end to the subversive struggle within universities. Thus, the death of the prime minister, Carrero Blanco, in a terrorist bomb attack in 1973, was seen by those parts of the power bloc as an opportunity to increase pressure for reform; these pressures included demands for the resignation of Franco. The death of the dictator in November 1975 led to the gradual dismantling of the apparatus of the dictatorship, which was accelerated by the Suarez government after July 1976, following seven months of intense political confrontation. This process of change was presented by the new regime as an achievement of a legal/reformist strategy, and by the organizations of the left as the gradual outcome of their strategy of 'democratic rupture'.

The opposition between the 'reformist' and the 'ruptural' conceptions must not be seen from a short-term perspective. The general election of June 15, 1977 was only the provisional result of this new struggle. It is of course obvious that there is no necessary correspondence between the militant capacity of an organization of the left and its electoral support, even among the working class. However, these first elections after forty years do have a few implications for some of the arguments that have been presented in this book. First of all, the elections demonstrated the strong continuity of political forces since the Republican defeat in 1939, in spite of four decades of dictatorship. This continuity was particularly visible in the case of the Socialist Party, whose success seems to have been the result of persisting ideological loyalties in working-class communities, of lingering ideological traditions within families, and of organizational politics. Second, the geographical distribution of political cleavages also showed similarities with the political situation under the Republic. The most notable exception was Catalonia, where socialism and, to a lesser degree, communism, were now the most powerful forces. Finally, the results of the election indicated that although the Basque, Catalan, and Galician nationalism was a crucial political issue, it did not fragment the underlying ideological cleavages in the country as a whole nor the unity of working-class politics. These seem to be relevant points, notwithstanding the basic difference between electoral competition and underground organized struggle – a difference dramatically underlined in the relatively poor electoral results of the Communist Party, which had been such an important force in the underground struggle. But the study of electoral results takes us away from the subject-matter of the book, in so far as they mark the beginning of a new historical period.

Notes

Chapter 1

1 Both researches provided materials for two doctoral theses. J. M. Maravall, *El Desarrollo Económico y los Trabajadores. Un estudio sociológico de los conflictos obreros en España*, Ph.D. thesis, University of Madrid, 1969; *Political Power and Student Radicalism. A study of student radical politics and leaders in Spain from 1940 to 1970*, D.Phil. thesis, University of Oxford, 1975.

2 Poulantzas (1970); Vajda (1976); Kitchen (1976). Trotsky's writings on Fascism have also recently been re-edited (1975).

3 The interpretation of the Francoist regime using the 'authoritarian' type has been defended in particular by Linz (1964). See also Almond and Powell (1966: 217); Almond (1966: 49); Hermet (1971); Ramirez (1972). The interpretation of the Francoist regime using the 'Fascist' type – which could adopt 'totalitarian' or 'authoritarian' political 'forms' – has been presented by Germani 1970; also Solé-Tura (1968).

4 Poulantzas (1970). An interesting discussion of Poulantzas' work is provided in Giner and Salcedo (1977).

5 This approach is thus notably different from that of theories of 'totalitarianism', as it tries to provide a theoretical link between the political economy, the system of class relations, and the capitalist state. The formalism of the theories of totalitarianism/authoritarianism is evident in the following definition of Fascism that Linz provides in his very important empirical contribution to a sociology of Fascism. 'We define Fascism as a hypernationalist, often pan-nationalist, anti-parliamentary, anti-liberal, anti-communist, populist, and therefore anti-proletarian, partly anti-capitalist and anti-bourgeois, anti-clerical or at least, non-clerical movement, with the aim of national social integration through a single party and corporate representation not always equally emphasized; with a distinctive style and rhetoric, it relied on activist cadres ready for violent action combined with electoral participation to

gain power with totalitarian goals by a combination of legal and violent tactics.' See Linz (1976). 'Notes towards a Comparative Study of Fascism in Sociological Historical Perspective', in W. Laqueur (ed.), *Fascism: A Reader's Guide*, University of California Press, 1976 (pp. 12–13).

6 Germani has stressed these similarities (1970: 340). See also Germani (1968).

7 *26 Puntos de la Falange*: point 6.

8 *Ley de Principios del Movimiento Nacional* (a constitutional law promulgated in 1958), point 6.

9 See for example the *26 Puntos de la Falange*: 'our regime will make class struggle utterly impossible, through the integration of every contributor to production within an organic totality' (point 11); 'We shall assure the corporatist organization of Spanish society through a system of vertical unions in the different branches of production, at the service of national economic integrity' (point 9).

10 *Ley Constitutiva de las Cortes* (1942).

11 National Youth Law of December of 1936, quoted in Shirer (1959: 253).

12 After modifications by laws of 1946 and 1966 it was still the case that only 19 per cent of deputies (108 out of 564) were elected by direct universal suffrage between heads of households and married women; 53 per cent were designated within the single party, the official trade unions and local authorities; and 28 per cent were designated by the Head of State or automatically appointed due to the post they were holding.

13 Trotsky, 'What Next'? (1932) and 'Bonapartism and Fascism' (1934), in Trotsky (1975: 125, 166, 456).

14 Cf. Report of the Second National Assembly of the Workers' Commissions, December 1967; Declaration of the Workers' Commissions Regarding the Present Crisis, Madrid, January 1968; Communication of the National Workers' Commission of Catalonia, March 1968; Report of the Fourth National Assembly, April 1969; Conclusions of the Interindustrial Commission of the Workers' Commissions of Madrid, November, 1969.

15 On the use of 'strategic informants', see Dexter (1970).

16 As a processual approach which centres on 'those crucial interactive episodes in which new lines of individual and collective activity are forged', see Becker (1970: 68–70).

17 See Lane (1962: ch. 24); Matza (1964: 66, footnote 23); Becker (1963: 46); Keniston (1968: 8–19).

18 As Arensberg and Kimball use this concept (1967).

Chapter 2

1 See Merton (1968: 73). See as classic treatments of the connection between different institutional areas in processes of development, Weber's discussion of the relationship between a bureaucratic type of administrative organization, a monetary economy and a tax system in Gerth and Mills (1947: 204–209); also Parsons' concept of 'evolutionary universals' (particularly the 'bureaucratic administration' and the 'money and market complex') in his article 'Evolutionary Universals in Society' (1964).

2 Cf. Ros Hombravella et al. (1973).

3 Ministerio de Trabajo, *La Dimensión de la Explotación Industrial en España*, Madrid: 1960.

4 See the estimates of post-war repression in Jackson (1965: Appendix D).

5 See Blanc (1966), E. Fuentes (1966), and Semprún (1966). See also Hermet (1971: 56–76) and Amsden (1972: Chapter 5).

6 Those years have been described in Ros Hombravella et al. (1973) and Tamames (1969). Gallo (1969) gives a descriptive and more political account.

7 Dirección General de Empleo, *Dinámica de Empleo*, (periodical publication).

8 See Anderson (1970). Anderson concludes his analysis pointing out that the circulation of criticism and of alternative proposals to the official economic policies had been quite extensive and that the amount of information available to the Public Administration was very wide. Anderson lays stress on the critical involvement of different groups in the analysis

of economic policies within Spanish society, but this element of limited pluralism in economic decision-making should not obscure the fact that the choice of a particular policy and the responsibility for it were independent from any form of democratic participation and representation. Anderson tends to underestimate the latter point. For a very interesting analysis of the 'circulation of elites' and the changes in economic policies, see Moya (1972 a and b).

9 From the villages of San Martín del Rey Aurelio, Laviana and Infiesto.

10 Instituto Nacional de Estadística, *Anuarios Estadísticos*, Madrid (annual publication); Fundación FOESSA 1967; Sanchez-López (1969: 26); Pascual (1970).

11 See Bulnes (1966: vol. II). The clandestine unions created in the postwar were then: (1) The AS (*Alianza Sindical*) composed by socialist, anarchist, and Basque groups (the *Solidaridad de Trabajadores Vascos*, which abandoned the coalition in 1965); (2) the AST (*Acción Sindical de Trabajadores*) which was composed of left-wing Catholics and later joined the 'Workers' Commissions'; (3) the ASO (*Acción Sindical Obrera*) which integrated in 1962 a dissident group from the AS, the small SOCC (*Solidaridad de Obreros Cristianos de Cataluña*) and, from 1965, important elements of the STV; (4) the USO (*Unión Sindical Obrera*) with a socialist orientation and some left-Catholic influence (it was originally composed of old members of *Acción Catolica* – an official Catholic organization). ASO and USO were unified in a single organization by the end of 1965; (5) the FST (*Federación Sindical de Trabajadores*), another left-confessional organization, also strongly linked with *Acción Católica*; (6) the OSO (*Oposición Sindical Obrera*) which had been created by the Communist Party and which progressively disappeared as the 'Workers' Commissions' developed. These organizations made indeed a very confusing jigsaw.

12 See on these attitudes of parts of Spanish management Linz and de Miguel (1963: 131 and 140); Pinilla de las Heras (1968: 193) and the survey made by *España*

Económica, February 27, 1965.

13 *Evolución Socioeconómica de España, 1964*, Vice-Secretaría Nacional de Ordenación Económica, Madrid, 1965.

14 See on the economic crisis of the mining industry Bulnes (1966) and the information provided by the publications *Perspectivas de Desarrollo Económico de la Provincia de Oviedo*, Consejo Económico Nacional, Organización Sindical, 1962, and *Estudio de Reconversión de la Mano de Obra en Asturias*, SADEI, Oviedo, 1967.

15 See the study of industrial strikes in this period in Blanc (1966).

16 As important documents on this subject, 'Ante el Futuro del Sindicalismo', Comisiones Obreras de Madrid, March 1966; 'Declaración de las Comisiones Obreras de Madrid', June 1966; 'Las Actuales Tareas de las Comisiones Obreras' Comisiones Obreras de Barcelona, February 1968; 'Conclusiones de la Comisión Interindustrial de las Comisiones Obreras de Madrid', November 1969. These clandestine documents have been published in *Cuadernos de Ruedo Ibérico*, 8 August–September 1966; 21–22, August–November 1968; and 25, June–July 1970. See also Hermet (1970); Romano (1973); Sartorius (1975); Camacho (1976); Ariza (1976); Calamai (1975).

17 Declaration of Julián Ariza to *Cuadernos para el Diálogo*, 138, March 1975.

18 From the annual statistical reports of the Ministry of Labour (*Informe sobre los Conflictos Colectivos de Trabajo*) and *Cambio 16*, No. 229, April–May 1976.

19 See on these political differences 'El Año X de las Comisiones Obreras', *Cuadernos de Ruedo Iberico*, 31–32, June–September 1971 (pp. 53–67). See also Amsden (1972: 99–104, 163–165), which much too prematurely wrote off the PCE's strategy within *Comisiones*.

20 'Solidarity' was of two kinds: support for other conflicts and support to workers who had suffered sanctions because of their activities. It must be noted that these claims were overt and that, because of the harsh measures taken against 'non-economic' [sic] conflicts, many wage

political questions. Conflicts over democratic unionization have been included
with the 'political-solidarity' class.

21 Report of the Third National
Assembly of the Workers' Commissions,
July 1968.

22 Document of the Provincial Strike
Committee of the UGT, Madrid, January
1976.

23 As a study of the differences between
'administrative' and 'political' reforms at
the end of the 1950s and beginning of
the 1960s, see Moya (1972b).

24 Touraine has developed his description of Phase B of capitalist industrialization in many different places. See for
instance, Touraine (1955) and a short
account of the typological cases (1966:
43–51).

25 This is, of course, a traditional point
of academic political science. For a general
discussion of the problem of the control
of change in non-democratic regimes, see
Apter (1965: 256–265, 402–405) and from
the same author, (1963: 135–159). Also
Huntington, 1968 (on the consequences
of non-legal political parties, vid. p. 404).
An interesting study of Ethiopia as a
paradigm can be found in Hess and
Loewenburg (1964). The whole theory of
the difficulty of absorbing change in such
political contexts is of course close to
Coser's well-known argument (1956: 44–
54, 79–80, 151–157).

Chapter 3

1 In connection with this, see Mallet
(1963: 28).

2 For an account of socialist and anarchist
groups see Tuñón de Lara (1972); Ramirez
(1966); and Brennan (1950) provides a
good account of the socialist and anarchist
distribution of influence.

3 Data calculated from the annual statistical reports of the Ministry of Labour:
Informe Sobre Conflictos Colectivos de
Trabajo, Madrid: Ministerio de Trabajo,
1963–1974. The reports are based on
secret information from the local branches
of the Ministry of Labour – in particular
the Inspecciones de Trabajo, which are sup-

posed to play a conciliatory role in
industrial disputes – and of the Ministry
of the Interior (Gobernación). All data on
industrial conflict used in the first section
of this chapter are based on the information
provided by these annual reports of the
Ministry of Labour, which have a very
restricted circulation. This information
had to be re-elaborated as it is presented
in a very raw form. All tables given in the
chapter are mine.

4 It could of course be that this concentration of conflict is simply the consequence
of the geographical distribution of the
active population. But these four areas are
still the areas of working-class militancy if
what is considered is the number of disputes per 1,000 inhabitants for the twelve-
year period or the ratio of the average
annual number of disputes/working-class
population in each area. From the point
of view of the incidence of industrial conflict in relation to density of the population, working-class militancy appears to
have been weak in the rest of the country
until the late 1960s.

5 See Martínez-Cuadrado (1969); Beca-
rud (1967); Aguilar (1968).

6 In 1964, when the working-class movement was gathering strength, and
considering as basis (100) the Spanish per
capita income average, Vizcaya reached
167, Madrid 162, Guipúzcoa 161, and
Barcelona 149. Source: Economic Reports
of the Banco de Bilbao for 1957, 1962,
1964, and 1971.

7 Whereas the percentage for the whole
country was 28.0 in 1967, the percentage
for Vizcaya was 52.2, for Barcelona 51.5,
for Guipúzcoa 51.3, for Madrid 35.8, and
for Asturias 34.9.

8 Source: Instituto Nacional de Estadística, Censo Español Industrial de 1958
(p. 21). This association was already
anticipated by K. Marx in The Communist Manifesto and in Capital (volume
1), and later by M. Weber in Economy and
Society (volume 1). See as recent studies
Ingham (1970 and 1969); Durand (1967).

9 Source: Ministerio de Comercio, 1958.

10 If the annual average number of
immigrants per 1,000 inhabitants in the
period 1964–67 is considered, the rate of

Barcelona was 35.3, that of Vizcaya 34.3, of Madrid 21.2, and of Guipúzcoa 20.2. Data collected from Vicesecretaría Nacional de Ordenación Económica, *Evolución Socioeconómica de España – 1967*, Madrid, 1968.

11 Data collected from *Informes sobre Conflictos Colectivos de Trabajo*. After 1972 these reports no longer provided information that could be used for secondary analysis.

12 Employed in electric machinery and machine-tool production, construction of transport material, and engineering.

13 Between 1961 and 1963 production decreased by 9.7 per cent and in 1967 the decrease was 3.0 in nine months. In 1962 the labour force was only 88 per cent that of 1959, and in 1967 alone there were 6,653 redundancies. The crisis was due to the competition of other sources of energy, to a liberalization of coal imports, to obsolescent instalations, and to low investment and productivity (in 1961, the daily output per worker was kg.709, substantially lower than that of other European coal-producing countries). Data and calculations from Organización Sindical (1962a and b); Ministerio de Industria (1961); Comisaría del Plan de Desarrollo Económico y Social (1965); Bulnes (1966); Montes (1963); SADEI (1967).

14 Most of the miners' struggle was carried out by the workers from HUNOSA (in particular from the pits *Polio, Riosa, San Victor, Mosquitera, Nicolasa, Tres Amigos,* and *Sotón,* which had between 350 and 700 workers each), and secondly from the private companies of *La Camocha* in Gijon (1,300 workers), *Minas Figaredo* in Mieres (1,640), and *Veguín y Olloniego* (313).

15 See as a comment on the increasingly overt political nature of strikes the article 'Llegaron las Huelgas', in *Cambio 16*, 161, December 22, 1974. An example would be a co-ordinated strike in Pamplona, Estella and Tafalla (Navarra), and Irún (Guipúzcoa) in 1973, in solidarity with workers involved in a dispute in Motor Ibérica in Pamplona. Also, a strike in 18 factories in Beasaín, in the zone of the *Bajo Goyerri* (Guipúzcoa), which ex-

tended in December 1974 to 80,000 workers from Irún to San Sebastián, all over Guipúzcoa, involving 16 towns, and reaching Pamplona (Navarra), where 70 factories and 25 per cent of the active population stopped.

16 The main centres in the development of the working-class struggle in Barcelona were SEAT (25,000 workers), Siemens (2,200), Maquinista Terrestre y Marítima (2,530), Pegaso-ENASA (3,065), AEG – Telefunken (1,898), Hispano – Olivetti (4,000), Rockwell-Cerdáns (600), Unidad Hermética (1,000), Matacás (200), FAESSA (1,000), Soler Almirall (700).

17 The strike started in the factories of Siemens and Pirelli, extended to the localities of Cornellá, Sant Joan Despí, Molins de Rei, Sant Vicent dels Horts, Viladecans, Gavá, Sant Feliu de Llobregat Esplugues, and reached Barcelona (where the wave of strikes started in SEAT and Pegaso-ENASA).

18 An example would be a strike in the factories of Solvay in Martorell, and Elsa in Cornellá, in 1974, which started because of a deadlock in a wage negotiation followed by sackings and economic sanctions against militant workers, and which resulted in a general strike in the area of the *Baix Llobregat* and the industrial periphery of Barcelona, where 87 factories closed.

19 The main factories were: Citroën, Forjas del Minor, M. Alvarez, Freire, and the shipbuilding companies of Barrera, Vulcano, Santo Domingo, and Astilleros y Construcciones.

20 Survey of the *Instituto de Estudios Sociales del Empleado* (IESEM) to a national sample of 1,117 bank employees, Madrid: 1969-1970. 65 per cent supported the nationalization of the banks, 69 per cent agreed with an interpretation of the legal system in terms of class domination.

21 The main companies involved in the strike were Dragados y Construcciones, Izarco SA, Copisa, Construcciones Bermúdez, Huarte, Agromán, Caviles, Comylsa, and Entrecanales y Tavora.

22 Thus, the three following quotations are illustrative:

'Mining had been very important, with outstanding leaders ... I met them in prison: very good, very able. But you see, it was something a bit apart from the rest. It was important still because the miners were always ready to go on strike, to face anything ... In the Basque Country things were more difficult for the Workers' Commissions, we found more problems, perhaps because other organizations were strong – UGT, USO. There was an organized movement there, many strikes, but it was difficult for us to build up connections.' (Member of the Madrid Inter-industry Co-ordinatory Commission, Workers' Commissions)

'We had difficulties in the mines because other groups had strong political roots and the Workers' Commissions, well, they didn't have the same meaning as in Madrid, which somehow was the centre which disseminated all the ideology of the Workers' Commissions. In Madrid the metallurgy was the strongest point by far. And overall I think that the metallurgy was the vanguard.' (Member of the National Secretary, Workers' Commissions)

'The Basque Country has always been a feud for the UGT, as Asturias. There, the strength of the UGT has survived. The origins of the Workers' Commissions were in Madrid, and later Catalonia, then Sevilla, Valencia, Alcoy, Elche ... Basically in the metal industry and later in the building industry.' (Member of the Provincial Committee of Madrid, UGT)

Chapter 4

1 The suppression of autonomous working-class organizations has been generally acknowledged to be a central characteristic of the different types of non-democratic capitalist states. It would be partly a requirement of a labour repressive organization of the economy, partly an aspect of a policy of elimination of political dissent, and partly the practical enforcement of a corporatist view of society. For a discussion on the nature of these states see Poulantzas (1970) and the discussion in Chapter 1 of this book.

2 The use of 'strategic informants' in the research – in order to study the working-class as well as the student movements – is discussed in the Introduction.

3 Miguel Hernández, a major Spanish poet, was born in Orihuela in 1910, and died in prison in 1942.

4 A bridge over the river Manzanares in the south-west of Madrid which leads to a major working-class area, Carabanchel.

5 The *Red Nacional de los Ferrocarriles Españoles*, a State monopoly of railway transport.

6 The *Campo de los Almendros* was a concentration camp set up in the outskirts of Alicante, in the road to Valencia.

7 The PCE moved quickly from support of guerrilla warfare to mass penetration in 'core' institutions (such as the official trade unions, the universities, etc.), while the PSOE, which had suffered terrible losses in the war and repression as the main party of the left, was slowly adjusting to what it considered a treason from the Allies after the post-1945 non-intervention in Spain. See Hermet (1971a); Preston (1976); Fuentes (1966); Flores (1966); Claudín (1966).

8 In particular the *Juventudes Obreras Católicas* (JOC – Catholic Workers' Youth) and the *Hermandades Obreras de Acción Católica* (HOAC – Workers' Fraternities for Catholic Action).

9 *Juventud Obrera* is a publication of the JOC (see note 8).

10 A large shipbuilding company, with two important shipyards in El Ferrol and Cartagena (this is the one the interviewee is referring to).

11 On the concept of 'system contradiction', see Lockwood (1964); Parkin (1972); Mouzelis (1974).

12 Pegaso-ENASA is a large truck factory in Madrid (with a smaller plant in Barcelona) employing 5,200 workers.

13 The 'Trial 1,001' (*proceso* 1.001) involved ten leaders of the Workers' Commissions arrested in 1972 and who

received prison sentences of up to twenty years; their trial coincided with the death of the president of the government, Admiral Luis Carrero Blanco, in a bomb attack carried out by the Basque nationalist group ETA on December 20, 1973.

14 For an account of the PCE's history and politics after 1939, see Hermet (1971a: chapters 2, 3, 5), and Preston (1976: chapter 6).

15 The *Casas del Pueblo* were local centres of the UGT which were the premises of the local administration of the union, of a public library run by the union, a coffee-room, and a hall for union meetings.

16 Within the Workers' Commissions, the ORT and the PTE opposed this unitary platform on the grounds that it delayed the creation of a single trade union through a constituent congress of the Spanish working class.

17 For example, the *Programa Mínimo de la UGT* and the book *Unión General de Trabajadores*, Colectivo Sindicalista de la UGT (1976).

18 Relevant documents are the publications *Qué es la USO* and *Carta de la Unión Sindical Obrera*.

19 The main documents consulted have been *Qué son las Comisiones Obreras?* June 1966: *Ante el Futuro del Sindicalismo*, March 1966; *Las Actuales Tareas de las Comisiones Obreras*, February 1968; *Conclusiones de la Comisión Interindustrial de las Comisiones Obreras de Madrid*, November 1969; *Comunicado de la Comisión Obrera Nacional de Cataluña*, March 1968; *Declaración de las Comisiones Obreras de Vizcaya*, no date; *Declaración de Principios de las Comisiones Obreras de Guipúzcoa*, no date; *Declaración de las Comisiones Obreras sobre la Crisis Actual*, January 1968; *Propuestas de las Comisiones Obreras sobre la Nueva Ley Sindical*, no date; *Declaración de la Reunión General de Comisiones Obreras*, (for the first seven general assemblies of the Workers' Commissions), June 1967, December 1967, July 1968, April 1969, November 1969, August 1970, October 1971.

20 E.g. the following descriptions of the regime: 'dictatorship of the large capitalists and landowners', 'ferociously anti-

worker dictatorship', 'Spanish monopoly capital through its present instrument, the Franco regime', 'regime of robbers and criminals ... The Franco dictatorship which crushes the whole people and which we can and must get rid of as soon as possible' (respectively in *Comunicado de la Comisión Obrera Nacional de Cataluña*, March 1968; *Conclusiones de la Comisión Inter-Industrial de las Comisiones Obreras*, November 1969; *Declaración de la Cuarta Reunión General*, April 1969; *Declaración de la Sexta Reunión General*, August 1970).

21 The following quote may be illustrative: '... convocation of a Constituent Labour Congress in which norms will be established regulating the future trade-union life in the country ... The system of affiliation and its possible compulsory character, together with the amount to be paid in contributions, will be determined by Workers' Congresses' (*Propuestas de las Comisiones Obreras Sobre la Nueva Ley Sindical*, no date. See also *Declaración de las Comisiones Obreras sobre la Crisis Actual*, January 1968).

22 This assumption is further discussed in Maravall (1976).

Chapter 5

1 Among others, the national president (Rafael Carrasco), the secretary general (Juan Lopez), a member of the executive Committee (Emilio de la Loma).

2 From *Universidad, Escalafón de Catedráticos Numerarios*, Ministerio de Educación Nacional (1964).

3 See Chapter 2 about this first wave of strikes.

4 See the discussion in Lenin, *What is to be Done?* (1902).

5 On the organization and the politics of the Spanish Communist Party, see Hermet (1971a).

6 For example see Bernal (1967: 3–25).

7 ETA (*Euzkadi Ta Azkatasuna* – Basque Homeland and Freedom) was created in 1960–1961 as a strictly clandestine party to fight for Basque national independence and socialism. It turned into a revolutionary group resorting to urban guerrilla tactics. Its support in the Basque Country appears to be important, and repression has been particularly harsh (state of emergency in the Basque provinces of Vizcaya and Guipúzcoa in August 1968, national state of emergency in January 1969 after strikes and demonstrations in the Basque Country, national state of emergency in December 1970 on the occasion of a military trial of ten leaders of ETA and the kidnapping of a German consul by ETA, etc.). The ETA–Berri group defended against the ETA–Zarra group a programme in which Basque national freedoms were not the exclusive claims, but were inserted in the context of a socialist revolution.

8 Enrique Ruano was a radical student leader from the Faculty of Law, who was killed falling through a window when arrested by the Security Police in January 1969.

9 For supplementary information on the evolution of the student movement see Farga (1969); Giner (1972); Tierno Galván (1966); Peña (1966); Tuñon de Lara (1969); León (1972); Formentor (1972); different articles in *Cuadernos de Ruedo Ibérico*, Nos. 2, 3, 4, 6, 12, 20/21 and in *Realidad* since 1964.

Chapter 6

1 The sequential interpretation of deviance seems to be suggestive in interpreting political dissent. For such an approach to deviance see Lemert (1951 and 1967); Becker (1963); Matza (1964 and 1969). An interesting use of elements of this approach may be found in Downton (1973: chapters 3 and 5).

2 As contributions to the study of political orientations in terms of political subcultures, see Kirby (1971); Parkin (1967 and 1968).

3 This would allow for an easier fulfilment of crucial requirements for conversion underlined by Lofland and Stark: namely, 'encountering the doctrine', 'bonds with other converts', 'neutralization of extra-cult attachments', 'exposure to intensive interaction'. See

Lofland and Stark (1965); also Wilson (1973: chapter 3).

4 See as examples, Maccoby, Matthews, and Morton (1954); Campbell, Gurin, and Miller (1954); Nogee and Levin (1958); Converse and Dupeux (1962).

5 Parkin (1968: 146–150); Denver and Bochel (1973).

6 See as examples referred to US students Lipset (1967 and 1972 – see particularly the two chapters 'Sources of Student Activism' and 'Who Are the Activists'); Flacks (1967); Keniston (1968: 349–350 and Chapter II); Westby and Braungart (1966). Data for British students are presented in Mott and Goldie (1971). Data for Chilean students are given in Glazer (1968a and b); Bonilla (1960). For Latin-America as a whole, see Silvert (1964).

7 On political indoctrination as a preventive mechanism against political deviance, see Germani (1970).

8 25 per cent of the interviewees within the 'higher education' category selected 'legalization of political parties'. The results, together with information about the sample and about the realization of the surveys, were published in *Revista Española de la Opinión Pública* (9) July September 1967, and (18) October–December 1969.

9 The term *'Nacionales'* (Nationals) refers to the Francoist side in the Civil War, and it has a patriotic connotation which is here used sarcastically.

10 The *Carnet de Familia Numerosa* (Card of the Large Family) is granted to families with more than 3 children and entitles them to a number of economic benefits.

11 The 'elections of the Popular Front' refer to the legislative elections of February 16, 1936 that concluded with the victory of the Popular Front.

12 See Linz (1970); also, Payne (1962).

13 The *'Frente de Juventudes'* ('Front of the Youth') is a youth organization of Falange that combines a para-military and a boy-scout character. Children from lower-middle and lower status families provided a large affiliation between 1940 and 1960, particularly for the benefits of summer camps.

14 José Antonio Primo de Rivera was

the son of the General Miguel Primo de Rivera, dictator between September 1923 and January 1930. José Antonio Primo de Rivera founded in October 1933 the '*Falange Española*'. Ramiro Ledesma-Ramos and Onésimo Redondo were the founders in October 1931 of the 'Juntas de Ofensiva Nacional Sindicalista' – JONS ('Juntas of National-Syndicalist Offensive'), a syndicalist movement of a nationalist, corporativist, and populist ideology. The Falange and the JONS merged in a single organization in February 1934. Its programme appeared as strongly anti-liberal, anti-democrat and authoritarian (it presented itself as 'revolutionary', anti-conservative, and anti-capitalist). The organization had little support until the Civil War, after the deaths in 1936 of the three founders, when it was used as the main mobilizing ideology of the Francoist side.

15 Angel Pestaña was one of the principal leaders of the '*Confederación Nacional del Trabajo*' – CNT ('National Confederation of Labour'), the anarchist union. He was a 'moderate' and opposed the revolutionary programme of the small anarchist organization FAI ('*Federación Anarquista Ibérica*') on the basis of a purely syndicalist ideology, and by 1932 he had lost almost all influence.

16 'The three' were Ramiro Ledesma Ramos, José Antonio Primo de Rivera, and Onésimo Redondo.

17 The 'National-Syndicalist Revolution' refers to the 'radical' programme of social reforms of '*Falange Española y de las JONS*': basically nationalization of Banks and industries and agrarian reform. These 'radical' reforms were the populist elements of an overall political programme that included a corporatist organization of the workers, a non-democratic authoritarian regime and a strongly nationalist ideology.

18 Ground (1967: 31); Fundación FOESSA (1970: 442).

19 Flacks (1963); Block, Haan, and Brewster-Smith (1968); Westby and Braungart (1966); Watts and Whittaker (1968).

20 Flacks (1963); Westby and Braungart

(1966); Lyonns (1965); Watts and Whittaker (1966).

21 See the discussion in Lipset (1972: ch. 3, esp. pp. 109–110). Evidence is presented for example in Lammers (1971); Glazer (1968: 347–403); Mott and Goldie (1971).

22 The survey is part of Fundación FOESSA, *Informe Sociológico Sobre la Situación Social de España* (1967). Thanks to the director of the research, Professor A. de Miguel, a set of the IBM cards was available to me and secondary analysis of the data was carried out with the help of Nuffield College Research Services Unit in the autumn of 1973.

23 As also seems to be the case for American radical students. See Braungart (1971).

24 The *Cara al Sol* is the official hymn of the Falange.

25 The course roughly corresponding to 'O' levels in English Secondary Education.

26 See Easton and Dennis (1969: chapter 9); Hess and Torney (1967); Merelman (1971).

27 For example, the *Encuesta de la Juventud Española* (1968) indicated that 86 per cent of students between 15 and 29 years of age were 'practising Catholics'. This was a survey of a representative sample of the Spanish population between the ages of 15 and 29, on the basis of data from the 1960 Census. 1,931 interviews were completed between May and June 1968. See *Revista Española de la Opinión Pública* (15) January–March 1969. By 'practising Catholicism' was meant assistance to mass and taking Communion with some regularity.

28 Julián Grimau was a member of the Central Committee of the Spanish Communist Party, who was arrested and executed in 1963.

29 For certain similarities in the US student movement, see Mankoff and Flacks (1971).

30 On the use of the concepts of 'affiliation' and 'affinity' see Matza (1969: 90–142).

31 Admiral Luis Carrero Blanco was vice-president of the Spanish government from September 22, 1967 to June 9, 1973, when General Franco delegated on him the presidency of the government. He was killed in a terrorist bomb attack on December 20, 1973.

Chapter 7

1 This double analysis of recruitment, focusing on the recruiting organization and on the recruits, has a number of similarities with Jarvie's discussion of why people join cargo cults. See Jarvie (1967: 68–73, 162–168).

2 As examples of other social movements with some similarities see Lofland (1966: 51–57); Gerlach and Hine (1970: 82); Pinard (1971: 182–200).

3 *Cristianos viejos* (Old Christians) were the traditional non-converted Christians in Medieval Spain for whom 'purity of belief' was associated with 'purity of blood': admission into that category was therefore based on strictly 'exclusive' criteria.

4 Walzer (1965: 317–20). See also for an analysis of other movements with similar characteristics of 'exclusiveness', Hobsbawm (1959: 152–62, *passim*). .

5 See Bittner (1963). Bittner, however, does not discuss the basis of 'common-sense' assessments.

6 See Almond (1954). 29 per cent of the group studied by Almond mentioned strains in personal relationships as cause for disaffiliation from the Communist Party.

Bibliography

The different sources of evidence (interviews, political documents, press reports, and secondary statistical material) are described in the Introduction.

AGUILAR, M. A. (1968) *Geografía de la Participación Electoral.* Madrid 31 January.

ALMOND, G. (1954) *The Appeals of Communism.* Princeton: Princeton University Press.

—— (1966) Comparative Political Systems. In H. Eulau (ed.), *Political Behavior.* New York: Free Press.

ALMOND, G. A. and POWELL, G. B. (1966) *Comparative Politics. A Developmental Approach.* Boston: Little, Brown & Co.

AMSDEN, J. (1972) *Collective Bargaining and Class Struggle in Spain.* London: Weidenfeld and Nicolson.

ANDERSON, C. W. (1970) *The Political Economy of Modern Spain – Policy Making in an Authoritarian System.* Madison, Wis.: University of Wisconsin Press.

APTER, D. (1963) *System, Process and the Politics of Economic Development.* The Hague: Mouton.

—— (1965) *The Politics of Modernization.* Chicago: University of Chicago Press.

ARIZA, J. (1976) *Comisiones Obreras.* Barcelona: Avance.

ARENSBERG, C. and KIMBALL, S. (1967) *Community and Culture.* New York: Harcourt Brace and World.

BARBANCHO, A. G. (1967) *Las Migraciones Interiores Españolas.* Madrid: Instituto de Desarrollo Económico.

BARCELÓ, L. (1974) Convenio de la Construcción de Madrid. *Gaceta de Derecho Social* 38–39, Madrid.

BÉCARUD, J. (1967) *La Segunda República Española.* Madrid: Taurus.

BECKER, H. S. (1963) *Outsiders.* New York: Free Press.

—— (1970) *Sociological Work.* Chicago: Aldine.

BERNAL, A. (1967) En el Corazón de la Violencia. *Cuadernos de Ruedo Ibérico* 12, April–May.

BITTNER, E. (1963) Radicalism and the Organization of Radical Movements. *American Sociological Review* 28(6).

BITTNER, E. (1968) Radicalism. In D. L. Sills (ed.), *International Encyclopedia of the Social Sciences*. London: Macmillan.

BLANC, J. (1966) Las Huelgas en el Movimiento Obero Español. *Horizonte Español, 1966*. Paris: Ruedo Ibérico.

BLOCK, J. H., HAAN, N. and BREWSTER-SMITH, M. (1968) Activism and Apathy in Contemporary Adolescents. In J. F. Adams (ed.), *Contribution to the Understanding of Adolescence*. Boston: Allyn and Bacon.

BONILLA, F. (1960) The Student Federation of Chile: Fifty Years of Political Action. *Journal of Inter-American Studies* 2.

BRAUNGART, R. (1971) Family Status, Socialization and Student Politics – A Multivariate Analysis. *American Journal of Sociology* 77(1).

BRAUNGART, R. and WESTBY, D. L. (1966) Class and Politics in the Family Backgrounds of Student Political Activists. *American Sociological Review* 31(5).

BRENNAN, G. (1950) *The Spanish Labyrinth*. Cambridge: Cambridge University Press.

BRZEZINSKI, Z. K. and HUNTINGTON, S. P. (1964) *Political Power: US/USSR*. London: Chatto and Windus.

BULNES, R. (1966a) Del Sindicalismo de Represión al Sindicalismo de Integración. *Horizonte Español 1966*. Paris: Ruedo Ibérico.

———— (1966b) Asturias frente a su Reconversión Industrial. *Cuadernos de Ruedo Ibérico* 4, December 1965 – January 1966.

CALAMAI, M. (1975) *Storia del Movimento Operaio Spagnolo dal 1960 al 1975*. Bari: De Donato.

CAMACHO, M. (1976) *Charles en la Prisión*. Barcelona: Laia.

CÁMARA DE COMERCIO, INDUSTRIA Y NAVEGACIÓN DE BILBAO (1968) *Informe Económico*. Bilbao.

CAMPBELL, A., GURIN, G., and MILLER, W. (1954) *The Voter Decides*. Illinois: Row Peterson.

CLAUDÍN, F. (1966) Dos Concepciones de la 'Via Española al Socialismo'. *Horizonte Español 1966*. Paris: Ruedo Ibérico.

COLECTIVO SINDICALISTA DE LA UGT (1976) *Unión General de Trabajadores*. Barcelona: Avance.

COMISARÍA DEL PLAN DE DESARROLLO ECONÓMICO Y SOCIAL (1965) *Memoria sobre la Ejecución del Plan de Desarrollo en 1964*. Madrid.

CONVERSE, P. and DUPEUX, A. (1962) Politicization of the Electorate in France and the United States. *Public Opinion Quarterly* 26.

COSER, L. A. (1956) *The Functions of Social Conflict*. London: Routledge & Kegan Paul.

CROZIER, M. (1962) Sociologie du Syndicalisme. In G. Friedmann and P. Naville (eds.), *Traité de Sociologie du Travail*. Paris: Armand Colin.

Cuadernos de Ruedo Ibérico. Numbers: 2, 3, 4, 6, 8, 12, 20–21, 21–22, 25–31, 32.

DELAMOTTE, Y. (1962) Relations Collectives et Règles Juridiques du Travail et de la Sécurité Sociale. In G. Friedmann and P. Naville (eds.), *Traité de Sociologie du Travail*. Paris: Armand Colin.

DENVER, R. T. and BOCHEL, J. M. (1973) The Political Socialization of

Activists in the British Communist Party. *British Journal of Political Science* 3(1).

DEXTER, L. A. (1970) *Elite and Specialised Interviewing*. Evanston, Ill.: Northwestern University Press.

DOWNTON, J. V. (1973) *Rebel Leadership*. New York: Free Press.

DURAND, C. (1967) Conditions Objectives et Orientations de l'Action Syndicale. *Mouvement Social* 61.

EASTON, D. and DENNIS, J. (1969) *Children in the Political System*. Chicago: McGraw.

EMERSON, D. K. (ed.) (1968) *Students and Politics in Developing Nations*. London: Pall Mall Press.

FARGA, M. J. (1969) *Universidad y Democracia en España*. México: Era.

FLACKS, R. (1963) The Liberated Generation: An Exploration of the Roots of Student Protest. *Journal of Social Issues* 23(3).

FLORES, X. (1966) El Exilio y España. *Horizonte Español 1966*. Paris: Ruedo Ibérico.

FORMENTOR, D. (1972) Universidad: Crónica de Siete Años de Lucha. *Horizonte Español, 1972*. Paris: Ruedo Ibérico.

FRANCO, F. (1943) *Palabras del Caudillo (19 abril 1937 – 7 Diciembre 1942)*. Madrid.

FRIEDRICH, C. J. and BRZEZINSKI, Z. K. (1956) *Totalitarian Dictatorship and Autocracy*. Cambridge, Mass.: Harvard University Press. (Reprinted by Praeger, New York, in 1966.)

FUENTES, E. (1966) La Oposición Anti-Franquista de 1939 a 1955. *Horizonte Español 1966*. Paris: Ruedo Ibérico.

FUNDACIÓN FOESSA (1967) *Informe Sociológico Sobre La Situación Social de Madrid*. Madrid: Euramérica.

—— (1970) *Informe Sociológico sobre la Situación Social de España*. Madrid: Euramérica.

GALLO, M. (1969) *Histoire de l'Espagne Franquiste*. Paris: Robert Laffont.

GARCÍA, E. (1965) El Movimiento Obrero en Madrid: Los Metalúrgicos. *Cuadernos de Ruedo Ibérico* 3, October–November.

GERLACH, L. and HINE, V. (1970) *People, Power and Change. Movements of Social Transformation*. New York: Bobbs-Merrill.

GERMANI, G. (1968) Fascism and Class. In S. J. Woolf (ed.), *The Nature of Fascism*. London: Weidenfeld and Nicolson.

—— (1970) Political Socialization of Youth in Fascist Regimes: Italy and Spain. In S. P. Huntington and C. H. Moore (eds.), *Authoritarian Politics in Modern Society*. New York: Basic Books.

GERTH, H. H. and MILLS, C. W. (1947) *From Max Weber: Essays in Sociology*. London: Routledge & Kegan Paul.

GINER, S. (1972) Spain. In M. S. Archer (ed.), *Students, University and Society*. London: Heinemann.

GINER, S. and SALCEDO, J. (1977) The Ideological Practice of Nicos Poulantzas. *Archives Européennes de Sociologie* 27.

GLAZER, M. (1968a) Student Politics in a Chilean University. *Daedalus*. Winter.

—— (1968b) Chile. In D. K. Emerson (ed.) 1968.

GOFFMAN, E. (1969) *Where the Action Is*. London: Allen Lane.

GROUND, L. (1967) *Sociología del Catolicismo Europeo*. Barcelona: Nova Terra.

HERMET, G. (1970) Les Espagnols devant leur Règime. *Revue Française de Science Politique* 20(1).

—— (1971a) *Les Communistes en Espagne*. Paris: Armand Colin.

—— (1971b) *La Politique dans l'Espagne Franquiste*. Paris: Armand Colin.

HESS, R. L. and LOEWENBURG, G. (1964) The Ethiopian No-Party State. *American Political Science Review*, December.

HESS, R. D. and TORNEY, J. V. (1967) *The Development of Political Attitudes in Children*. Chicago: Aldine.

HOBSBAWM, E. (1959) *Primitive Rebels*. Manchester: Manchester University Press.

HUNTINGTON, S. P. (1968) *Political Order In Changing Societies*. New Haven, Conn.: Yale University Press.

INGHAM, G. (1969) Plant Size: Political Attitudes and Behaviour. *Sociological Review* 17.

—— (1970) *Size of Industrial Organization and Worker Behaviour*. Cambridge: Cambridge University Press.

INSTITUTO NACIONAL DE ESTADÍSTICA *Anuarios Estadisticos*. Madrid (periodical publication).

INSTITUTO NACIONAL DE ESTADÍSTICA *Censo Español Industrial de 1958*.

JACKSON, G. (1965) *The Spanish Republic and the Civil War*. Princeton: Princeton University Press.

JARVIE, I. C. (1967) *The Revolution in Anthropology*. London: Routledge & Kegan Paul.

KENISTON, K. (1968) *Young Radicals*. New York: Harcourt, Brace and World.

KERR, C. (1964) *Labour and Management in Industrial Society*. New York: Doubleday.

KIRBY, D. (1971) A Counter-Culture Explanation of Student Activism. *Social Problems* 19(2).

KITCHEN, M. (1976) *Fascism*. London: Macmillan.

LAMMERS, C. J. (1971) Student Unionism in the Netherlands: An Application of a Social Class Model. *American Sociological Review* 36(2).

LANE, D. (1976) *The Socialist Industrial State*. London: Allen and Unwin.

LANE, R. E. (1959) Fathers and Sons: the Foundations of Political Belief. *American Sociological Review* 24.

—— (1962) *Political Ideology. Why the American Common Man Believes What He Does*. New York: Free Press.

LAQUEUR, W. (ed.) (1976) *Fascism*. University of California Press.

LEMERT, E. M. (1951) *Social Pathology*. New York: McGraw Hill.

—— (1967) *Human Deviance. Social Problems and Social Control*. Englewood Cliffs: Prentice Hall.

LENIN, V. I. (1902) *What Is to Be Done?*

LEÓN, S. (1972) Notas sobre el Movimiento Estudiantil en España. *Horizonte Español 1972*. Paris: Ruedo Ibérico.

LINZ, J. J. (1964) An Authoritarian Regime: Spain. In E. Allardt and Y. Littunen (eds.), *Cleavages, Ideologies and Party Systems*, Transactions of the Westermaark Society, X, Helsinki. Reprinted in E. Allardt and S. Rokkan (eds.), *Mass Politics*. New York: Free Press (1970).

—— (1970) From Falange to Movimiento Organization: the Spanish Single Party and the Franco Regime, 1936–1968. In S. P. Huntington and C. H. Moore (eds.), *Authoritarian Politics in Modern Society. The Dynamics of Established One-Party Systems*. New York: Basic Books.

—— (1974) Opposition In and Under an Authoritarian Regime: the case of Spain. In R. A. Dahl (ed.), *Regimes and Oppositions*. New Haven, Conn.: Yale University Press.

—— (1976) Some Notes towards a Comparative Study of Fascism in Sociological, Historical Perspective. In Laqueur (1976).

LINZ, J. J. and DE MIGUEL, A. (1963) Los Problemas de la Retribución y el Rendimiento Vistos por los Empresarios Españoles. *Revista de Trabajo* 1.

—— (1966) Within Nations Differences and Comparisons: The Eight Spains. In R. L. Merrit and S. Rokkan (eds.), *Comparing Nations*. New Haven, Conn.: Yale University Press.

LIPSET, S. M. (1967) Students and Politics in Underdeveloped Countries. In S. M. Lipset (ed.), *Student Politics*. New York: Basic Books.

—— (1972) *Rebellion in the University*. London: Routledge & Kegan Paul.

LOCKWOOD, D. (1964) Social Integration and System Integration. In G. K. Zollschan and W. Hirsch (eds.), *Explorations in Social Change*. London: Routledge & Kegan Paul.

—— (1966) Sources of Variation in Working Class Images of Society. *Sociological Review* 14(3).

LOFLAND, J. (1966) *Doomsday Cult. A Study of Conversion, Proselytization and Maintenance of Faith*. Englewood Cliffs: Prentice Hall.

LOFLAND, J. and STARK, R. (1965) Becoming a World-Saver: A Theory of Conversion to a Deviant Perspective. *American Sociological Review* 30(6).

LOGAN, J. R. (1964) *Industrialization, Repression and Working Class Militancy in Spain*. Unpublished Ph.D. dissertation, University of California (Berkeley).

LYONNS, G. (1965) The Police Car Demonstration: A Survey of Participants. In S. M. Lipset and S. S. Wolin (eds.), *The Berkeley Student Revolt*. Garden City: Doubleday.

MACCOBY, E., MATTHEWS, R. and MORTON, A. (1954) Youth and Political Change. *Public Opinion Quarterly* 18.

MALLET, S. (1963) *La Nouvelle Classe Ouvrière*. Paris: Seuil.

MANKOFF, M. and FLACKS, R. (1971) The Changing Social Base of the American Student Movement. *The Annals* 395.

MARAVALL, J. M. (1969) *El Desarrollo Económico y los Trabajadores. Un Estudio Sociológico de los Conflictos Obreros en España*. Ph.D. thesis, University of Madrid.

—— (1975) *Political Power and Student Radicalism. A Study of Student Radical Politics and Leaders in Spain from 1940 to 1970*. D.Phil. thesis, Oxford University.

MARAVALL, J. M. (1976) Subjective Conditions and Revolutionary Conflict: Some Remarks. *British Journal of Sociology* 27(1).

MARAVALL, J. M. and MARTÍNEZ-LÁZARO, U. (1977) *La Distribución de los Conflictos Obreros en España: Factores Económicos y Políticos* Unpublished manuscript.

MARTINEZ-CUADRADO, M. (1969) *Elecciones y Partidos Políticos en España.* Madrid: Taurus.

MARX, K. (1943) *The Communist Manifesto.* London: Lawrence and Wishart.

—— (1961) *Capital,* vol. I. Moscow: Foreign Languages Publishing House.

MATZA, D. (1964) *Delinquency and Drift.* New York: Wiley.

—— (1969) *Becoming Deviant.* Englewood Cliffs: Prentice Hall.

MERELMAN, R. M. (1971) The Development of Policy Thinking in Adolescence. *American Political Science Review* 65(4).

MERTON, R. K. (1968) *Social Theory and Social Structure.* New York: Free Press.

MIGUELEZ, F. (1977) *La Lucha de los Mineros Asturianos Bajo el Franquismo.* Barcelona: Laia.

MINISTERIO DE EDUCACIÓN Y CIENCIA (1964) *Universidad. Escalafón de Catedráticos Numerarios.* Madrid.

MINISTERIO DE INDUSTRIA (1961) *Energía en España. Evolución y Perspectivas.* Madrid.

MINISTERIO DE TRABAJO (1960) *Dimensión de la Explotación Industrial en España.* Madrid.

—— (1963) *Informe sobre los Conflictos Colectivos de Trabajo* (periodical report since 1963).

MINISTERIO DE TRABAJO, DIRECCIÓN GENERAL DE EMPLEO, *Dinámica de Empleo* (periodical report).

MONTES, J. L. (1963) Minería del Carbón. *Madrid,* November 3.

MOTT, J. and GOLDIE, N. (1971) The Social Characteristics of Militant and Anti-Militant Students. *Universities Quarterly* 26(1).

MOUZELIS, N. (1974) Social Integration and System Integration: Some Remarks on a Fundamental Distinction. *British Journal of Sociology* 25(4).

MOYA, C. (1972a) Las Elites Económicas y el Desarrollo Español. In *La España de los Años 70: La Sociedad.* Madrid: Moneda y Crédito.

—— (1972b) *Burocracia y Sociedad Industrial.* Madrid: Edicusa.

MUÑOZ, J., ROLDÁN, S., GARCÍA DELGADO, J. L., and SERRANO, A. (1973) *La Economía Española, 1972.* Madrid: Cuadernos para el Diálogo.

—— (1974) *La Economía Española 1973.* Madrid: Cuadernos para el Diálogo.

NOGEE, P. and LEVIN, M. B. (1958) Some Determinants of Political Attitudes Among College Voters. *Public Opinion Quarterly* 22.

OCDE (1966) *Croissance Economique 1960–1970.* Paris.

ORGANIZACIÓN SINDICAL, CONSEJO ECONÓMICO NACIONAL (1962) *Perspectivas de Desarrollo Económico* (for the provinces of Alava, Guipúzcoa, Navarra, Vizcaya, Oviedo). Madrid.

ORGANIZACIÓN SINDICAL, SECCIÓN ECONÓMICA PROVINCIAL (1962)

Plan de Expansión de la Minería Asturiana de Hulla. Oviedo: Sindicato del Combustible.

ORGANIZACIÓN SINDICAL (1965) *Resúmen Estadístico de Convenios Colectivos Sindicales*. Madrid.

ORGANIZACIÓN SINDICAL, VICE-SECRETARÍA NACIONAL DE ORDENACIÓN ECONÓMICA (1965) *Evolución Socioeconómica de España*. Madrid.

——— (1968) *Evolución Socioeconómica de España*. Madrid.

PARKIN, F. (1967) Working Class Conservatives. A Theory of Political Deviance. *British Journal of Sociology* 18.

——— (1968) *Middle Class Radicalism*. Manchester: Manchester University Press.

——— (1972) System Contradiction and Political Transformation. *Archives Europeènnes de Sociologie* 13(1).

PARSONS, T. (1964) Evolutionary Universals in Society. *American Sociological Review* 29(3).

PASCUAL, A. (1970) *El Retorno de los Emigrantes*. Barcelona: Nova Terra.

PAYNE, S. G. (1961) *Falange. A History of Spanish Fascism*. Stanford: Stanford University Press.

PEÑA, A. (1966) Veinticinco Años de Luchas Estudiantiles. *Horizonte Español, 1966*. Paris: Ruedo Ibérico (Vol. II).

PÉREZ-DIAZ,V. (1972) *Emigración y Cambio Social*. Barcelona: Ariel.

PERNOUD, R. (1962) *Histoire de la Bourgeoisie en France*. Paris: Seuil.

PINARD, M. (1971) *The Rise of a Third Party. A Study of Crisis Politics*. Englewood Cliffs: Prentice Hall.

PINILLA DE LAS HERAS, E. (1968) *Los Empresarios y el Desarrollo Capitalista: El Caso Catalán*. Barcelona: Península.

POULANTZAS, N. (1970) *Fascisme et Dictature*. Paris: Maspero.

PRESTON, P. (ed.), (1976) *Spain in Crisis*. London: Harvester Press.

RAMÍREZ, M. (1966) Las Huelgas Durante la Segunda República. *Anales de Sociología*.

——— (1972) Modernización Política en España. *Revista de Estudios Sociales 5*.

Revista Española de la Opinión Publica (1967) 9 July–September.

——— (1969) 15 January–March.

——— (1969) 18 October–December.

ROLDÁN, S. (1966) *Evolución de la Norma de Obligado Cumplimiento*. Unpublished manuscript, Madrid.

ROMANO, V. (1973) *Spain. The Workers' Commissions*. Toronto: The Canadian Committee for a Democratic Spain.

ROMERO-MAURA, J. (1971) The Spanish Case. In D. Apter and J. Joll (eds.), *Anarchism Today*. London: Macmillan.

ROS HOMBRAVELLA, J. *et al.* (1973) *Capitalismo Español: De la Autarquia a la Estabilización*. Madrid: Cuadernos para el Diálogo.

SADEI (1967) *Estudio de Reconversión de la Mano de Obra en Asturias*. Oviedo.

SÁNCHEZ-LÓPEZ, F. (1969) *Emigración Española a Europa*. Madrid: Confederación Española de Cajas de Ahorro.

SARTORIUS, N. (1975) *El Resurgir del Movimiento Obrero*. Barcelona: Laia.

SEMPRÚN, J. (1966) La Oposición Política en España, 1956–1966. *Horizonte Español 1966*. Paris: Ruedo Ibérico.

SHIRER, W. L. (1959) *The Rise and Fall of the Third Reich*. New York: Fawcett, World.

SILVERT, K. H. (1964) The University Student. In J. J. Johnson (ed.), *Continuity and Change in Latin America*. Stanford: Stanford University Press.

SOLÉ-TURA, J. (1968) The Political Instrumentality of Fascism. In S. J. Woolf (ed.), *The Nature of Fascism*. London: Weidenfeld and Nicolson.

TAMAMES, R. (1969) *Estructura Económica de España*. Madrid: Guadiana.

TEZANOS, J. F. *et al.* (1973) *Las Nuevas Clases Medias. Conflicto y Conciencia de Clase entre los Empleados de Banca*. Madrid: Cuadernos para el Diálogo.

TIERNO GALVÁN, E. (1966) Students' Opposition in Spain. *Government and Opposition* 1(4).

TOURAINE, A. (1955) *L'Evolution du Travail Ouvrier aux Usines Renault*. Paris: CNRS.

—— (1965) *La Sociologie de l'Action*. Paris: Seuil.

—— (1966) *La Conscience Ouvrière*. Paris: Seuil.

—— (1969) *La Société Post-Industrielle*. Paris: Denoel.

—— (1970) Crise et Conflict. *Cahiers Internationaux de Sociologie* 48.

TOURAINE, A. and MOTTEZ, B. M. (1962) Class Ouvrière et Société Globale. In G. Friedmann and P. Naville (eds.), *Traité de Sociologie du Travail*. Paris: Armand Colin.

TROTSKY, L. (1975) *The Struggle against Fascism in Germany*. Harmondsworth: Penguin Books.

TUÑÓN DE LARA, M. (1969) Le Problème Universitaire Espagnol. *Esprit* 5, May.

—— (1972) *El Movimiento Obrero en la Historia de España*. Madrid: Taurus.

VAJDA, M. (1976) *Fascism as a Mass Movement*. London: Allison and Busby.

WALZER, M. (1965) *The Revolution of the Saints*. Cambridge Mass.: Harvard University Press.

WATTS, W. A. & WHITTAKER, D. (1966) Free Speech Advocates at Berkeley. *Journal of Applied Behavioral Science* 2.

—— (1968) Profile of a Non-Conformist Youth Culture. *Sociology of Education* 41(2).

WEBER, M. (1968) *Economy and Society*, vol. 1. New York: Bedminster Press.

WILSON, B. (1961) *Sects and Society*. London: Heinemann.

—— (1967) An Analysis of Sect Development. In B. Wilson (ed.), *Patterns of Sectarianism*. London: Heinemann.

—— (1971) *Religious Sects*. New York: McGraw Hill.

WILSON, J. (1973) *Introduction to Social Movements*. New York: Basic Books.

ZALD, M. N. and ASH, R. (1966) Social Movement Organizations: Growth, Decay and Change. *Social Forces* 44.

Name Index

Subject Index